Cockleshell Heroes

'Peter' Lucas Phillips was born in 1897 and educated at St Lawrence College and King's College, London University. In the First World War he served in the Royal Artillery in France and Flanders, becoming a Major before he was twenty-one. During the Second World War he fought in the campaigns of Dunkirk, the Western Desert and Italy. He became a Brigadier and was awarded the MC, the OBE and the Croix de Guerre. He was the author of several successful war books, including *Cockleshell Heroes, The Greatest Raid of All, Escape of the* Amethyst, *Alamein* and *Springboard to Victory*.

Lucas Phillips was a passionate gardener and also wrote several books on gardening. He died in 1984.

Also in the Pan Grand Strategy Series

OVERLORD
Max Hastings

BOMBER COMMAND
Max Hastings

THE KOREAN WAR
Max Hastings

THE DAM BUSTERS
Paul Brickhill

THE SOMME
A. H. Farrar-Hockley

THE OTHER SIDE OF THE HILL
B. H. Liddell Hart

THE IMPERIAL WAR MUSEUM BOOK OF
1918: YEAR OF VICTORY
Malcolm Brown

CHRISTMAS TRUCE
Malcolm Brown and Shirley Seaton

DEFEAT INTO VICTORY
Field-Marshal Viscount Slim

THE IMPERIAL WAR MUSEUM BOOK OF
WAR BEHIND ENEMY LINES
Julian Thompson

THE 900 DAYS: THE SIEGE OF LENINGRAD
Harrison E. Salisbury

THE GREATEST RAID OF ALL
C. E. Lucas Phillips

TRENCH WARFARE
Tony Ashworth

C. E. LUCAS PHILLIPS
OBE MC
with the co-operation of Lieut-Col H. G. Hasler, DSO OBE

COCKLESHELL HEROES

With a Foreword by
Admiral of the Fleet the Earl Mountbatten of Burma, KG

PAN GRAND STRATEGY SERIES

PAN BOOKS

First published 1956 by William Heinemann Ltd

This edition published 2000 by Pan Books
an imprint of Pan Macmillan Ltd
Pan Macmillan, 20 New Wharf Road, London N1 9RR
Basingstoke and Oxford
Associated companies throughout the world
www.panmacmillan.com

ISBN 0 330 48069 3

3 5 7 9 8 6 4 2

A CIP catalogue record for this book is available from the British Library.

Typeset by SX Composing DTP, Rayleigh, Essex
Printed and bound in Great Britain by
Mackays of Chatham plc, Chatham, Kent

This book is dedicated to

THE ROYAL MARINES

And especially to the memory of the brave men
whose names are inscribed below

Marine James Conway
Marine Robert Ewart
Corporal A. F. Laver
Lieutenant J. W. Mackinnon
Marine W. H. Mills
Marine David Moffat
Corporal C. G. Sheard
Sergeant Samuel Wallace

CONTENTS

PART TWO: THE WEAPON STRIKES

PART THREE: WHAT HAPPENED AFTERWARDS

APPENDICES

List of Photographs

List of Figures in the Text

Author's Note

This story of the raid upon enemy shipping in Bordeaux Harbour carried out by a small party of Royal Marines in 1942 is compiled from official documents, from the diary and personal narrative of Lieutenant-Colonel Hasler and from the narratives of others concerned with the planning and execution of the raid. There is no fiction.

The titles and ranks that are used are those appropriate to the time. The anonymity of men and women in the French escape organizations has been preserved.

The Admiralty and the War Office in their several branches and the Headquarters staff of Amphibious Warfare have been most helpful in searching out much deeply buried information hitherto designated as very secret and a great deal of what is here related has never before been made public. I am very grateful to those who have sanctioned the publication of these details and to those who have been to so much trouble to help me to discover it.

I tender my warm thanks likewise to all others who have helped me in this task – to the Commandant General Royal Marines, Major J. D. Stewart, Major-General G. E. Wildman-Lushington, CB, CBE, Major-General Sir Robert Neville, KCMG, CB, Quartermaster-Sergeant J. M. King, DSM, Major W. H. A. Pritchard-Gordon, Mr Eric Fisher, the mothers of the men lost in the raid, Warwick Films and Columbia Pictures, and above all to Lieutenant-Colonel Hasler.

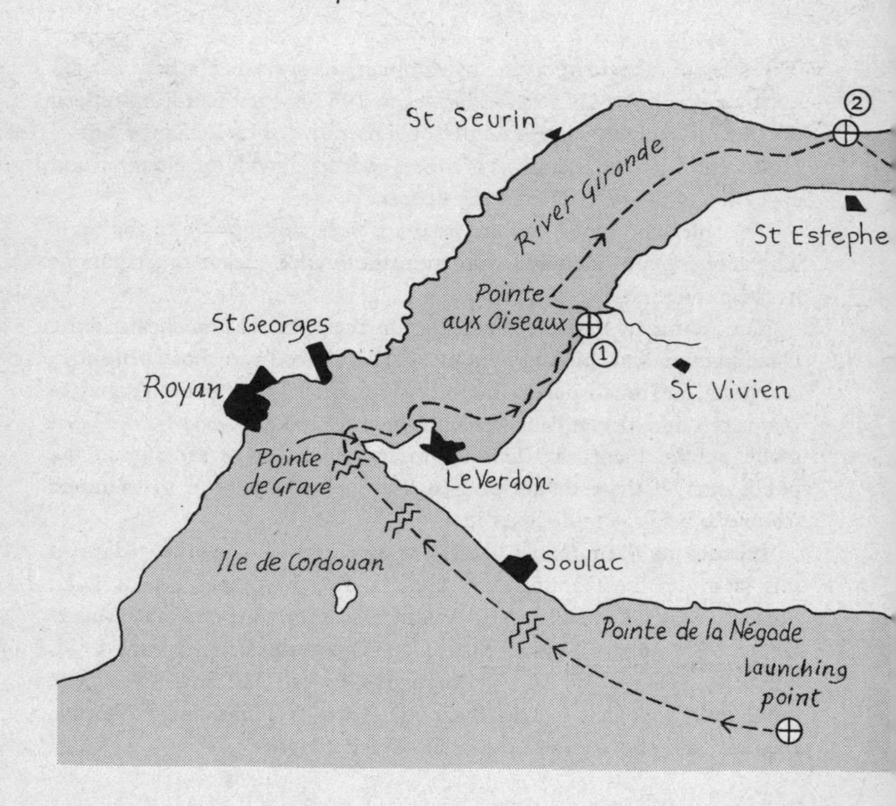
N
St Seurin
River Gironde
St Estephe
Pointe aux Oiseaux
St Georges
Royan
St Vivien
Pointe de Grave
Le Verdon
Ile de Cordouan
Soulac
Pointe de la Négade
Launching point
1
2

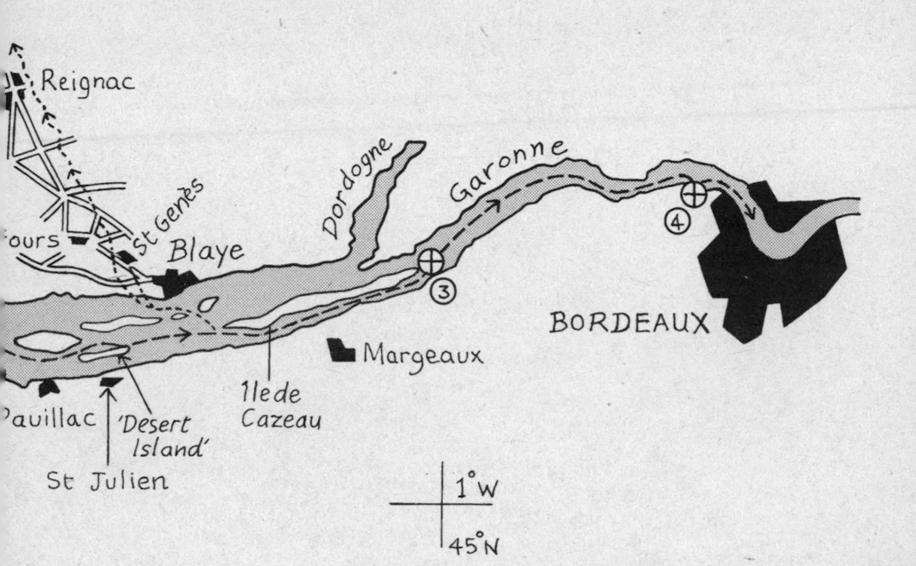
Reignac
St Genès
Blaye
Dordogne
Garonne
3
4
BORDEAUX
Margeaux
Ile de Cazeau
'Desert Island'
St Julien
1°W
45°N
Legend
Course of the Canoes
Escape route
Daytime 'Hides'
Tide Races
0
5
10
Sea Miles

Foreword

By Admiral of the Fleet the Earl Mountbatten of Burma, KG

Of the many brave and dashing raids carried out by the men of Combined Operations Command, none was more courageous or imaginative than Operation 'Frankton'.

An immense amount of trouble was taken over the training of the small handful of picked Royal Marines who took part under the indomitable leadership of Lieutenant-Colonel Hasler. They maintained their object in spite of the frightening losses of the first night and the subsequent ever-increasing difficulties encountered. Although the force had been reduced to four men, the object was finally achieved.

The account of this operation brings out the spirit of adventure always present in peace and war among Royal Marines. It emphasizes the tremendous importance of morale – pride in oneself and one's unit – and what a big part physical fitness plays in creating this morale. It also stresses the need for careful detailed planning of operations.

I commend it to all as an account of a fine operation, carried out by a particularly brave party of men.

PART ONE

FORGING THE WEAPON

1. A WAR OF SHIPS

On 30 October 1942, Vice-Admiral Lord Louis Mountbatten, Chief of Combined Operations, took up his pen and signed a letter to the Chiefs of Staff Committee.* Forwarding for their approval the outline plan of an operation designated by the code-name 'Frankton', he said:

MOST SECRET

Secretary,
Chiefs of Staff Committee
October 30, 1942

Operation 'Frankton' has been planned to meet Lord Selborne's requirements, referred to in COS (42) 223 (O) and subsequent papers, that steps should be taken to attack Axis ships which are known to be running the blockade between France and the Far East.

2. Both seaborne and airborne methods of attacking the ships have been carefully examined and the plan now proposed is the only one which offers a good chance of success.

3. On an average, between six and ten blockade runners are usually to be found alongside the quays at Bordeaux, in addition to other shipping. It is hoped to deal with at least six blockade runners.

4. Briefly, the plan is for one officer and five other ranks of the Royal Marine Boom Patrol Detachment to paddle up the River Gironde in cockles, moving during the hours of darkness only, and to place 'limpets' on the waterline of the ships they find at

* Admiral of the Fleet Sir Dudley Pound, General Sir Alan Brooke, Air Chief Marshal Sir Charles Portal and Lord Louis himself.

Bordeaux. The cockles will be carried to within nine miles of the mouth of the river in a submarine which will be on passage to normal patrol duty and thus will not require to be specially detailed.

5. Twelve copies of the summary of this outline plan are attached.

[sgd] Louis Mountbatten
Chief of Combined Operations

Thus was put in train one of the minor operations of the Second World War which in boldness of conception, care in planning and courage in execution was not excelled by any other of its kind, and one that a German officer described as 'the outstanding commando raid of the war'. For in this operation four men accomplished a task that would have required a very large force by conventional methods of attack, with very heavy loss of life.

With only two exceptions the men who adventured out upon this task and accomplished it were very ordinary young men from the streets of our industrial cities. They were little more than boys and had engaged in the Royal Marines for the period of 'hostilities only'. None of them had ever before in his life handled a boat; yet, after only a few months' training, they accomplished a task that would have daunted many a man who has lived with boats since infancy.

Theirs is the story of how men engaged in the humdrum occupations of modern industrial society can, under inspired leadership, attain an ampler status and fulfil a braver purpose. Yet it is not a story of shot and shell, of battlements stormed at bayonet point, of artillery that 'did affright the air'. If it had been, they would surely have failed. It is, on the contrary, the story of how all these things must be avoided. Tenacity of purpose, physical endurance, a cool nerve and courage under natural and unseen perils, a high training in the skills of stealthy and unobserved movement – these, rather, are the qualities that this story reveals. For nearly all who took part it is also a story with a dark, satanic end, illuminated only by their own defiant heroism. Above all, we shall see shining through all these pages a wonderful 'morale', a high *esprit de corps*, a pride of warriorship in which each man, developing with calculated training the qualities of self-reliance, not only fulfilled himself but also served, under discipline, the common purpose of his team.

Behind this story lies the personality of the leader of these young men – a man of marked modesty and reserve, who, inheriting and enriched by all the traditions of the Royal Marines, added to them his own strong personality and devoted to his task a concentrated singleness of purpose that alone could have led him to his dark goal on that bitter night of December deep in the heart of enemy territory. We shall meet him presently and judge for ourselves.

It all began with a letter to the Prime Minister, Mr Winston Churchill, from Lord Selborne, Minister for Economic Warfare, on 9 May 1942. In this letter Lord Selborne showed that enemy ships, sailing between the Far East and German-occupied ports in Europe, were beginning to run our blockade. This traffic was likely to increase. He specially mentioned cargoes of rubber. Since Japan's entry into the war, a few months earlier, traffic between Germany and Japan had shown signs of development and if it were not checked would seriously benefit the war efforts of both our enemies.

On 22 June Lord Selborne wrote again on the same subject, this time to the Deputy PM, Mr Attlee, Mr Churchill being then on a visit to Washington. Lord Selborne emphasized the scale of traffic between Germany and Japan planned for the next twelve months, and its effect on the war potentials of both countries.

Lord Selborne's ministry was now studying the matter and, in a paper prepared in July, showed that the particular resort of the enemy blockade runners was Bordeaux. In the previous twelve months some 25,000 tons of crude rubber had passed through that port to Germany and Italy. If that were kept up, the enemy's requirements in rubber would be met. Other important cargoes were tin, tungsten and animal and vegetable oils – all most important for the German war effort. Cargoes in the reverse direction – to Japan – were less certain, but were thought to be mainly equipment for manufacturing processes and prototypes of various weapons and equipment that the Japs did not possess.

On 5 August Lord Selborne wrote again to Mr Attlee, Mr Churchill this time being away on his momentous visit to Cairo, when Alexander and Montgomery were appointed to the Middle East commands in which they were to be famous. 'Hardly a day passes', wrote Lord Selborne, 'without my seeing convincing proof of the determination of both countries (Germany and Japan) to execute their programme.' Fifteen potential blockade runners were awaiting cargoes in French Atlantic ports, three were believed now to be on their way from the Far East and three more were expected to sail shortly.*

Mr Attlee passed this letter to Brigadier L. C. Hollis, who was Senior Assistant Secretary of the War Cabinet, asking him to place the matter before the Chiefs of Staff.

These developments were occurring during one of the blackest periods of the war, and indeed of our whole history. Throughout the spring and summer of 1942, one disaster after another befell the Allied arms, one new peril upon another threatened our cause. In the Pacific the treacherous attacks of the Japanese had inflicted grave reverses on the Americans, and on 15 February, following our grievous losses in Malaya, came the terrible blow of the fall of our fortress of Singapore – 'the worst disaster and the largest capitulation in British history', as Sir Winston Churchill has described it.

About the same time came the apparent blow to our naval prestige and pride in the escape through the Straits of Dover of the German warships *Scharnhorst, Gneisenau* and *Prinz Eugen*. In February, too, the world heard with astonishment of the new submarine fury unloosed by the Germans in the Atlantic and of the huge losses that our ally was suffering off the distant American coasts.

As the weeks followed, we in our own country listened daily to the gloomy record of continued Japanese success, and the loss, piece by piece, of all the East Indies, British and Dutch, as well as of Burma, while at sea and in the air great quantities of ships, aircraft and men – British, American, Dutch and Australian – were added to our deprivations. In March and April there had

* It is also possible that, about the time our raid took place, the enemy ships may have been carrying models or blue-prints of radar equipment, which the Japanese did not possess; but this does not appear in the records.

followed the furious onslaughts by the Germans and Italians upon our little isle of Malta, where the heroic and half-starved garrison, under the leadership of Lieutenant-General Sir William Dobbie and later of Lord Gort, daily scanned the infested seas for that succour which the Navy and the Merchant Service, unshaken by fearful losses, brought to them in their extremity in the face of bomb, torpedo, shell and mine. Only the impotence of the Italian Navy, which had had too many lickings from our own, saved Malta from actual invasion.

Then in May and June a hard-tried Britain writhed as it listened to the record of Rommel's success in Egypt, when he broke our Gazala line, forced Tobruk to surrender and drove us back by hard stages to the line of Alamein. Though it was only a victory of movement in waste spaces, the blow to our pride, especially the unaccountable fall of the once heroic Tobruk, was galling. The public demanded to know why these things had happened.

Throughout that same summer, the German armies away in Russia continued to surge further forward, penetrating deep into the Caucasus and reaching the gates of Stalingrad. The Allied fortunes everywhere seemed indeed on an ebbing tide, and the wonderful dramas of Eighth Army's 'Desert Victory' and the defeat of Paulus before Stalingrad – those two great events that Sir Winston Churchill has called 'The Hinge of Fate', when the whole course of the war swung and, after never having a victory, we never had a defeat – had yet to be played by their inspired actors.

Only in a few isolated places had our darkness so far been lightened. In March there had been the gallant and successful raid on St Nazaire by Commander R. E. D. Ryder and Colonel A. C. Newman in which both won the Victoria Cross. In May, Vice-Admiral Sir Neville Syfret and the Royal Marine general Robert Sturgess, by a bold and well-handled expedition, had secured Madagascar against the Japanese, while away in the far Coral Sea, the American Navy had taught the Japs their first sharp lesson.

This was the atmosphere in which the deed we are going to relate was conceived and born. Everywhere we were suffering reverses – reverses which, in distant Britain, and in a world in which the blanket of 'security' necessarily smothered the facts that would have helped us to form a balanced judgment, seemed unexplainable and indeed shocking. The barometer of events read at its lowest.

Yet the black clouds and threatening seas to which it too clearly pointed were accompanied by no fall in the temperature of the people's will and spirit. We were not so much dismayed as puzzled and angry. Everywhere imaginative minds were stirred to a new activity (and in the last analysis it was by brains and inventiveness that we won the war). In 'the quick workshop and forge' of men's brains new ideas were being worked out, new paths were being traced and caverns hitherto measureless to man were beginning to be lit. Much that was thrown into this busy workshop was valueless, much was mad, many tools broke in our hands, many little private 'empires' were built by the unworthy; yet from the assembly lines there came at last the golden weapons of victory.

One of these new ideas – Churchill's own – was 'Combined Operations'. A doctrine and policy for operations that required the participation of all the Services had been formulated long before the war in the 'Manual of Combined Operations', an able document for which Admiral Sir Sydney Fremantle had been largely responsible. There had, however, been no organization to give practical effect to this doctrine, and, apart from some valuable but limited work in developing landing-craft types, 'combined ops' had remained a theoretical subject for interesting but sterile discussions at staff colleges. Even at the Imperial Defence College, that post-graduate course for senior Service practitioners, they had said that these things were very desirable but quite impossible.

The Prime Minister had determined that they should be possible. From the small beginnings of a purely 'advisory' role, Combined Operations had at his direction assumed step by step a higher importance, a more positive function and a stronger staff. When the time came, as it shortly would, for us to throw off the garments of defence and go forward equipped for the attack, we should be faced with the fact that wherever we might decide to strike our main blows at our enemies, whether in Europe or Asia, we should be obliged first of all to fight for a foothold on alien soil. We should have to fight for it, moreover, against seemingly impregnable coastal defences equipped with every modern preventive device and stratagem. It was a situation almost unique in our military history, though the Dardanelles had proved the need and taught the first lesson. Technical problems of the most formidable magnitude confronted us, together with problems of tactics, transport and administration. 'Co-operation' between the Services was not enough; there must be complete integration of thought, planning, experimentation and executive action. Besides these weightier military propositions, it was also important that we should develop the new techniques and equipment for smaller operations – for raids and sudden sallies and expeditions to destroy the enemy's installations, to harass his shipping and to discover his defences.

Thus the special organization of Combined Operations was evolved and at the time of which we write its head was Lord Louis Mountbatten, who, though in substantive rank still no more than a Captain RN, had been singled out by the Prime Minister by reason of his special qualities of heart and mind. As captain of the destroyer *Kelly*, which had gone down with her guns still firing, he had shown qualities of daring and leadership; he was keenly interested in scientific invention and had knowledge of many of its more abstruse mysteries; he had prestige and could command loyalty from all ranks; he worked swiftly and overrode obstructions. In March 1942 the Prime Minister had given him the new status of Chief of Combined Operations, with a seat on the Chiefs of Staff Committee.

The headquarters of Combined Operations (which we shall in future call COHQ) were in Richmond Terrace, which lies between Whitehall and the Embankment. Here in this hive had been gathered together a small swarm of enthusiasts from all three British Services, together with an American element and civilian specialists. There were few drones. Their busy and wide-ranging brains examined innumerable schemes and ideas, storing the military honey tidily into their secret cells. They hatched plots and scrutinized plots submitted to them by all sorts of people. Their scientific side, under Professor J. D. Bernal, experimented and tested. Small inter-Service syndicates prepared plans for innumerable operations, large and small, and gradually developed new techniques that were to prove themselves on the beaches of

Africa, Italy, France and the Far East. The intelligence staff collated information from innumerable sources, and representatives of that very secret lodge known as Special Operations Executive, whose business was to feed the flames of the Resistance movements in enemy-occupied lands, maintained here an active agency.

The Chief of Staff of this busy machine was an accomplished Royal Marine officer, Brigadier G. E. Wildman-Lushington, who, besides his knowledge of operations 'by sea and by land', was also an experienced flying officer, and may therefore be said to have combined in his person all three elements. Royal Marines were peculiarly appropriate in such an organization and were to inherit special responsibilities; they were well represented at all other levels also. Colonel Robert Neville was Chief Planning Co-ordinator, Lieutenant-Colonel Cyril Horton was the senior of a staff of Royal Marine planners and Captain the Hon. David Astor (later Editor of the *Observer*) was on the public relations staff.*

In the somewhat complicated hierarchy of this organization, there were two committees of special importance to us. The first was a small Search Committee, whose task was 'to speed up the search for targets'. Lord Louis had laid down the policy that 'small raids should be carried out on an average of once every two weeks', and this little committee had to devise them and consider those submitted by other people.

More important was the Examination Committee, who, after their submission to Neville, considered proposals put forward by the Search Committee. Wildman-Lushington presided over the Examination Committee, which also included Colonel Antony Head, afterwards Secretary of State for War. Any expeditions they approved were passed forward to the Council of COHQ – the highest of the many committees, and later termed the Executive. When sanctioned, the project was committed to a special 'syndicate', charged with preparing an outline plan of the methods by which the operation would be carried out, for the final seal of approval of the Chiefs of Staff Committee itself.

To COHQ Lord Selborne's problem of the Bordeaux blockade

* Before August offices and their holders were slightly different.

runners had already been referred a few days after his first letter to Mr Attlee. It is not clear from existing records through what other channels the proposition was passed, but it seems clear from personal narratives that it was referred to both the Admiralty and the Royal Air Force, and that both of them declined the target as one for a punitive expedition. For the Navy, Bordeaux was obviously much too far within the heart of enemy-held country. For the RAF, the target was within bombing range, but it would have been impossible, with instruments and skills then available, to identify and pin-point the ships to be attacked and it would have been necessary to bomb the whole dock area, causing great destruction and loss of life to French civilians, many of whom were friendly to us, and with results that could not be guaranteed. The Foreign Office was also reluctant to agree to the bombing, taking the view that it would adversely affect public opinion in France and have a bad effect on the Free French overseas.

To intercept the enemy ships while at sea by naval or RAF craft was, of course, an obvious consideration, but the heavy calls made upon our ships and aircraft in all the seas of the world made it impracticable to divert special craft to the interception of lone ships on uncertain dates. Preventive or harassing methods by means of submarine patrols and by mining the mouth of the Gironde by air were possible and these were in fact carried out.

It was therefore to Combined Operations that the problem was now sent, and the Examination Committee was asked to study means of attack upon Bordeaux itself, either to destroy the enemy ships in harbour or to make the port unusable.

Look for a moment at the map on pages xii and xiii. You will see that the great port of Bordeaux, in the Bay of Biscay, lies deep in the heart of France. It is some 500 miles from Plymouth, the nearest British port of magnitude. Moreover, to reach it from the coast one must travel about 62 land miles up the broad, many-isled estuary of the Gironde and on into the narrower waters of the Garonne. This is approximately as far as from Margate to the Tower of London on the Thames, from North Berwick to beyond Stirling on the Forth, from Holyhead to Dublin across the Irish Sea. Thus it is strongly protected by nature herself from any hostile approach by water.

The approaches to Bordeaux were well, if not heavily, guarded by the Germans. Their naval and air forces patrolled the approaches to the Gironde estuary, and their submarines crept out from their pens in Bordeaux itself upon their murderous missions. Batteries of coast defence forces threatened the approaches and anti-aircraft guns kept watch along the likely air routes.

Obviously, therefore, an attack on Bordeaux was an enterprise 'of great pith and moment', not to be undertaken lightly. A combined operation would, the Committee thought, require at least three divisions of troops (about 50,000 men) with a large force of warships and transports and a heavy commitment in aircraft. This constituted a major operation, and the forces for it were not available, in view of the heavy demands in the Desert, the Far East, Malta and the forthcoming landings in French North Africa under Eisenhower, now in active preparation. The Examination Committee therefore turned down the idea of a combined operation.

This meeting took place in the first week of July and three weeks later, in accordance with their instructions, the Search Committee, sitting under the chairmanship of Commander J. H. Unwin, examined what courses were open to achieve the object without the employment of a large combined operation. They thought that the area was much too large for bombing, that effective submarine patrolling would require a great many craft unless our intelligence was so good that we knew when ships were going to arrive, that mining the mouth of the Gironde could be done, or that a mission might be carried out by submarine or canoe.

But no action ensued.

2. THE SEARCH FOR NEW WEAPONS

Meanwhile, known to only a very few, a new instrument had begun to take shape, which in due time was to carry out the task for which an armada had been thought necessary – a small instrument, an insignificant one, the plaything of one man who had seen in his own pet enthusiasms a means of adapting them to warlike uses.

Ever since he had been a boy in shorts, a passion for small boats had ruled the heart of H. G. Hasler, at this time a substantive Regular captain and temporary major in the Royal Marines of some ten years' service, who had been granted the OBE for his services in the Norway campaign, from which he had returned with a considerable reputation. He was the son of Lieutenant-Quartermaster A. T. Hasler MC, Royal Army Medical Corps, one of the very first winners of the Military Cross in the First World War, who had been killed in May 1917 when the troopship *Transylvania*, in which he was returning to the Salonika campaign after leave, had been torpedoed off Genoa. His mother, with the determined resourcefulness of maternal affection, had somehow contrived, on the pittance of her pension, to send both her boys to public schools – the elder to Christ's Hospital and thence into the Royal Engineers and the younger, with whom we are concerned, to Wellington and afterwards the Royal Marines.

At the age of twelve young Hasler became part-owner of his first boat – a canvas-covered two-seater canoe which he and his friend Colin Ellum built in the school workshop with help from one of the masters. In it, he learnt the rudiments of seamanship while navigating the relatively safe waters of Langstone Harbour, Hampshire, and visiting the more exposed beaches of Southsea and Hayling Island. In it he hoisted his first primitive sail, and promptly became obsessed with sailing – an obsession with which he became seized even more tenaciously with the passing of the years.

At fourteen, just after he had entered Wellington, he found it imperative to own a 'proper' sailing boat. He could not afford to buy one, so once again he started to build – this time by himself, in a small open yard attached to his mother's flat. The new boat was curious to look at. The lower part was a sort of flat-bottomed river punt, chosen because it looked the simplest of all the designs in a little book called *How to Build Canoes, Dinghies, and Sailing Punts*. Then, after a few trials, it 'sort of grew upwards' as he gave it more freeboard, some decking, a great iron centreboard bought for five shillings from a junk dealer, and a proper mast and sail.

Everything was chosen for cheapness. She was built of match-boarding, fastened with iron screws and nails, and the rudder hangings – bought at a time when financial difficulties were unusually pressing – were a couple of iron gate hinges. But she was strong, and she sailed – she even sailed well. Also, she proved stiff and seaworthy, and carried him, sometimes alone and sometimes with a school friend, all over the Solent and into every corner of the shallow, marshy backwaters of Portsmouth, Langstone and Chichester Harbours. In the summer, the boy would often disappear from home for days at a time, spending each night sleeping in the boat with a tent rigged over it, anchored in some quiet creek or tucked in among the clumps of sea grass on the mud flats.

His mother soon learnt that he was able to look after himself. 'I knew,' she says, 'that he would always turn up' – just as she was to say when, before long, he disappeared on a mission much more perilous.

A few years later, when serving in the Royal Marines as a second lieutenant, he bought a good twelve-foot centreboard sailing dinghy, and cruised single-handed in her from Plymouth to Portsmouth, a stretch of 180 miles of open coast, in five and a half days, hauling the boat up on open beaches for the night if there was no harbour adjacent, and waking to the rustle of the restless shingle and the cry of the seabirds overhead. A few months later he made the return passage in six days, and by this time there was scarcely a mile of this coast that he did not know by heart. He learnt how the current set from Selsey Bill to the Needles, and how the sea built up into dangerous tide-races at Start Point, at St Albans and above all at the dreaded Portland Bill. He learnt the signs of cloud and wind and

> All the swift importings
> On the wilful face of skies.

The impulse of the moving waters was in his veins.

Together with this passion went an ardour for contriving and devising things. He was not content to accept things ready-made, but worked them out for himself, and they had to pass every test. He was fascinated by 'all trades, their gear and tackle and trim'. He loved making things with his own hands, from the beginning up, and to whatever problem he turned – whether it was a point of ceremonial drill, the rig of a dinghy, the fastenings of a ski, the modifications of a car, the diet needed for a long cruise – he devoted to it an intensity and singleness of purpose that was not satisfied with any ready-offered solution but impelled him to probe the smallest details of invention, whether it were a screw, a cord, a strap or a grain of wheat.

All this means that Hasler was, and remained, very much an individualist; in both senses of the term, he liked to paddle his own canoe.

Early in this year of 1942 Major Hasler was twenty-eight years old, some six feet tall, of a strongly-built frame and a spare, athletic mould, with pale red-gold hair, most of which he had already lost, and a flowing mane of a moustache of the same colour; these had earned for him throughout the Corps the name of 'Blondie'. He had just become (26 January) a member of a small team, based on Southsea and under the command of Captain T. A. Hussey RN, known as Combined Operations Development Centre (CODC), where he was able to do the sort of work he enjoyed. Under its earlier title of Inter-Services Training and Development Centre, this little body, with great foresight and acuteness of judgment, but no money, had prepared excellent paper plans before the war and had evolved the first of the assault landing craft that were to prove so valuable.

The special task to which Hasler was assigned was the study

and development of all methods of attacking enemy ships in harbour by stealth. He had already, in the previous year, written a paper on methods of attacking enemy ships by canoe and underwater swimmers, but he was before his time and the equipment did not exist. The paper was rejected by Combined Ops. Then the Italians had set us all thinking by their attack on our ships in Alexandria Harbour with 'human torpedoes', when they had seriously damaged HMS *Queen Elizabeth* and *Valiant* on 19 December 1941. Earlier still (26 March 1941), with somewhat different equipment, they had damaged the cruiser *York* and the Norwegian tanker *Pericles* in the Mediterranean and they had been pursuing guerrilla warfare against merchant shipping lying off Gibraltar. Someone at Combined Ops then remembered Hasler's paper and he was sent for.

*

All this dark and deadly realm of sea-wolf warfare – human torpedoes, explosive boats, underwater wreckers, miniature submarines and so on – was by no means unknown to the Admiralty, but hitherto the Navy had had small use for such methods of guerrilla warfare. Not so the Italians. Ever since 1935 they had been actively experimenting with such toys, under the original stimulus mainly of Commander Belloni; and after Mussolini, stealing in jackal fashion upon the trail of the lion Hitler, when the fight seemed to be all over and done with, declared his claim to share the carcase of a dying Europe, they pursued their hazardous experiments with ingenuity and daring. It was the only element in which the Italian navy was to distinguish itself. A small band of officers of lively inventive ability and fighting spirit found in this marauder type of warfare their adventurous vocation. They were the originators of many diverse methods of attack by surface and underwater swimmers as well as of midget craft. Throughout the war they were a lap ahead of us in all these methods of attack, and indeed sometimes we were reduced to copying Italian equipment and technique after it had been successfully used against us. For some years a bold group of these men carried out periodical underwater sorties against Allied shipping at Gibraltar, launching their raids, unknown to the Spaniards as to ourselves, from their secret lair in the hull of the interned *Olterra* at Algeciras, whence they crept out by way of doors cut in the ship's side underwater.

Fortunately for us, the Italian technique and equipment were partly counterbalanced by their faulty intelligence and their inefficient planning. These failings were starkly illuminated in the shining fiasco of their mass raid on Malta, when a small armada of pigmy craft, including nearly every weapon that they had developed, left Sicily to attack Grand Harbour. They were picked up by our shore-based radar while yet a long way off, and by the time that they were assembled outside the boom in the dark, every finger of our defences was on its trigger. No attacker succeeded in penetrating the harbour and no Italian boat got away.

The very first day of Hasler's joining CODC he went to Gosport with Hussey to inspect the Italian 'explosive motorboat' which we had captured during the enemy's attack on Crete. The next day he visited COHQ and had an interview with Mountbatten himself. Tom Hussey introduced him.

'Well,' said Mountbatten, 'we've got you in because you know a lot about small boats and seem to have some ideas about using them. Are you keen to have a shot at the job?'

'Very keen, Sir,' replied Hasler eagerly.

'Good. I'm sure you are going to fit in well at the CODC under Captain Hussey, and I'm sure we shall get some results out of you soon.'

He then read and approved the proposed terms of reference that Hasler had drafted. These were to study, co-ordinate and develop all methods of stealthy seaborne attack by very small parties. 'In particular,' said Mountbatten, 'you will be responsible, under Captain Hussey, for the development of a British version of the explosive motorboat, and pay particular attention to methods of attacking ships in harbour.'

It was the first time that Hasler had met Mountbatten. He at once became devoted to him and ever remained so. Mountbatten's open-mindedness appealed to him and his sporting approach to every difficulty captivated him. Mountbatten, he found, never played for safety, never cramped other people's ideas, and always kept his eyes resolutely on the objective instead of on the difficulties in front of it.

Hasler therefore plunged into the uncertain waters of his new mission with delight. He gave to it also that meticulous attention to detail that characterized anything he undertook. He had an inquisitive mind and his thought was orderly and disciplined. He had also great energy and a frame not easily fatigued. He examined all sorts of devices and travelled far and wide to see various specialists both military and civilian. He was supplied with a small 'Experimental Party' for his work at Southsea and these he had to train. In accordance with his instructions, he was occupied at first with the 'explosive boat', working closely in touch with Vosper's, the boatbuilders, in bringing out the British version of it.

The Italian invention was a high-speed planing motorboat, carrying a formidable 500-lb charge in the bows. The pilot, having aimed the boat at his target, pulled a lever and was ejected over the stern together with a folding raft, on to which he climbed to avoid being killed by the subsequent underwater concussion. Italian operators, after this acrobatic performance, gave themselves up as prisoners – indeed they could do little else – but this idea was abhorrent to us, and our plan was to provide the man with some means of escape, however difficult. Our own version on which Vosper's were now working was very soon given the code-name of Boom Patrol Boat (BPB).

There was also a new device called a 'chariot', which was the British version of the Italian 'human torpedo'. This was a slow-speed torpedo-shaped underwater craft, manned by two men sitting astride it. They attacked the enemy ship under water, attached the 500-lb charge to the bilge-keel and then withdrew on the remaining portion of the machine – or if Italians, scuttled it and surrendered.

Whatever kind of device was to be used in this dangerous kind of game, Hasler was faced very early with the problem of how any such craft were to be transported to within a measurable distance of their objective. At a very early stage he was examining various kinds of air transport. Air approach had many disadvantages, but it had valuable potentialities for launching small craft and swimmers close to their objective, in waters that no surface ship or submarine could penetrate. He had frequent discussions with the RAF and with civilian designers.

A feature of our version of the explosive motorboat was that it was designed to be dropped by a huge trefoil parachute, with its driver strapped inside it cheek by jowl with the 500-lb explosive charge. Numerous trials, which Hasler attended, were carried out of this parachute and the release equipment, some of them successful, but later in the war Lieutenant David Cox, of Hasler's unit, was awarded a more than merited MBE for being the first man to carry out a live drop in this alarming equipment. The parachute development was being handled by Raymond (now Sir Raymond) Quilter, the dynamic head of G.Q. Parachutes Ltd, and himself a celebrated parachutist.

Hasler went to Avro's to see if the explosive boat could be loaded into a Lancaster, to Slingsby Sailplanes, to Airspeed and to the Parachute Training Centre. Commander (E) Peter Du Cane, Managing Director of Vosper's and a member of COHQ scientific staff, was his frequent companion in these enquiries and tests. Together they also made dropping tests from derricks to discover the height at which a boat of about the same weight as the BPB could be dropped on to the surface of the water without breaking up. The BPB remained for a long time in a state of infancy, largely because we were not content to accept the Italian idea of surrender.

An even more dangerous toy was the Rotachute, which was at that time under development by the RAF. This was a parachute that used free-spinning rotor blades, like an autogyro, instead of a canopy. It was intended to enable a parachutist to glide down at a steep angle, with some control over his course and selection of landing place. Hasler attended many conferences and tests on the Rotachute. 'But I only knew,' he said, 'one RAF officer brave enough to fly the thing and after a trial demonstration flight he had to use both hands to hold a glass.'

Extract from Hasler's diary:

> *11th March, 1942.* A.m. at CCO's offices. Saw Lushington re Trondheim and studied data. Tried idea of explosive tadpole on Hussey – NOT well received . . .

But all the time that he was investigating the explosive motorboat, Hasler's thoughts were never far from the canoe. To many it may well appear fantastic that so small and frail a craft as a canoe should be considered to have any important place in modern war. It savours rather of quiet backwaters and summer streams under slumbrous foliage; and if it savours also of boyhood Red Indians, that was a long time ago and was of a piece with bows and arrows. So, in some distant century, may future warriors perhaps look back and find again a warlike use for the horse. The canoe, besides being frail, is slow, cannot ride out a rough sea, nor make headway against a strong current, nor carry a heavy load. But, to Hasler, and to many others dwelling on the same problems, its very defects were to its advantage. If small, it is inconspicuous; if underpowered, silent; if frail, light enough for men to carry. These were the very qualities needed for stealthy penetration into enemy waters. Unseen, unheard, the canoe could carry men who had the wits, the cunning and the daring into many a fastness where a big ship, with all its guns, would have no chance to penetrate.

Hasler's rejected proposals of 1941 had already specified the use of canoes. Now he found that various 'private armies' both in England and in the Middle East, had been employing canoes for clandestine operations against enemy coasts. Among the highly individual personalities who had led these sorties were Lieutenant-Commander Nigel Willmott, Major Roger Courtney (the big-game hunter) and Captain Gerald Montanaro; and one of Hasler's early tasks was to seek out these elusive people and learn what he could from them. For the most part, he found that they had been using canoes of a German type called a 'Folbot', covered with a rubberized fabric skin stretched over a wooden frame. They could be dismantled and packed into two or three large kitbags, but the process of reassembling them was not a rapid one, especially on a dark night. They also, for Hasler's purposes, had other disadvantages: they could not be dragged over a beach without tearing the skin, and, since they were not rigid, they could not be lifted and carried if loaded with heavy equipment without straining the frame. Nor would they go, as might be required, down the torpedo hatch of a submarine without being partly dismantled.

For these reasons Hasler made an exhaustive study of all known types of canoe available in England, including the German 'Klepper', Canadian canoes, types that raced in peace-time under the auspices of the Royal Canoe Club, and the Eskimo kayak, in which he was specially interested and over which, later, he had a long and important discussion with Professor Debenham of the Scott Polar Research Institute at Cambridge, where they had an authentic kayak with full equipment.

None of them showed the characteristics that Hasler was looking for, particularly in respect of stowage in the limited space inside a submarine and launching through its circular torpedo hatch, which was only about twenty-nine inches in diameter. He therefore came to the conclusion that it would be necessary to develop a new design of canoe for his purposes.

Of all the adventurous characters whom he met, he learnt most, probably, from Gerald Montanaro, a Regular officer of the Royal Engineers who combined an adventurous spirit with remarkable technical qualifications. He was one of the earliest of all war-time canoeists, and his men, who had all been hand-picked early in the war from Commando units of the First Special Service Brigade, had already undergone long and rigorous training in Scottish waters, learning to handle their craft (of the Folbot type) in strong currents under the most arduous conditions of weather and learning to move by night and remain concealed all day, sometimes nearly up to their necks in water. They had made great progress in navigational methods and evolved their own technique of attacking enemy ships with 'limpet' magnetic mines, which they attached to the hull of an enemy ship below the waterline by means of a six-foot rod. They had also evolved a magnetic holdfast by which they clung to the enemy ship while carrying out the operation. They had developed their own camouflage technique, using an 'octopus suit' and reversible flaps for the canoes by which they could instantaneously change their colour outlines from light to dark when they came to the critical angle of sight of a sentry standing on a quay or ship. Montanaro himself later underwent an extraordinary metamorphosis from Captain RE to Lieutenant-Commander RN for three years, an example that must have been without parallel, and he also did some very interesting work on a submersible mothership for raiding canoes called the Mobile Flotation Unit, these craft forming part of a Naval flotilla under Montanaro's command.

Montanaro's 'private army' – 101 Troop of the Army Commandos – paid a visit to Portsmouth early in 1942 and Hasler saw something of them. When his ideas began to crystallize he paid a return visit to them in Dover, where another part of the unit had been transferred and whence Montanaro himself carried out a brilliant raid on Boulogne Harbour, in which he plastered a large enemy tanker with limpets and sank her.

The Folbot type of canoe which Montanaro used, and which according to Combined Ops classification appears to have been the Cockle Mark I, did not interest Hasler. What interested him most was Montanaro's method of attack with limpet and placing-rod. On 31 March 101 Troop laid on a special attack demonstration for him in Dover Harbour and the same night Hasler himself did a two-hour exercise with the boat in the dark.

On his return from Dover, Hasler, his ideas now crystallized, went at once to see Hussey and told him what he had seen and that he wanted a new type of canoe without the disadvantages of the Folbot – a strong craft, with flat, rigid bottom that could be hauled over shingle and lifted up, fully loaded, without breaking its back. On Hussey's advice he took his problem to Mr Fred Goatley, the Works Manager of Saro Laminated Woodwork Ltd, who had just won a War Office competition for the design of a new river-crossing assault boat, and whom Hasler had already met a few days before. Thus, from the marriage of these two minds, was born the famous Cockle Mark II, whose achievements are the loom on which the fabric of this chronicle is woven.

The Cockle Mark II was soon under construction and a prototype or pilot model produced. During the next few months Hasler carried out exhaustive and stringent tests of it in all conditions, making improvements little by little in conjunction with Goatley, and it was some time before a 'production model' was available to the unit that was formed later on. We shall have a close look at this famous Cockle Mark II in due time.

'Cockle' was a name to which Hasler always had a strong objection and at one time he wrote an indignant letter about it. To him it seemed contemptuous and derisory, but today, like 'tank' in the First World War, it has won an honourable meaning in men's minds.

Boats, however, were by no means the only objects of study. Closely associated with them was the new craft of 'operational swimming'. To many people today, when the waters of the world's seaside resorts are made horrid with youths and maidens arrayed in ghoulish masks and the very water is made perilous by the darting spears of fish-hunters, it may seem hard to realize that such antics were merely beginning to be known in 1942, and harder still to apprehend how dangerous were the early attempts at them. Although 'swim fins' had been in use in California just before the war, and although at some time we sent an inter-Service party there to study them, Hasler had never heard of them until he received a pair captured from the Italians who had raided Alexandria. Until that moment, operational swimming, whether on the surface or underwater, involved using the traditional breast stroke. Underwater swimming had interested him for many years, and in addition to his other talents he was a qualified diver, both in the conventional heavy diver's dress with air hose and leaden boots, and in the celebrated Davis Submerged Escape Apparatus, which, with its oxygen supply, enables men to escape from sunken submarines.

To Sir Robert Davis, inventor of the DSEA gear and one of the world's foremost authorities on diving, Hasler paid an early visit. He asked him whether he considered it feasible for a man to swim underwater in the gear. Sir Robert replied: 'Perhaps a few strokes, but not for any distance.' The invention of the swim fins was to revolutionize this state of affairs and before very long, when the summer evenings came, one of Hasler's relaxations was to put on fins and a DSEA set, arm himself with a home-made spear and prowl about along the bottom of the Solent, off Southsea, searching for flatfish in the cloudy water. It was also possible, he found, to catch pipefish (a close relative of the sea-horse) by hand and bring them home to dry off as amusing ornaments for desk or shelf.

Extracts from Hasler's diary:

19th March, 1942. A.m. to office by motorcycle. 1000, left for Blockhouse. Discussed 'chariot' equipment with Shelford. Had dip in tank, using Italian mask on DSEA. Used escape chamber for the first time. Lunch at Blockhouse. P.m. had a look at torpedo hatch of 'H' class submarine. Discussed submersion and trimming with Shelford. Returned to office at 1530. Evening – sunshades.*

13th April, 1942. To office by motorcycle. 1045, visited Dr Powell re explosive effects. 1130, train from Havant. 1430, visited Cdr Shears re supersonic defence, Godwin re German MTB carrier and Todhunter re Cockles. 1600, discussion with Alan Muntz and Baynes re glider wing for COHQ. Saw Price re Special Boat Section organization. 1845, train back, picked up staff car and brought it home.

15th April, 1942. Started paper on BPBs. . . . a.m. Experimental Party swimming and dishing up inflatable boat. P.m. rough-water launching and testing new camouflage cream.

22nd April, 1942. . . . Went down in the 'Chariot' suit in 20 ft of water in the Basin.

A busy and varied life. On 26 April he recorded:

Set out for 2 hours in 'Cranthorpe' – boom dodging and warping off in smart S.E. wind. Glorious day. Got arrested on arrival back.

We have seen that on 15 April Hasler 'started on BPBs'. This was an important development paper that Hussey was anxious to present to COHQ, summing up the situation as it stood and proposing the future lines of development. It laid special emphasis on the need to develop means of transporting and launching the BPB by air, while the boat itself was under construction and trial at Vosper's. This kind of document caused Hasler much sweat and anguish, but out of it was born a great idea.

Finally, after it had been amended and approved by Hussey, he took the paper to COHQ personally and elaborated verbally on the matter of transport by air. A definite stage had been reached.

The next morning, back at Southsea, from the bright heaven of invention an idea shone out. The diary records:

Birth of embryo idea for more Active Service role for yours truly (in bath).

He was not attracted by the idea of hanging on for ever in an

* An invention of his own for waterproofing vehicles.

experimental unit. After experiment should come operation. 'Here,' he said to himself as he bathed, 'is a new weapon, a very specified weapon. But who is going to man it? There is not any existing unit suited to it – why not yours truly?

Fired with this idea, he discussed it with Hussey, who agreed that the formation of a unit to develop the tactical use of this and other craft was a logical and necessary development.

'There is also this point, sir,' Hasler added. 'I don't see how these BPBs are going to act on their own against an enemy harbour if they have to pass over any surface obstruction like a boom in the dark.'

'What do you suggest, then?'

'I think there should be a unit which includes canoes as well as BPBs. The canoe could do two things – it could clear surface obstructions and it could take the chaps off after they had fired their charges.'

After a little thought, Hussey said:

'Well, why not form a Royal Marine unit to run the thing?'

'That's just what I'd like, sir.'

'We should have, of course, to invent some apparent reason or excuse for the existence of a unit of that kind.'

'A cover-name of some sort?'

'Yes. If these things are buzzing about all over the Solent, a lot of people will ask what are they supposed to be doing? We are calling these things Boom Patrol Boats; so the obvious thing seems to be to form a unit for patrolling the boom. We could call it the Royal Marine Harbour Patrol, or something of the sort.'

They discussed it further and Hussey said:

'You had better shoot up to COHQ and see if you can put it over.'

Hasler shot. On 24 April he saw Lushington and 'put across the basic idea'.

He had to fight for it, however, not only seeing COHQ repeatedly, but also bidding for the support of the Commander-in-Chief Portsmouth by emphasizing that the proposed unit would have 'a genuine defence role'. The proposals, which were for a unit with the title of Royal Marines Harbour Patrol Detachment, were put formally into writing on 12 May by Lieutenant-Colonel

H. F. G. Langley RA, who was then commanding CODC. This paper emphasized that the BPB (still not evolved) had difficulty in negotiating boom defences and could not pass over surface obstructions in the darkness without assistance.

To overcome this, it was proposed 'to develop Cockles in conjunction with the BPB'. The Cockle was to accompany the BPB to clear surface obstructions, using either explosive or silent cutters. It was then to follow up the BPB to its target area and take off the driver of it after he had shot his bolt. Both craft could also, of course, act independently for certain operations, and the men in the proposed unit would be trained in both. The highest standard of individual morale was needed when the men were selected.

Then we read, on 20 May:

> To office by motorcycle. 1100, Goatley arrived for a discussion on modifications to Mk II Cockle. Caught 1324 train without having had time for lunch and proceeded to Manchester with Laidlaw, calling at COHQ and DTSO on the way through London. Heard the glad news that ALL our BPB proposals had been approved. Slept at Antrim Hotel, Manchester.

Mountbatten personally approved the proposals but with the title of the unit amended to 'Royal Marine Boom Patrol Detachment', and forwarded them to the Director of Training and Staff Duties at the Admiralty on 26 May.

Hasler therefore threw himself ardently into a course of self-training – not only in the handling of the craft in all conditions, but also in physical endurance and in the vital business of learning the technique of stealth. For it was obvious that, if you were intending to get right inside an enemy harbour, and get away again safely, you must do so unobserved by the most vigilant eyes and ears. So, night after night, Hasler went out alone in a canoe or in his own sailing dinghy into the dark waters. Twice he was arrested by patrol boats, but on 4 June he successfully made an all-night patrol and got ashore unchallenged. He practised the 'stealthy approach' on land also. He went for long walks, kept up his swimming and took revolver and Bren-gun practice.

All the time he was thinking out and testing new ideas in the technique of using canoes and the explosive boat and worrying over endless detail – the right sort of varnish for the boat, camouflage cream for the men's faces, fluorescent paint for locating important pieces of equipment in the dark, how to eat, sleep and relax while spending the whole day concealed in a hedge under a camouflage net, what shape of paddle showed the least silhouette and was best for pushing a canoe off the beach, how to navigate without chart table or instruments, how to make signals to other boats in the dark, and so on.

This was the period when the fortune of the Allies all over the world was at its lowest ebb. Tobruk fell on 2 June and by the end of the month our Desert Army had been forced back to the Alamein line. The Germans were continuing their conquering way through South Russia. The U-boat sinkings in the Atlantic reached their maximum, attaining a figure of 627,000 tons in June, two-thirds of them off the American coast, whose waters the enemy ravaged almost uncontrolled. In Asia the Japanese had swept right up to the gates of India.

It is at times when fortune is at its lowest that the thoughts of commanders, for want of any means of massive action, turn to such operations as small-scale raiding. If you cannot knock out with a bludgeon, you can still hurt with many needle-pricks. So it had been in the Desert, where the audacious 'Jock Columns', ranging far and wide, damaged and worried the enemy, though with no tactical effect. For a like reason the Italians had developed their small clandestine craft to make good the failure of their larger forces. For us, during the period while in Western Europe we were obliged to remain largely on the defensive, they were a means of making offensive sallies, of damaging the enemy's technical equipment and of discovering information of his dispositions.

3. 'HASLER'S PARTY'

The new unit came into being officially on 6 July under the title of the Royal Marine Boom Patrol Detachment. It was a great day, for from this tiny spring significant waters were to flow. It so happened, quite by chance, that at this period the problem of the blockade runners, on which Lord Selborne had written to Mr Attlee on 22 June, had just reached COHQ and had been before their Examination Committee, who had considered it on 1 July and rejected it as a full-scale combined operation.

The new unit numbered only thirty-four Royal Marines all ranks, but before the war ended one man in every five was to be decorated and the lessons that it established were to be embodied in the permanent teaching, training and equipment of the Royal Marines.

Other units of both Army and Navy were also working or experimenting with canoes and other small craft. There were the Royal Marine and the Army Commandos, from which branched the Small Scale Raiding Commando and the Special Boat Section. There was Montanaro's unit, there were, later, the naval Combined Operations Pilotage Parties that did such brilliant reconnaissance work under Nigel Willmott, and there were the Chariot and X-craft Parties under the Admiral (Submarines). But the work of Hasler's RMBPD was to have its own special significance and interest.

After approval of the formation of the RMBPD had been given, a call was sent out by the Royal Marines Office at the Admiralty for 'volunteers for hazardous service'. The call had been for men 'eager to engage the enemy', 'indifferent to personal safety', 'free of strong family ties'. The response was prompt, but not overwhelming, for most of the adventurous men in the Corps had already volunteered for Commando service. It embraced all sorts and conditions of men, including, as always happens on such occasions, a certain number of scallywags, for in the armed services there are always types of men to whom military discipline is irksome but who are ready for colourful adventure, especially if it promises to bear something of a piratical nature. The 'private army' or 'private navy' is always looked upon with suspicion by generals, admirals and the like, and rightly so, for if these things became a law unto themselves they have little military value and become instead a military nuisance. But when they are under proper control and directed to a particular purpose they can be valuable aids to a commander's intent, as was shown by the Long Range Desert Group, by Wingate's Chindit jungle-fighters, and by others. Hasler, as a Regular officer, bred in a Corps with the highest possible traditions of steadfast discipline and soldierly bearing and behaviour, had no intention that his new unit should become a gang of pirates. There was a deadly serious task to be done and their training must also be deadly serious. But he did require a special type of man, and from among those who volunteered he selected his officers and marines with great care.

He wanted no 'taproom commandos', nor film-type 'tough guys', who too often prove soft inside when scratched. 'Care I for the limb, the thews, the stature, bulk, and big assemblage of a man? Give me the spirit, Master Shallow.' Your really tough man under stress is more often of homely and simple exterior, and nearly always modest. What Hasler wanted was young men, unmarried, who were individualists with natural intelligence and a fighting spirit, men who perhaps had had to bear a little rough-and-tumble in the struggle of life and who would have developed resourcefulness and self-reliance. From the very beginning such men would have to face the likelihood that they might find themselves working alone inside enemy territory, where their mission and their lives might depend as much on their own wits as upon their training.

Before the unit was formed he had already fixed on his second-in-command – Captain J. D. Stewart, who had served with him in the Royal Marines Fortress Unit in Norway, and in whom he saw all the qualities that he needed for a No. 2. 'Jock' Stewart was a London-bred Scot, dark-haired and of strong physique (though he was to suffer in due time from the constant exposure and immersions that were to be the lot of all these hardy and adventurous young men). Besides his physical aptitude for the task, he had the steady solidity and administrative competence that are so useful in a 2 i/c, and it was to be found that, as a learner himself, he was invaluable as a trainer of the men, whose difficulties he had experienced himself. Stewart, not a Regular officer, was in private life an advertising agent, and, although scarcely any older than Hasler's twenty-eight years, he was known as 'the old man' among all these high-spirited youngsters. He won the entire admiration of the men, for, although they knew right well that his lot was mainly 'admin', he willingly participated in the full rigour of their training. He never 'ducked out' of anything but laughed and came back for more. In consequence, as Sergeant King said, 'he got a brand of loyalty that was reserved for him alone'.

There were, at first, only two other executive officers, each of whom was to command one of the two operational sections into which the unit was divided. One of these was Lieutenant J. W. Mackinnon, who was put in command of No. 1 Section. He came from Glasgow of a humble home, his father being a groundsman, and before joining the Royal Marines he had been employed in a coal merchant's office. Jack Mackinnon was quite an exceptional young man. A little below medium height, broad and athletic, brown-haired, he was full of fun and bursting with keenness. He was a scout master, very fond of open-air life, a good swimmer and played all games with ardour. Indeed, he did all things with ardour. He had served in the ranks before earning a commission, and had passed out of the officer training school almost at the top of his course – a fine achievement for a lad of his origin. His qualities of initiative were strongly developed, backed by imagination and natural intelligence. A patriot to his fingertips, Mac would dare anything with a laugh and was dying to get into action against the enemy. He drank little, smoked not at all, yet had a passion for enjoyment, and when the unit had a 'party', as it frequently did, he always played the jazz drums. He was a fine messmate and everybody loved him. In training matters he could be quite 'tough' with the troops, taking them out to sea in an assault boat and from time to time ordering: 'Over the side, So-

and-so', whether they could swim or not, and making all alike dive or jump from an extemporized diving-board erected on the boom. 'So we were not,' says Eric Fisher, 'non-swimmers very long!' A jolly, debonair and bonny fighter was Mac. 'He was,' says Hasler, 'a terribly nice boy – a real gem.' There could be no better epitaph.

No. 2 Section was commanded by Lieutenant W. H. A. Pritchard-Gordon, a tall, dark and good-looking young officer of dash and polish, educated at Shrewsbury. He was a fine athlete and there was keen rivalry among all ranks to see who could do things better than he could, but he was more fleet of foot, swift of arm and keen of eye than most of them. He does not come much into our story, and his special interest, at this stage, is that he and Mackinnon, who had done their young officer training together, were ardent and inseparable friends.

The sergeant-major of this band of brothers was Colour-Sergeant W. J. Edwards. He was a Regular soldier recalled from the reserve and was a steadying influence and a great help to the other NCOs. 'He kept sanity in our ranks,' says Sergeant King, 'when we ran amok; and although he sometimes had to hound us, he also helped us no end.' To his peers he was known as 'Bungy'.

There were only seven other Regulars. One of them, Sergeant Samuel Wallace, senior NCO of No. 1 Section, we shall meet more intimately later on; but we may note here that, as a Marine of twelve years' service, 'Sailor' Wallace was a tower of strength to young Mackinnon, to whom he was quite devoted. He told his sister: 'I would follow Major Hasler and Mr Mac anywhere in the world.' They made a splendid combination, this eager-spirited young officer and the handsome, friendly sergeant, who was tremendously looked up to by the men who, by his cheerful example and his light-hearted rallying of men at times of strain, was a potent influence in creating that high-spirited morale for which the unit became famous. When the Royal Marines Office at the Admiralty wanted to ascertain how long a man could keep afloat in the sea in full marching order, it was Wallace who at once came forward and jumped in, steel helmet and all, and kept going for nearly five minutes before he sank.

In No. 2 Section, under Pritchard-Gordon, there was Sergeant

J. M. King, who had a specially important part to play as P.T. Instructor and who, together with Marine P. N. Ruff, was later to win the Distinguished Service Medal in the raid on Leros. Other Regulars were Corporal Robert Johnson, Corporal Evans, Marine Lawrence Ashton and the very young Corporal Laver, of whom we shall hear a great deal – a quiet, stocky fellow of great physical stamina and with little more service than the non-Regulars.

To the sergeant-major and the other Regular NCOs fell naturally the task of instilling and maintaining the normal disciplines of behaviour and turn-out among the lads who gathered together that war-time summer. One thing the sergeant-major was careful to impress on all – 'If you do have to come up for punishment before Major Hasler,' he said, 'you may expect the punishment to be severe; but in this unit we do not expect you ever to come up.'

For it was very soon learnt that Hasler, in spite of the way he drove himself, was a kindly man. 'I can never,' he said, 'bring myself to punish anyone if it can possibly be avoided.' Indeed, it was himself that he punished the most. He regarded troops as being creatures who needed rather to be encouraged, like overgrown boys, as long as there was any hope that they would improve without punishment. He expected a great deal from his men, but he knew that they were in for an exacting time and so long as they put their heart and soul into their training, he was pleased. He was immensely admired throughout the unit, for they saw in him a complete master of his craft, who could do everything better than they could and who always insisted, before expecting them to undertake any hazard, overcome any difficulty or practise any kind of equipment, weapon or action, on doing so himself first. If circumstances prevented him from doing so, then Jock Stewart had to be the first to face the bowling.

The men who gathered together that critical July were not, to the eye, any collection of supermen. 'They were,' says Hasler, 'just a good cross-section of average young fellows, and we had to do the best we could with what was offered to us.' It was odd, perhaps, that for this task for which they were to be trained, not one had had any experience of small boats. Hasler liked the types of men who came forward, but he very much regretted this lack of boating experience: it would make training so much the longer. Stewart said to him:

'Surely there must be plenty of men in the Commando Brigade who have small-boat knowledge?'

'There are,' Hasler answered, 'but they won't be allowed to volunteer for us. They have to do boat work themselves.'

'I suppose that everyone with a knowledge of boats is already doing a boating job?'

'So far as the Corps is concerned, yes, but what is maddening is that there must be thousands of keen young yachtsmen wasting their time in the Army and the RAF, but of course we can't tap them.'

Some of these volunteers could not even swim, and some never learnt, though Marine Turfrey was to show, paradoxically, that it was not necessary to be a surface swimmer to become a competent underwater 'frogman'. Marine Eric Fisher was another such example; Mackinnon taught him to swim only tolerably on the surface, but below water he became really efficient. On the other hand, husky Marine Ellery, a really fine surface swimmer, hated the underwater gear and its claustrophobic effects and could make no headway.

The officers were as ignorant as the men, and one of Hasler's problems was that there was no instructor in boat work but himself. As he had to spend a great deal of time on development, worrying out all sorts of problems, and later on operational planning, this was a serious difficulty. Those who should be instructors had themselves to be instructed and at first Hasler had to take the whole unit in a single class for many subjects, instructors and all, or else somehow to get the instructors together while the rest were kicking their heels – not an ideal system of training. However, he was able to get his officers and a nucleus of others together for three weeks before the main body of troops arrived on 23 July and to put them through a stiff initiation; later on he found that he was able to leave a great deal of the training to Jock Stewart. It was greatly to the credit of these young officers, especially as they lived on such very close and intimate terms with the men, that in these circumstances they sustained their positions as leaders. But Pritchard-Gordon and Mackinnon were both above the average – intelligent, tremendously keen, good leaders and good mess-mates.

Initially, there was the problem of how much this 'private army' should conform to conventional military practices, habits and disciplines. Hasler, less of an expert in men than in things, therefore paid an early visit to Lieutenant-Colonel J. P. Phillipps, who was then training the first Royal Marines Commando in the Isle of Wight, and who was soon to be killed leading his Commando into action in the Dieppe Raid. 'Tigger', one of the Picton Phillipps' family long known in the Corps, was a very fine type of officer, and Hasler, who, as a subaltern, had served under him in HMS *Queen Elizabeth*, now came to ask his advice. Phillipps said that in his opinion it was essential to maintain forms of parade-ground discipline in all units of this sort, since the traditional forms of training developed instincts that came naturally into play when in action. Troops who do not instantly obey their leaders or remain steady on parade are not likely to obey or remain steady in battle. Hasler therefore decided to follow this course, nor was it discordant with his own instincts, for he had always himself been a model on the parade-ground and had often been specially selected for those ceremonial drills for which the Royal Marines have a standard and a reputation surpassed by none. In the new unit, therefore, parade-ground behaviour and the traditional bearing of the Royal Marines became a necessary formative part of the curriculum, in which the teaching of the Regular NCOs, such as Wallace and King, had a lively and positive influence.

From the very first, the RMBPD was a completely happy unit and developed a tremendous spirit and pride in themselves. They looked on themselves as something very special and set apart from the rest. Their superlative physical fitness was one of the mainsprings of this pride, as it always is. Though routine drills filled only a small part of the weekly training programme, the Regulars in the unit led the way in setting an example, which was followed eagerly by those known in the Corps as 'HOs' or 'hostilities only'. When they marched into Eastney Barracks they took a particular pride in displaying that style and polish which made them look like a squad of Regulars. They used to attend barracks for lessons at the Signals School, and as their programme was pretty tight,

Sergeant Wallace devised for them a special rapid march, which they all delighted in and called the 'Southsea Stroll'. People in barracks used to say: 'Here comes Hasler's Party', and the name stuck, a symbol of unit pride and of the good name they made. Their turn-out off duty was nearly always excellent and they held their heads high. Yet they wore no distinguishing marks. Though they all in due course, in addition to their other accomplishments, became qualified parachute-jumpers (with exceptionally high marks), they did not until much later wear the parachutist's wings; nor did they wear the admired green beret of the Commandos. They were sufficient to themselves.

This smartness and self-pride were encouraged. Hasler thought, by the fact that they did not sleep in barracks but lived out in the Commando subsistence scheme; it gave them not only greater independence but also greater responsibility, as well as removing some tedious administrative work in the unit. When off duty they wore the handsome 'blues' of His Majesty's Jollies – a tremendous stimulus to a smart bearing. Service 'welfare' had no placc in Hasler's Party – the men were expected to be self-reliant and look after themselves. 'I don't mind,' said Hasler, 'what you do with yourselves off duty, within reason, so long as you appear on parade next morning *fit*.' Fitness was to be the first thing above all othcrs, as we shall see presently.

One of the hostesses of these youngsters was Mrs Leonora Powell, whose husband was also in the Royal Marines – a long-service Regular – and was now at sea in HMS *Aurora*. She had a guesthouse called 'White Heather' in Worthing Road, where No. 1 Section, with whom our story is most concerned, were lodged. Mrs Powell grew very fond of them and cherishes their memory still. She had a daughter, scarcely sixteen, a girl of gentle ways and disposition and older than her tender years. When an NCO, arriving to arrange the men's lodging, advised Mrs Powell to take up her stair-carpet and put away her best blankets, Heather was furious. 'Mother,' she said, 'supposing one of them had been Dad? Should we have to take up our carpets because of him? They must have the best.'

To Heather, all these strapping young men, older than herself, became 'our boys'. If they helped to peel the potatoes, she darned their socks and mended their clothes. When anxious mothers wrote to Mrs Powell, saying that they had had no news of their sons, Heather would put paper, pen and stamped envelope in front of the delinquent and stand over him while he fulfilled his filial duty; then she would go out and post the letter herself.

She kept a sharp eye on their turn-out, too, and, trained by her father in all the old traditions, would say if anything were not right: 'That's not the way for a proper marine; just you do that again.' She idolized her father and to her there was nothing in the world like a Royal Marine.

Young as she was, there grew up a special attachment between Heather and young Robert Ewart from Glasgow. When he told his mother of his feelings for Heather, she accused him of 'kid-napping'; but when, later on, she met her in the days of her distress, Mrs Ewart understood why her son had been attracted. Theirs was a 'young love' story of an old-fashioned kind, im-mature, no doubt, but painful in the telling.

No. 2 Section, with whom, unfortunately, our story has few dealings, were lodged with Mrs Montague at 35 St Rownan's Road, where they were equally well looked after. No. 2, as they themselves admitted, were a little 'rougher' lot, but were later to do a fine job in the Middle East.

While the men lived in lodgings, the officers lived at first in Eastney Barracks, but later they rented a small furnished house in Spencer Road – No. 9 – and organized their own little mess there. Hasler himself had been living with his mother at Catherington, twelve miles out from Portsmouth, where of an evening, after the day's work, he would mow the lawn or do other tasks in the garden, which he cordially disliked. But when the mess was established he moved in there to be with the others. Whenever he had an opportunity for relaxation he would take out his own fourteen-foot sailing dinghy *Mandy*, resorting very often to various stratagems to defeat the increasingly severe war-time restrictions on private sailing. To make his excursions appear legal, he would wear a few items of uniform, and he kept a Wren's hat handy as a disguise when he wanted feminine company. No one was deceived, but the patrol boats got to know him so well that they used to say: 'There's Blondie again, out with a popsie. Shall we pull him in or look the other way?' If the breach of rules were not too flagrant, they looked with a Nelsonic eye.

Relations between officers and men in the RMBPD were of a quite unusual nature. It is much more difficult to preserve a satisfactory discipline in a small 'private army' than in a normal unit, and in Hasler's Party officers and men were thrown together particularly intimately. Their training was almost identical and when embarked, two to a canoe, each manned a paddle. Afloat, the man was his officer's mate and companion. Ashore, on exercises, they slept together, ate the same food, kept watch and watch. Yet the distinction and the mutual respect remained. They were not on 'Christian name terms', as the crews of some of the RAF bombers were. They were friendly, but strict, and at the basis of their relationship was that fact that no officer ever called on a man to do anything that he had not done first himself. It is true that the junior officers and the men used frequently to meet in the Eastney Tavern for a gay evening of song, singing 'Suda Bay' or 'On the Jetty Stands a Sailor', much to Hasler's alarm, but he did not forbid it. 'They have built up a tremendous spirit,' he said to a brother officer, 'and I think if I were to interfere, it would damage their morale. Of course, it would be disastrous with poor officers, but my officers seem to be able to fraternize like this without losing respect or lessening their authority. Still, it is a little worrying.'

He kept out of these parties himself, except for a brief appearance when specially invited. All the same, he liked an occasional party himself and every now and then would have a 'run around town' of an evening, expelling the next morning's hang-over with the exhilaration of exercise on the water and in it. Breathing pure oxygen under pressure he found to be a sovereign 'hangover' cure, and training in underwater swimming with the Davis Escape Gear at the submarine base, Blockhouse, was commonly arranged to kill two birds with one stone!

In addition to the young men destined for operational tasks, the unit had a very happy small Headquarters staff. Marine 'Dicky' Drew and Marine Jock Brown were two Regulars who were invaluable as storemen. Drew was a real old soldier. Nothing was too much trouble for him, whether it was drying your wet clothes or patching up your boat after a tip-up. He was always happy. Brown was the dourest of Scots, but as soon as he lit his pipe you knew he was going to help you. There was also 'Flash' Phelps, whose heart lay in his truck and his motorcycle and, some say, in a more tender passion. It was his boast that he was never late at a rendezvous to pick up 'the boys' after a gruelling exercise. Then there were the three Marine Officers' Attendants (MOAs), as batmen are called in the Jollies – Hoy, Todd and Oxley – and last, but far from least, there were Wren Keech, tiny, blonde, shy, but a terrific worker in the small but very busy office, and Wren Brenda Reed, the staff car driver lent from the Dockyard 'pool', who, though not a member of the unit, was attached to it for a considerable time and became a great favourite.

There was also a small naval workshop unit, whose business it was to look after the mechanically propelled boats, mainly the explosive boats; it was formed and commanded by Lieutenant (E) R. W. Ladbrook, RNVR, who had been serving before at the landing-craft base on Hayling Island. He and his ratings, who assumed a greater importance later on, were a tremendous asset to the whole team and there was no trouble to which they would not go, and no ingenuity that they would not practise to maintain and improve their equipment.

Such was the raw material from which this splendid little band of raiders was to be moulded. Their training headquarters were two Nissen huts on the sea front of Southsea, beneath the old grass ramparts of Lumps Fort, immediately at the end of the boom, and, appropriately enough, hard by Canoe Lake, where, by the providence of a beneficent Corporation, the young disport themselves in holiday time and where, indeed, Hasler himself as a boy had first learnt to handle a canoe. Their offices were just behind Canoe Lake, at 24 Dolphin Court, where they took over the luxury flat vacated by CODC, who, under Hussey, were now transferred to COHQ in London and rechristened the Directorate of Experiments. At Dolphin Court, Hasler's Party showed that, though they had no intention of following the worst precedents of private armies, they had no objection at all to seizing the benefits. As a new, uncatalogued and rather mysterious product of COHQ, of whom no one knew anything, they were in a delightful position to play off Jack against Tommy. Many of the authorities in the

Dockyard and elsewhere never really discovered that there had been a change of tenants at Dolphin Court, so Hasler's Party were always able to draw lots of 'useful stores' without any authority. Another luxury in Dolphin Court was that, whenever he felt 'frustrated', Hasler could wallow in a hot bath in a smart modern bathroom. He also discovered quite early that, oddly enough, if you needed a car you asked the Navy, but if you wanted a boat you asked the water transport section of the Royal Army Service Corps. The point was that in both instances the authorities concerned were a little out of their elements!

However, before Brenda Reed came they did have their own staff car, a legacy from CODC. It was an Army car, with an ATS driver, who was changed from time to time. Coming back late one night, Hasler said to Jock Stewart: 'I'm afraid the Army are really not giving us the cream of the ATS.'

'Why, sir, what happened – or perhaps it was a case of didn't happen?'

'Not a bit of it. She was driving me along a country road and I was sitting in the back reading a map. When a fork appeared ahead she asked, "Which way, sir?"

'I was a bit slow in answering, so she, in the absence of orders, drove straight on and rammed the car up the bank right at the road junction.'

In Southsea they lived a life curiously compounded of war and peace. While Portsmouth, with its great Naval Dockyard, can quite naturally don a war-time cloak, its neighbour Southsea is one of the most agreeable seaside resorts, with a splendid promenade and a fine beach. Nearly all this tranquil shore, however, redolent with memories of crowding holiday-makers, was a grim tangle of barbed wire and defence works, its animation suspended and its sparkle fled. Yet these were but a mask worn upon a cheerful face. There was still plenty of night bombing by the Germans, but the daytime dive-bombing was over and the immediate threat of invasion was passing. The Civil Defence organization was now fully set up and uniformed and in the country Home Guard were in great form but beginning to feel that they had been swindled out of their invasion. Civilians still lived under drastic shortages and restrictions. The night black-out was complete, petrol for private purposes was virtually non-existent, nearly everything was rationed. Yet many things of life went on much as usual. Hasler found that the early pattern 'Molotov cocktail' provided a satisfactory substitute for petrol for his motorcycle. The inns were doing a roaring trade, though there was often nothing to drink but beer, and there were plenty of dances where the uniforms of men and women gave a vicarious Strauss atmosphere to many a ballroom whence the sparkle of evening dress had departed. Civilians and Service men, despite the gloomy news from abroad and the irritation of bombing by night, were in good heart and high fettle and Hasler's men in the billets got on famously.

The task of the new unit was to train for the destruction of enemy shipping in harbour. One of its main weapons was to be the Boom Patrol Boat, but to begin with the prototype was not yet at the trials stage and the operational craft could not be ready for some time to come. Meanwhile, training was carried out in all sorts of small craft, for the first thing to do was to make all ranks efficient seagoing boatmen and navigators. If that could be achieved, they could be trained to any particular craft very quickly. Except until the war had been going on for another two years, few, if any, of either the officers or men ever really attained the standard of a first-class amateur yachtsman in seamanship or navigation. In the early days Hasler was never really confident that in a matter of seamanship or navigation, any of the officers or NCOs would ever, in a difficulty, do the right thing instinctively. This worried him a great deal, and was one reason why he trained the unit to make their approaches to an objective in formation, rather than each craft separately. However, they certainly had a lot to learn besides seamanship.

Besides the explosive Boom Patrol Boat, they trained as well in canoes, Army assault craft, surf boats, inflatable boats of all sizes, swimmers' floats and later on a creature called the 'Sleeping Beauty', or Motor Submersible Canoe. What ideas were thought up in those inspiring times! The 'Sleeping Beauty' was a brilliant idea worked up, in complete disregard of the advice of naval constructors, by the late Quentin Reeves, so recently lost to us in a dreadful accident while working on a silencer for jet aircraft. The 'Sleeping Beauty', which was the product of Special Operations

Executive at Welwyn, one of the development establishments under Professor Newitt, was an electric canoe manned by one man wearing underwater gear. The RMBPD were the main uniformed users of it and carried out many of the trials during the development period, in which one of its officers lost his life.

In spite of their ignorance, the high-spirited youngsters of Hasler's party took to all this boating with gusto. 'This,' said one of them, 'is the sort of thing we used to pay for in civvy-street; now we get it all free!' It would, however, be quite a mistake to say that they 'took to it like ducks to water', for on their very first outing they all got a bad wetting. On the first day the whole unit was at last assembled (24 July), Hasler gave them an address in the morning and then straightaway had them on the water. They were very soon in it, and the afternoon was spent in salvaging the boats, when training was again continued.

Extract from Hasler's diary:

> *24th July, 1943*: 0815–0910, addressing new troops. A.m. new troops almost drowned themselves. P.m. salvaging boats and continue training.

From the very first day it was a strictly enforced rule that all ranks when training on the water must wear life-jackets, and as a result the unit never had a casualty.

Extract from Hasler's diary:

> *26th July, 1942*. Police had removed my motorcycle, so had no breakfast. Troops doing Mk I lesson and finishing by sinking one Mk I and one 12-man assault boat, held against the boom by a spring tide. P.m. salvaged boats with Duty Section. Home early. Rural walk. To local with Adams.

4. MEET THE COCKLE

Though they were intended to train specially for the explosive boat, the unit very early, and fortunately, took to canoes.

Let us look therefore, before we go further, at the famous canoe in which our passage throughout the story will be undertaken; so far as we are concerned, we shall lose interest in the explosive BPB. It was never, in fact, used in operations.

The first month or two of the training of Hasler's Party was carried out in the old Mk I canoe, in addition to various other craft. The Mk I, they found, was always developing small leaks and broke up easily. The Mk II canoe, designed by Goatley and Hasler, was still in the prototype stage and Hasler was putting it through its trials. To simplify our story, however, let us confine our study to the Mk II, bearing in mind that it was not in use by the men until quite late. In fact it was not until the eve of their departure on their great adventure that No. 1 Section received the model that incorporated all the modifications resulting from their experiences.

The Mk II, then, was a fully-decked two-man canoe, designed to carry two men and about 150 lb of equipment through rough water. Its measurements were:

Length 16 feet, beam 28½ inches, depth 11¼ inches, collapsed depth 6 inches. Weight about 90 lb.

The beam was restricted by the need to pass the canoe, fully erected, through the forward torpedo hatch of a submarine; otherwise she would have been a few inches wider and more stable, but slightly slower.

The canoe had a flat wooden bottom of ⅛-inch plywood with shallow bilge keels, or runners, underneath, so that it could be dragged across mud, sand or shingle, fully loaded, and in rough weather launched from the beach itself.

The sides were of canvas or rubberized fabric, and the deck was of 1/8-inch plywood on rigid wooden gunwales. When folded, the sides collapsed and the deck lay flat on the bottom. Erected, the deck was held up by eight hinged struts, three each side and one each at bow and stern. The central cockpit, where the men sat, was covered by a waterproof fabric cover, held together along the centre line by spring clips which would disengage if the men started to struggle out – for example, after a capsize. The men's anorak jackets had elastic round the bottom, which fitted over the circular edge of the cockpit cover, thus making an almost watertight joint. This was very necessary, as in rough water wave tops would wash right over the deck. There was a folding breakwater on the foredeck, to help deflect water when going into a head sea.

The men sat on wooden seats only an inch or so above the plywood bottom, and had wooden back-rests attached to beams behind them. Essential gear carried in each canoe included a grid-type magnetic compass, mounted on the foredeck inside the breakwater; a bow and stern painter, for towing or securing alongside; a bailer and sponge; and at least two pairs of double paddles. These paddles were jointed in the middle, so that the two halves could be pulled apart to make two single paddles.

The normal method of propulsion was for each man to use a double paddle, the aftermost man (No. 2) keeping time with No. 1, who was in command and responsible for steering. To alter course, he would simply take two or more successive strokes on one side only; No. 2, seeing what he was doing, would do the same. When manoeuvring in crowded water, it was sometimes necessary for No. 1 to take alternate forward strokes on one side and backing strokes on the other, but whatever he did, No. 2 followed suit.

The double paddles were invariably 'feathered', that is to say the central joint was so adjusted that one blade was at right-angles to the other. The effect of this was to ensure that the upper blade, which was high in the air and coming forward on the recovery, was flat and 'feathered', thereby decreasing its wind resistance in a head wind, and creating a less noticeable silhouette.

When proceeding in double paddles it was, of course, possible for either man to stop paddling for a little while, while the other continued to propel the boat. For example, No. 1 could pause to look at his chart, or No. 2 could do some bailing.

In any case, it was standard practice to stop entirely for five minutes at the end of every hour, to rest the muscles and allow each man to make any adjustments he needed. When two or more canoes were out in company, they would 'raft up' in this hourly rest, and in a long expedition, especially at night, this was a most welcome interlude and a psychological tonic. Rafting up meant that the canoes came up all together alongside each other, holding on to each other's gunwales. The leader would give his orders to the other Nos. 1 for the next hour's course, while the Nos. 2 would exchange audible remarks with each other on the behaviour of their Nos. 1. Nor was it by any means unknown in the early days, when Hasler himself was leading and setting a stiff pace, for his No. 2, whoever he was, to be badgered by the others to hold him back by not pulling his own weight. However, Blondie was quite up to that one!

When there was danger of being observed by the enemy, the canoe 'went into single paddles'; each man separated the two halves of his paddle at the centre joint, stowed the female half on the deck beside him, where there were special hooks for it, and used the other half as a single paddle, the recovery in this case being made feathered, a few inches above the water instead of overhead. This resulted in much less silhouette, and in less noise from the drips of the blade on the recovery. The men, obviously, paddled on opposite sides, and would occasionally change sides to rest their muscles.

Single paddles were much slower, and steering a good course was more difficult, since it was no longer possible for No. 2 simply to imitate No. 1. In fact No. 1 had to use hand signals to indicate which way he wanted the boat to be steered. There was also a full series of hand signals for every other normal manoeuvre, such as 'stop', 'go on', 'change to single paddles', etc., so that it was possible to do everything in complete silence.

In rough water everything depended on the two men working together in balancing the boat. Body balance was most important. The canoe was extremely seaworthy provided it could be kept the right side up, but unlike the Eskimo kayak, it was not possible to 'roll' it back again after a capsize by a stroke of the paddle – at any rate not with two men and stores in it. When faced with heavy breaking crests, as in surf or a tide race, it was, of course, essential to keep bows-on to them. In the case of a capsize, the only thing to do was for the two men to break out of their cockpit covers underwater, and float alongside the canoe. Then, with a quick movement, to try to turn it back again without taking in too much water. They then leant over the gunwale to bail out most of the water, and climbed in over the bow or stern.

The canoe had buoyancy bags in the bow and stern, which kept it afloat when fully swamped, but in rough water it was impossible to bail out, as the waves kept washing in, and the canoe had therefore either to be abandoned or left for subsequent recovery. It was so light and buoyant that, unless well weighted down, it was almost impossible to scuttle.

Extract from Hasler's diary on the day after an all-night patrol afloat:

> *28th July, 1942*. 0500, came ashore. 0545–0645, slept. 0900, boat to Cowes. 1000–1230, with Goatley, testing new seats, backrest and cockpit cover for Mk II. The end is almost in sight, I think. Also dealing with adaptations to 12-man assault boat for pulling and outboard motor. P.m., office work till 2000. Home.

Thus the Cockle Mk II, very narrow and very low in the water, was a very inconspicuous craft. It was a craft for stealthy and unobserved movement. When in double paddles there was a very audible and unavoidable drip, but in single paddle it could move noiselessly.

To young landsmen, the navigation of these little craft, especially on a dark night in the rain, was a sore trial and oppression. To know his position, to set his course by compass, estimating the strength of a tide running diagonally against him and making the right allowance for it, to assess the time of arrival at his set objective – all this without a chart table and with only a dim red torch for light – was the sort of problem that really required long study and experience. They had also to learn a little about the stars, to study the meanings of the face of the water, to take soundings and to judge the strength and direction of a tidal stream with a fishing line and lead. For those who are interested in such matters, and in order not to interrupt our story, and example of a typical navigational calculation, as done in these canoes, is given in Appendix A.

To propel these canoes for all the hours of a night was extremely arduous work. All the effort was thrown on the muscles above the waist, and the legs, unused and lying nearly flat on the bottom of the boat, could easily become senseless. The strain on the arms and shoulders was severe, and it was a rule to take five minutes' rest every hour, or whenever over-fatigued, and there was a risk of a muscle being pulled. The shoulder and arm muscles had to be specially worked up by all sorts of exercises.

Perhaps more serious was that on these lone, dark expeditions, when complete silence was the rule and no sound could be heard but the drip of your paddle or the slap of the waves on the boat's hull, the mind was apt to become dazed and even to entertain hallucinations. 'The eyes were made the fools o' the other senses.' These hallucinations often took strange forms, but the commonest were for men to see lighthouses, large ships, railway bridges or big buildings suddenly before them, though the conscious intellect knew that there was nothing but water all round. On one occasion Hasler himself, while acting as No. 2 at night, imagined that his No. 1, instead of paddling, was reading a large, illuminated newspaper and he actually began to reprimand the man before he came to his senses.

Moreover, before the end of a long passage, it was common for one of the men in a canoe to conceive an intense and unreasoning hatred for his mate. Usually this was the result of a sum of little irritations, often imaginary. You might, if a No. 1, become convinced that your No. 2 was not pulling his weight on the paddles, or not keeping the boat upright, or not keeping time or turning round to look behind him, and a childish irritation would be built up. Hasler himself confessed that, on one occasion, he with difficulty controlled an unreasoning impulse to take an extra back swing with his paddle and hit Marine Ned Sparks smartly on the side of the head.

Sometimes it was found that a No. 1 and a No. 2 could never get on at all together. Thus Sparks and the older Marine Eric

Fisher, though good friends ashore, were always at 'battle stations' with each other afloat, and consequently always getting tangled up in the barbed wire of the boom and having either to swim for it or be rescued by a patrol boat. Thus there was a good deal of sorting-out to be done before all the crews were satisfactorily matched. Eventually, Sparks became No. 2 to Hasler and Fisher to Ellery.

5. TOUGH TRAINING

The demands made on the young officers and men were certainly exacting. 'These crews,' said an experienced naval officer, Captain H. M. C. Ionides, before in due time they set off on the Frankton expedition, 'ought to be all officers.' It was certainly asking a lot of a city lad to learn to navigate by night without lights, handle his craft in all conditions, exercise initiative, cunning and deception, swim underwater, handle explosives, draw maps and find his way about on land, and have the wits to get away from an enemy either overland or on the water.

But that was the requirement, and they went to it with a will, sometimes sadly befogged, often dog-tired and frequently very wet. Very bad at navigation, many times in the early days they would all capsize and be found clinging to the boom, whence they had to be rescued in an assault boat. The 'cover' purpose for which the unit had been created – the patrol of the defensive boom – was itself excellent and sufficiently arduous training at first, especially at night. The boom itself, stretching for six miles in a dog-leg course from Lumps Fort across to Sea View in the Isle of Wight, bristled with surface and underwater obstacles, and the patrolling of it, known under the code name of 'Margate', was the duty to which Hasler's Party grew most accustomed.

They were trained to work both in formation, especially arrowhead formation, and, as initiative tests, to go on longer and longer trips singly, finding their own way and fending for themselves in all circumstances, lying up by day and learning to escape observation. One night they would be ordered to find their way into Langstone Harbour, another they set out on the difficult course into Chichester Harbour, where they found themselves waist-deep in mud. Training in soft mud was very important, and they soon learnt that if you tried to walk in it, you 'had had it'. The trick was to lean on your canoe and use it as a sledge, by which means you could get along quite fast. As we have seen, the Cockle Mk II had been designed by Goatley and Hasler specially for this purpose, and this provision was to prove its value when in due time Hasler and his companions found themselves in the oozy mud of the Gironde.

Training in explosives meant learning first of all how to handle them coolly and confidently. Later the famous limpet mine was to be the chief operational weapon, but for early training Hasler obtained a supply of the small 5-lb anti-personnel depth charges that the Navy had concocted for use against the Italian underwater swimmers who had been making a nuisance of themselves. They were in fact apt and useful equipment for the unit in their 'cover' rôle of a boom patrol detachment, in the unlikely event of any Italians ever reaching Portsmouth.

The method of actuating these depth charges was to squeeze the igniter on the end of the time fuse with a pair of pliers, wait for it to start fizzing, then drop it over the side, when it would explode in about ten seconds. On the very first occasion of their use, the object lesson was handsomely realized. The canoes were out in formation, each in turn dropping a charge as they paddled slowly along. One No. 2, when his turn came, was so flustered that, before the horrified eyes of all, he squeezed the igniter, threw the pliers overboard and placed the fizzing explosive between his legs.

'We all,' said Hasler afterwards, 'yelled our heads off,' and in a moment the smoking charge was describing a huge parabola in the air, to plunge into the water very much further off than the pliers.

When they came to endurance tests, Jock Stewart and Corporal Laver paddled 34 miles in one night. Another night, before they were equipped with compasses, he and Corporal Laver went out into the Solent under a bright moon, when the air-raid sirens sounded and they found themselves completely lost in the thick pall of the smoke screen that the Army put up. To have moved in a direction that would have taken them out to sea would have meant disaster, and they could do nothing but remain where they were until, after some hours, they crept forward cautiously and, soaked to the skin, slept the rest of the night in a dummy barge anchored in the Solent.

Because of the endurance called for, it was a commandment that every officer and man should keep himself at a high pitch of physical fitness. This always means that, psychologically, there must be an occasional let-up, but if this meant that you had a 'hangover' next morning you had to grin and work it out of your system quickly. There would be an all-night march, followed by swimming in the early morning, then straight out in the canoes again to the Isle of Wight and back. There were feet-hardening exercises, running across the shingle in bare feet, which were usually won by Pritchard-Gordon or Marine Lambert, his No. 2, and there was Mackinnon's own speciality of jumping bare-footed on to the shingle from a height. There were diving exercises with the Davis escape gear, rope climbing, negotiating obstacles, including the trick of how to get through an iron railing, and training with weapons. They practised deliberately capsizing the canoe, to learn the drill of recovery. There was also the sober and tedious training in how to read charts, to calculate compass deviations, wind and tide allowances, repair and maintenance of the boats and gear, including emergency repairs to a canoe damaged in landing. The unit's boathouse opened on to the seafront road and to reach the beach one had to get down a vertical wall about five feet high. The Portsmouth Corporation had provided steps for this purpose for holiday-makers, but it was one of Hasler's standing orders that the steps were never to be used. The wall had to be climbed up or jumped down, regardless of what officer or man was carrying.

Next to physical fitness came stealth. Hasler's Party had to learn all the crafts of both the sea and the land scout – to move both on land and water without being seen or heard, to lie up under cover by day, and to escape in enemy country. By standing arrangement with the Boom Gate Vessels and the boats of the Solent Patrol, they regularly practised attempts to approach and board unseen. They learnt how to avoid being silhouetted against the moon and how, if in danger of being observed on a clear night, to adopt the 'lowest position', sliding down into the boat almost flat and simulating a floating log, or alternatively flopping forward from the waist, face downwards. When in the 'lowest position' the canoe would be propelled gently with single paddles, but if it was thought that it had been observed by an enemy, the invariable technique was to turn the canoe gently end-to to him, to reduce silhouette, and then to 'freeze' motionless, with paddles stowed close alongside, and allow the tide and wind to carry the canoe clear, as if it were driftwood. When canoes were operationally loaded, with stores between the men's legs, the forward face-down position was the only one that could be adopted. We shall see this technique being employed in action.

Stealthy movement on the water by night also required special training of the eyes. Various medical means of improving night vision were tested by Professor Solly Zuckerman, who was lent to the scientific staff of COHQ by the RAF, and for whom the unit acted as guinea pigs, but none of these was found to be of any real benefit. It was found possible, however, to bring about a great improvement in a man's natural vision by practice and training. One essential is to get the eyes fully 'night-adapted' and to keep them that way. If artificial light has to be used, either before or during a night operation, it must be a very dim red or orange light, and a torch of this nature should be used if you have to refer to charts or maps. A special 'dim' torch was devised and made by Major Sir Malcolm Campbell, who will be remembered as the one-time holder of the world's motorboat speed record, who was a member of CODC and who took a fatherly interest in these ardent young boatmen. Another essential of night vision is to look slightly to one side of a doubtful object, instead of staring at it. Veterans of the Eighth Army in the Desert will recall the similar trick of getting your head down to ground level to distinguish outlines. On the Frankton operation itself, they were to find that they could see a great deal and that all aids to navigation were quite secondary to direct vision.

Training in stealth in a country at war, when movement around the coasts was so much restricted, and when both professional and very amateur eyes were on the watch, was often lent a realistic touch. Official notification of their exercises did not always reach the right people. One dark night Corporal Johnston and his No. 2, in difficulties with their boat, landed on the beach at Hayling Island. In a very few minutes the crack of rifle-fire was heard and spurts of sand were kicked up at their feet. They took cover, but continued to be pinned down by fire. It was the work of watchful coastguards – and was excellent training for the two marines. On another occasion Hasler himself spent a ridiculous half-hour on the beach at Sea View with two Home Guards pointing Sten guns at his stomach, while their officer tried by telephone to get confirmation of his implausible story from the Commander-in-Chief's office.

They also frequently had battles of wits and stealth with the Solent Patrol. This service, one of the plums of the Navy, was provided by small private motorboats which had been requisitioned and which were manned by their owners 'disguised' as RNVR officers and well stocked with duty-free drink. As has already been shown, Hasler was more than once arrested by them, but none the less the Boom Patrol Detachment, when on 'legitimate' business, had a good liaison with them and often used to tie up astern and go aboard to assuage the summer's thirst.

Some of these naval patrol boats, especially those sent out to 'clear the course' for anti-aircraft gunnery practice, were manned entirely by Wrens. During the slack periods of this not very active duty, these young nereids, far from the observant crowd and tempted by the summer sun, were wont to strip for a course of sun-bathing. Here was a marvellous target for young marines whose duty it was to train themselves in the art of the stealthy approach (if their CO was not present). As their technique improved, it was impressive to observe how close they could get to their objective before the first scream rent the stillness of the summer air.

Training in stealth on land was combined with training for escape from enemy-occupied territory, for it was inherent in any raiding operations that men might be stranded among enemies (as they were in fact to be) and be obliged to find their way to safety by their own initiative and wits. The training was similar to that for infiltration tactics in the Army. Many little exercises were held by day and by night in the local countryside, learning how to move about inconspicuously and how to make use of maps. There were also light-hearted raids on the Home Guard in Lumps Fort.

Nor was their training in initiative always planned for them. One night, returning to 'White Heather' after a bad bombing raid,

Ewart (Heather's sweetheart), Conway and Mills and perhaps one or two more, heard cries for help from a side street. They turned down it, to be met by an air-raid warden, who tried to stop them, reminding them that rescue work could only be done by the civil defence bodies. 'Just you try to stop us,' they said. They found the cries to come from an air-raid shelter that had been buried by the fall of a bomb just outside it. From this, working with their hands and pieces of débris lying about, they rescued two or three children and finally an old lady. The old lady was unable to walk, so they tore down a door and used it as a stretcher to carry her away.

While this training was going on, Hasler himself was busy at many other tasks – what stores would be needed on an expedition, how they were to be stowed in the tiny spaces, what type of compass should be used and how it should be mounted, what was the best shape of paddle, how to devise a cockpit cover fitting close to the man's body to prevent flooding of the canoe in rough water, what clothing the men should wear ('nothing any use' he said after a visit to the stores depôt), what food they should carry and what were the best camouflage devices.

Extract from Hasler's diary:

> *30th July, 1942.* To Havant by motorcycle 0830, train to Waterloo. A.m. interviewing Douglas Fairbanks* re dummy boats. P.m., DNECO on Cockle II and paddles; DPQ re parent vessels, 1630–1715, Prof. Newitt re underwater glider [the 'Sleeping Beauty'], wire climbing, buoy sinking, etc. Then futile chase round. . . . 2045, train back

The compass finally decided upon was the RAF P8, a grid-type compass with luminous markings. As late as the end of August he was still making capsizing tests with the Mk II canoe and finding it 'highly lethal with the present cockpit cover'. He made frequent visits to COHQ in London, went to Cambridge to see Professor Debenham and Dr Brian Roberts of the Scott Polar Research

* The American film star was on COHQ staff; he was concerned first with landing craft and afterwards with camouflage and 'deception'. He took part in the Dieppe Raid.

Institute and inspect their Eskimo kayak. He visited Fordingbridge with Stewart to witness the first drop with the great trefoil parachute, in which a 400-lb iron weight was used to represent a loaded canoe, and saw the iron weight drop like a plummet to the earth, burying itself permanently in Hampshire, while the parachutes glided gracefully on to land long afterwards!

This problem of approach to the scene of a distant objective worried them a good deal, and all the time they were developing the parachuting of an explosive boat with a man in it. They also, as we have seen, experimented with dropping canoes, but at that time it could be done only on land, which meant dismantling the canoe and its gear, which in turn caused a long delay in reassembling it in the dark after the drop. Later an inflatable canoe was evolved for this purpose, which could be carried strapped to the leg of a parachutist-swimmer and inflated after he had been dropped in the sea. An adventurous pastime.

Another means of approach to a distant target area was by means of submarine, and this is the method that is going to interest us most. The use of submarines for this purpose had already been established in the Mediterranean by the Special Boat Sections and other adventurous bands. As we have seen, one of Hasler's main concerns in the design of the Cockle Mk II was that it should be of a size that would allow of its going through a submarine torpedo hatch. He was able to make adequate checks for this purpose by visits to HMS *Dolphin* (Fort Blockhouse) at Gosport, but no trials or training for the men with submarines were possible at Portsmouth and they had to wait until the time came for them to prepare for their great adventure. Nor had any solution yet been found to the problem of how the canoes, having been stowed away in a submarine, were to be launched from it in the open sea, and to probe this problem Hasler paid a visit on 21 July to the Third Submarine Flotilla in the Clyde.

6. PLANNING THE RAID

September came, and with it the news of Rommel's exemplary defeat at Alam Halfa, where, attempting his much-vaunted victory drive to Alexandria, he learnt his first sharp lesson from Montgomery.

The world did not apprehend the significance of this model battle and down at Southsea Hasler's marines, paddling, swimming, diving, puzzling over charts and compasses, no doubt thought of it as no more than another desert scrap. The water was now their element and they were beginning to conform to its moods, to understand its strange impulses and to harness it to their own uses. They worked hard, played hard and occasionally fought and drank hard. They were becoming superlatively fit and, by the community of their comradeship and the growing confidence in their own powers, were developing that gay and happy morale that characterized them – 'felt in the heart and felt along the blood'. Mackinnon wrote to his mother that he was enjoying every minute of it. Marine Conway said that he felt 'the proudest lad in the land'.

Such was the temper of the boys who were rapidly being welded by Hasler and his officers and the NCOs. He was not so sanguine as to think that they were yet fit for any major operation, but his mind was already beginning to shape itself to the notion that the next phase of training should be an excursion against the enemy. You cannot learn to play cricket by always practising in the nets. Their training needed to be tested against live bowling and a keen field. He therefore wrote to COHQ saying that he hoped the unit would be ready for a simple canoe operation by the end of August and resolved that next time he was in London he would call to see what matches there were that needed to be played.

He was to have that opportunity very soon, but immediately before it occurred a typical example of this phase in the training of his Party which is well worth our notice before we leave all such things behind us. It is told best in the terse words of his own diary:

> *16th September, 1942.* No. 1 Section to 7 days' leave. A.m., office work. 1200, Mother arrived to look after the house (9 Spencer Road). P.m., testing kicky fins and Sten Mk II. 1600, Zuckerman arrived. Organizing night vision and endurance tests for Paradrene and Dipthal. 2030, dope inserted in eyes. 2130–2230, Paradrene test. Not very convincing. 2325 onwards, Corporal Bick and self on exhaustion test. Marching all night.

> *17th September, 1942.* 0645, finish marching. 0745, swimming. 0920–1315, in Cockle Mk II to Isle of Wight and back. 1400–1600, being tested before and after Dipthal. Fairly convincing. Office work till 1830. Turned in early.

The next day after these illuminating entries marks the beginning of the new turn in the story. Hasler left early in the morning for Cambridge to see Professor Debenham and Dr Roberts about the kayaks and on his way back through London called in at Richmond Terrace to see Neville.

'We ought to be thinking of a live operation soon, sir. Have you got anything on the plate that we could tackle?'

'Already?' said Neville. 'You have only been going a couple of months.'

'They are shaping up, sir. Provided it is not a job needing very good navigation or seamanship, I think they'll soon be ready. Besides, we must put the equipment and the tactics to a live test as soon as we can.'

'All right. Let's see what there is.'

Neville sent for a few files, handed them to Hasler and said:

'Have a look through these.'

Hasler spent an hour going through the dockets, but it seems that there was nothing that suited him and he went back to Southsea.

A day or so afterwards, however, he had a note from Cyril

Horton, saying: 'I think we have got something that might interest you; it might be worth your while to come up.'

It will be remembered that the Bordeaux problem arising from Lord Selborne's letter to Mr Attlee of 22 June had been studied by the Search Committee of COHQ on 27 July, after the Examination Committee had turned down a combined operation, and that they had recorded their views very briefly and with no apparent enthusiasm. What happened immediately after Lord Selborne's further letter (the third in all) of 5 August, which Brigadier Hollis had forwarded to the Chief of Staff, is not clear from the existing records. But in mid-September Horton was about to write to say that this adventure was 'not on', when he learnt from Neville of Blondie Hasler's visit. He at once thought of the troublesome 'Frankton' problem.

Hasler hurried up to London on 21 September, examined the Frankton docket and was at once attracted. He spent all day in studying the problem. He had to study the charts, consider the 'time and distance' factors, how the raiding force was to be conveyed within striking distance, what information there was on the enemy dispositions and the topography of the Gironde Estuary. Tides and the state of the moon would also have to be discovered in order to find the best dates. It was essential to mount the operation during a 'dark period', that is to say, during the period of four to six days in each month that extends two or three days either side of the new moon. An additional implication of using the dark period was that at this time the tides would be at 'Springs'. During spring tides, which occur every fortnight, the high water rises higher than the normal and the low water falls lower, and the strength of the tidal stream in both directions reaches its maximum.

The information immediately available on all these points was far from complete, but Hasler thought there was enough for a start. That evening he spent discussing the problem with Neville, then he slept on it and in the morning worked out his 'Outline Proposals' and submitted them to Neville.

'The quickest outline plan of its kind on record,' said Neville afterwards.

> The attached outline plan [Hasler wrote in a covering letter] has been produced without close study of the natural features of the locality or of the defence measures which may be encountered.
>
> Before proceeding with planning, it is requested that I may be informed whether the proposal made in the outline plan, that a carrying vessel should drop three Cockles Mk II not more than five miles from the mouth of the river, in the dark, is practicable.
>
> At first examination, the Cockle side of the operation appears to have a good chance of success, and it is hoped that RMBPD may be allowed to carry it out.

His outline proposals were that only three Cockles should be employed and that they should be transported to the area in a submarine or such other vessel as the Admiralty would provide. The attack on the enemy ships would be made with limpet mines. It would take four nights to paddle from the open sea up the Gironde to Bordeaux, and the night of the attack (D4) must be within two days of the new moon, i.e. as dark as possible. As to the critical task of getting away after the operation, he hoped to be able to return down the estuary on successive nights and be picked up by the mother ship on D8, but if that were not possible the attacking force must destroy their canoes and equipment and escape overland.

Several interesting features appear in this rapidly produced outline plan. The use of canoes – on the face of things very frail and hazardous craft for such an ambitious operation – was governed mainly by the fact that the explosive Boom Patrol Boat was nowhere near ready for operations. Even if the operation had been delayed until the Boom Patrol Boat was ready, it would have suffered from the objection that, on account of its limited range, it would have had to be launched by parachute well up the Gironde, thus quite certainly raising the alarm long before it could reach its target. Canoes would certainly mean a great trial of endurance and fortitude, as well as of great skill in all the techniques of unobserved movement, but they would be silent and their range would depend only on the men's endurance and on how long they could remain unseen and unheard.

The second interesting point was the decision to use only three canoes – a tiny force. Hasler's proposal was based on the simple facts that three canoes would carry sufficient limpets to sink up to eight ships, which was as many as he expected to find, and that the smaller the number of canoes the better the chance to get through unobserved. We shall be looking at this point again.

The third point of interest in the outline proposals was the preference for a submarine as a carrying ship. A submarine was, from its construction, by no means the perfect carrier. To get the canoes through the narrow, sloping torpedo hatch, with only inches to spare, was a tricky operation; and to get them launched in the open sea was a problem not yet solved. But these handling difficulties could be overcome and to Hasler's mind it was an obvious submarine operation right from the start. Before the canoes were launched, in the dark, it would be quite essential for them, in order that they should be able to find their way, to know precisely where they were; and, to get a good 'fix' by triangulation, daylight was desirable. No vessel other than a submarine could fix its position in daylight close to an enemy coast and launch the canoes close inshore after dark. As we have seen, Hasler had already made sure that the Cockle Mk II could be got into a submarine (though launching from it was a problem still to be solved) and the only question that required to be answered was whether Flag Officer (Submarines), or the Admiral (S),* as the chief submarine officer in the Navy was now being called, could be persuaded to allow one of his valuable ships to be used for this purpose. The submarine service did not at all relish the frequent demands that were made upon them to carry out extraneous functions, such as landing agents and picking up generals, for not only did they imperil valuable craft and lives, but they also diverted the craft from their vital tasks of attacking enemy shipping. Still, that was Hasler's mission, too!

There was nothing new about these submarine-canoe exploits, for several had taken place elsewhere. The feature of Frankton that distinguished it from all other canoe raids hitherto was its deep penetration into enemy-held territory. Most raids so far had been tip-and-run sallies, the raiders withdrawing to a parent ship the same night. This was an expedition that was to call for great

* Admiral Sir Max Horton.

endurance, a sustained mental tension and the exercise of much skill in avoiding detection for so long a period in a very busy waterway and a well-populated countryside. Moreover, there was the deliberate decision, in the unlikely event of any vessel being able to pick them up after the raid, to put the raiders to the great hazard of having to make their individual withdrawals over a great distance overland through hostile and semi-hostile country. Lord Louis, with no small justification, regarded it as extremely unlikely that any of the men could ever get back.

As we have seen, Hasler knew that his unit, with only two and a half months' training, was hardly yet fitted for a serious operation, but he would have another month or two, and he could now concentrate on the training needed for the particular operation in view. The plan must, of course, be kept a dead secret, but training could be intensified. Meanwhile, he was now due for seven days' leave and, although he spent one day of it watching parachute tests, and another in the office 'telephoning madly in all directions', he spent most of the time 'digging holes' in his mother's garden at Catherington, which bored him, playing the saxophone, and sleeping in the autumn sun.

He said no word to his mother of what was afoot, nor did he ever have any difficulty about keeping secrets from her. Mrs Hasler was a woman with a strong sense of duty and made a point of never asking her son any questions about what he was doing. Whatever she may have been thinking or guessing in her own mind, she always accepted without curiosity whatever statements he made about his activities, and if he did not make any she left it at that.

Then followed several weeks of intense activity. Hasler took Jock Stewart into his confidence (and no one but him) and the two worked all hours of the clock, being obliged to take benzedrine occasionally when working late into the night. There were many modifications to be made to the canoes, a great deal of work to be done on stores, food and clothing, and the plan for the Frankton enterprise had to be revised, amplified and approved by various authorities. He went to see Captain S. M. Raw RN, the chief staff officer of the Admiral (S) at Northway in London, and succeeded in getting approval for the use of a submarine, but learnt it would have to sail from the Clyde, where the 3rd Submarine Flotilla, under the command of Captain H. M. C. Ionides, was based on the depot ship HMS *Forth*, anchored in Holy Loch off Kilmun. He learnt, however, that it would be impossible for them to expect the submarine, eight or nine nights after dropping them in enemy waters, to come back again and pick them up. The risks to the submarine, for which the enemy would certainly be looking after the explosion, would be altogether too great, and the likelihood of a canoe being able to find its way back to a pinpoint in the Bay of Biscay at night was almost as remote as the stars. The raiders would therefore have to put themselves deliberately to the peril of attempting to find their way overland for a great distance through territories occupied or dominated by the Germans and where all the police, under Vichy orders, were collaborating with them. Hasler was not deterred.

The requirement to embark in the Clyde provided a good 'cover plan' for the departure of the expedition. It was therefore decided to announce that No. 1 Section was being sent to Scotland 'for advanced training', which was in fact the truth though not the whole truth.

Meanwhile there was the detail planning of Operation Frankton. The Dieppe raid in August had shown the need for the most meticulous care in planning and Hasler was fortunate in that the Staff Officer at COHQ who was responsible for co-ordinating all the planning of the operation and acting as the link between himself and Whitehall was Lieutenant-Commander G. P. L'Estrange RNVR, a rubber planter from Malaya. L'Estrange did a most careful and painstaking job, providing Hasler with the fullest available information on the tides and currents in the Gironde and at its mouth, the dispositions and strength of the enemy and the local topography. With his own hands he prepared the reference cards which each canoe carried and which set out all the necessary data on tide, moon and the times of morning and evening twilight. On 12 October he and Hasler paid a further visit to see Raw at the headquarters of Admiral (S), when they tied up final details about the submarine, and on 18 October they sat down together and wrote out the first revised outline plan for submission to COHQ. It was still for the use of three canoes only.

Then occurred a most unexpected and disheartening check. Hasler had planned, from the beginning, to lead this raid himself. He now learnt to his dismay that, although Mountbatten had approved the plan, he had ruled that Hasler, as their chief canoeing specialist, was not to go on the raid himself, since it was too unlikely that anyone who went on the raid would return. Hasler, on 21 October, came to Neville almost with tears in his eyes. He said that it was out of the question for him to send his men on this first and very hazardous raid and not to go himself. 'If they go without me, sir, and don't return, I shall never be able to face the others in my Party again.'

Neville promised to intercede with Mountbatten, but Hasler took the formal step of putting his view in writing to Cyril Horton, in the following hurried memorandum:

FRANKTON

1. Operation is an important one, and appears to have good chance of success. Main difficulty is a question of small-boat seamanship and navigation on the part of the force commander. My 2nd-in-command has only been using small boats for about 4 months and chances of success would be materially reduced if the most experienced officer available were not sent.
2. A failure would prejudice all future operations of this type.
3. In a new unit, the OC can hardly gain respect if he avoids going on the first operation.
4. I am supposed to be no longer a member of the Development Organisation in general but simply the OC of an operational unit.
5. If I am not allowed to go on this operation, what type of operation will be permissible for me? The case of Major Stirling in Egypt is thought to be similar.

This memorandum Horton, who fully agreed with it, forwarded to Neville.

On 29 October, while the whole Empire was thrilling with the daily news of the great battle of El Alamein, where Eighth Army, under Montgomery, was breaking Rommel's forces with repeated blows, Mountbatten himself presided over a meeting at COHQ which Hasler attended.

At this conference the completed plan was put before Mountbatten, and considered in detail. They came to the 'command' paragraph and Mountbatten, looking at Hasler, said: 'I understand you want to lead this raid yourself?'

Hasler: 'Yes, sir.'

Mountbatten: 'Why?'

Hasler: 'Because it is an important operation, sir, and I think we should put our best team into it. Mackinnon and his men have been doing intensive boat training for a few months, but I have been using small boats all my life, and it is only natural that I'm better at it than they are.'

Mountbatten: 'What about the other half of your unit, which you would be leaving behind?'

Hasler: 'Captain Stewart is fully capable of carrying on the training and development work with No. 2 Section, sir.'

Mountbatten: 'The fact remains that this is a risky operation, with an unusually difficult withdrawal plan. If you go, there is a strong possibility that you won't come back. We originally got you into Combined Ops because you were well qualified to develop new ideas for us, and all that side of things will be prejudiced if you go.'

Hasler: 'Sir, I don't see how I can develop raiding technique and equipment properly if I've never been on a raid myself. And I don't see how I could go on commanding the unit if I sent No. 1 Section away in its present inexperienced condition without my guidance; and if the operation were a complete failure, and they didn't come back, I simply shouldn't be able to face the others, sir.'

Mountbatten then, in the usual 'staff conference' manner, went round the table asking the various senior officers their opinions. He looked at Neville: 'What's your view, Robert?'

Neville: 'I think he should go, sir. He's mad keen to. I know Blondie and I'm pretty confident he'll get back all right.'

Neville's, however, was a lone voice. One after another, all the rest said 'No'. Hasler's heart sank. He regarded the day as lost, when Mountbatten suddenly smiled and said:

'Well, much against my better judgment, I'm going to let you go.'

Hasler was on top of the world again, beaming all over his face. It was another step in cementing his devotion to Lord Louis.

Highly delighted, Hasler went on that night to Glasgow, and the next day Mountbatten, as related at the beginning of this story, sent forward to the Chiefs of Staff Committee a 'Summary of the Outline Plan'* for their approval, which they formally gave on 3 November. Very shortly afterwards Mountbatten decided that the number of canoes to be taken should be increased to six, 'in case of accidents'.

How right that decision was will appear.

Somewhat later the Admiral (S) issued his own orders for the operation. The submarine detailed for the mission was the *Tuna* (Lieutenant-Commander R. P. Raikes DSO, RN). Training for the raid was to take place under Captain Ionides, 3rd Submarine Flotilla, and the operation was not to proceed unless the standard of training met his requirements. *Tuna* was to sail about 30 November for a patrol in the vicinity of the Gironde Estuary after dropping the military party. She might attack enemy ships encountered, and if this endangered the Frankton exercise, then Frankton was to be 'off'. The number of Cockles that could be taken aboard was at the discretion of *Tuna*'s commander after consultation with Major Hasler.

*

Down at Southsea a lorry called at 'White Heather' to collect No. 1 Section. If Ewart felt any wrench at the separation from Heather, he concealed it in joining with the others in their display of high spirits. They had left their blues and other possessions still in their wardrobes and before they clambered into the lorry they called out: 'Heather, look after our things; we'll be back soon.'

It was a charge that she was to remember with peculiar significance in the time of despair that lay ahead. As the lorry drove away she and her mother turned back into the empty, silent house. Although she had no idea whatever that they were about to go on

* The full Outline Plan is given in Appendix B.

an expedition, Heather broke down on her mother's shoulder and cried: 'Oh, mother! They'll never come back. I know they'll never come back.'

This might have been only a young girl's emotionalism, but, as we shall see, she was not the only one to have a premonition. Very surprisingly, Mackinnon, who also had no idea whatever that an expedition lay ahead, taking leave of Pritchard-Gordon, said:

'Well, goodbye, Bill. I shan't see you again.'

'Oh, nonsense, Mac.'

'No, I don't think I shall, Bill.'

7. SUBMARINES AND LIMPETS

Extract from Hasler's diary:

> *30th October*. 0745, arrive Glasgow. Bath in gents' lavatory. Breakfast at Central. 0945, train to Gourock. Steamer to Dunoon. Bus to Ardnadam. Arrived HMS *Forth* 1230. P.m. saw S3 [Ionides] re object of visit. Fixed details of hoisting-out apparatus. Fixing up various preliminary arrangements. Rang Neville. Planned instruction for No. 1 Section. Evening, drinking with Bobby Lambert.*

He found the *Forth*, the submarine depot ship, which we have already seen him visit in July, anchored in Holy Loch, with several of her brood alongside, and had a most fruitful interview with Ionides, who was extremely quick off the mark in helping him solve his many difficulties. It was the beginning of eight days of intense activity, day and night, for No. 1 Section was due from Portsmouth the next day, and, in addition to many other matters, they had to be put through stringent training in two particularly important new techniques – how to get themselves, their canoes and their stores in and out of a submarine and how to handle and plant the limpet mines that they were to use on the operation.

How to get the canoe *into* a submarine was already known. It went down the forward torpedo hatch, a shaft of very narrow diameter that went down at an angle of about 45 degrees. The Cockle Mk II had been designed for this purpose, though the operation was a delicate one, with considerable risk of damage to the fabric of the canoe as it went down or up the hatch with only a few inches to spare. A new and more difficult problem, however,

* Son of the Royal Marine general Roger Lambert; he was a submarine officer and was later lost at sea.

was to develop a method of launching the canoes from the submarine in the open sea. Once launched successfully, they would be capable of withstanding a good deal of rough water, but getting away from the submarine was a critical stage in the operation. In previous canoe operations carried out in the calmer waters of the Mediterranean with lightly loaded canoes, it had been possible to lower the empty canoes over the side of the submarine's casing into the water, then haul them to the forward hydroplanes, which provided a sort of platform a few feet above the water. The men scrambled down into them from this platform, and their stores were passed down to them afterwards.

Neither Hasler nor the submarine officers had any hope that this method would work in the open Atlantic, particularly with the great weight of cargo which had to be loaded into the canoes. They would have been swamped alongside before their crews could get in and close their cockpit covers, and it was therefore necessary to develop an entirely new system.

Hasler wanted to hoist each canoe out over the side fully loaded, with its crew already sitting in it and their cockpit covers done up, thus in one stroke obviating the danger of swamping and leaving only the risk of capsizing. The longitudinal strength of the Cockle Mk II would enable it to be slung in this way without damage, so the new design was already beginning to pay off.

He designed a special sling consisting of two wooden spreaders connected together by two strips of broad, heavy webbing, and having a wire lifting strop attached to each spreader. In use, this sling was spread out flat on the casing of the submarine and the canoe – loaded only with its two end cargo bags – was carried on to it and lowered on to the webbing. The rest of the cargo bags were then loaded into it, and finally the two men got in and fastened their cockpit covers. The two wire strops were then brought together, and the canoe was ready for hoisting. On reaching the water, the canoe floated up off the webbing, and was quickly pushed backwards out of the sling, which could then be hoisted back in for the next canoe.

Since the submarine had no davits or derricks, it was necessary to develop some sort of hoisting gear as well, and this was achieved with startling simplicity by the staff of the 3rd Flotilla.

They clamped a steel girder to the underside of the muzzle of the submarine's gun, in such a way that it projected a long way ahead of the muzzle, looking rather like the bayonet on a rifle. A rope tackle shackled to the end of the girder provided the hoisting power, and the girder was canted up and down and swung from side to side by means of the gun's own training and elevating gear. This girder could be fitted before leaving base, since it did not interfere with firing the gun in an emergency.

Using this method, hoisting the canoes out in the open sea became feasible, though still far from easy if there was any swell running. It required a good deal of practice, both on the part of the canoeists and of the seamen handling the hoisting gear, and there was precious little time.

Nor was there much time for training in the handling and use of the actual weapon that Hasler's men were going to use in the operation, the magnetic limpet mine, and we must have a look at this weapon before we move on.

This dangerous little toy was another production of Special Operations Executive and it was designed specifically for attaching to the side of a steel ship. It consisted of a canister of explosive mounted on a frame to which were fitted six permanent magnets of the familiar horseshoe shape and it could be quite simply stuck on to a ship or other target and left to cling until the time set for its detonation. This was governed by a simple delay fuse with a chemical action. After breaking an ampoule of liquid inside the fuse, the washer holding back the striker pin was slowly dissolved and at the set time the pin sprang forward and fired the detonator.

They were highly affected by changes in temperature, but in each box of ampoules for the time fuses there was a chart showing roughly how the period of delay was increased by low temperatures. The limpet weighed only about 10 lb, but if placed against the side of an unarmoured ship about six feet below the waterline it would blow a hole about three feet in diameter. The subsequent inrush of water was far beyond the capacity of the ship's pumps. On the other hand, most cargo ships are divided into a number of watertight compartments, and in order to ensure sinking a large ship it was considered necessary to place three limpets on her, spaced out over different compartments. It was considered good

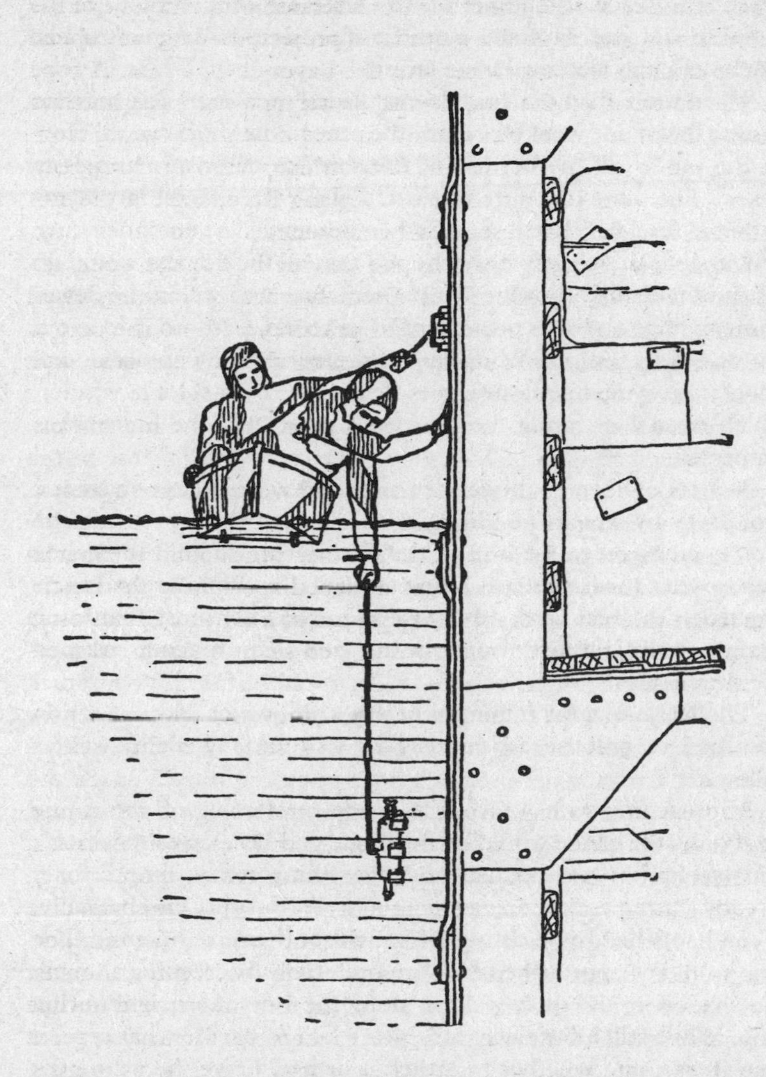

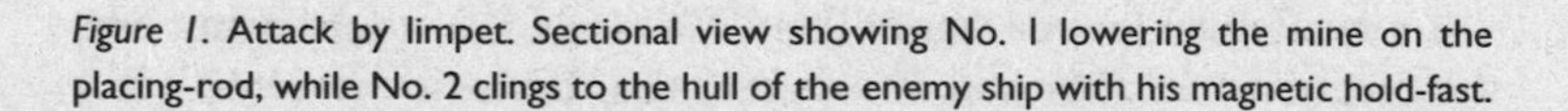

Figure 1. Attack by limpet. Sectional view showing No. 1 lowering the mine on the placing-rod, while No. 2 clings to the hull of the enemy ship with his magnetic hold-fast.

practice to place one limpet on the engine-room, so that even if the ship did not sink she would suffer serious damage to her machinery and electrical installation.

When more than one limpet was placed on a ship there was the danger that if one went off before the others, the shock would blow all the others off the bottom of the ship, to detonate harmlessly below. The mine therefore was fitted also with a secondary 'sympathetic' fuse, which was set off when influenced by an underwater concussion. In this way it was hoped that all the limpets would go off simultaneously, but the sympathetic fuse was still in the development stage and was not regarded as reliable. In order to avoid the risk of the limpets being set off prematurely by an accidental knock, the sympathetic fuse was held 'safe' by a soluble washer, which dissolved during the first hour or so that the limpet was immersed.

As handmaiden to the limpet, there was also a large magnetic 'holdfast', by which the No. 2 of the Cockle (or sometimes the No. 1) clung on to the hull of the enemy ship to hold the canoe steady while the limpet was being applied. This holdfast had to be applied with great care, otherwise there was the most shattering 'clang', reverberating throughout the ship, as the magnets grasped the ship's sides.

The technique for mining a hostile ship, which No. 1 Section now had to practise assiduously by day and by night, was as follows:

Approaching with a favourable tide, preferably of about one knot only, the canoe would be in 'single paddles, lowest position', with cockpit covers opened and everything ready, limpet fuses already started and fizzing away inaudibly (but very emphatically, if you happened to be sitting with eight of them round you). The ship would be approached end-on, preferably by creeping along in the shadow of the quay wall or along the side of a neighbouring ship. While still a little way off, No. 1 had to decide what type of ship it was, and whether to attack it or not. Once the canoe got close to it, it was more difficult to see the type of ship, because nothing was visible but a towering, overhanging steel side.

Once alongside, at a signal from No. 1, No. 2 would bring out the magnetic holdfast and attach it to the ship's side level with his shoulder. No. 1 then pulled one of a pair of limpets off its keeper plate by brute force, and hooked it on to the bottom end of the placing rod, a jointed steel rod six feet long which had already been assembled ready for use.

Then, leaning over the side of the canoe, No. 1 would carefully lower the limpet down, keeping it well out from the ship's side until it was at the required six feet depth. Then he would gently move it on to the ship's side until there was a slight – and very worrying – 'clonk' as it clung on. The rod could then be unhooked by pushing it downwards, and at a further signal from No. 1, No. 2 would pull off his holdfast and they would gradually drift on, aided occasionally by a few quiet strokes of the paddles.

The limpets, of which each canoe carried eight, and the hold-fasts, were a serious problem in navigation, for their powerful magnets set up a magnetic field that caused enormous compass deviation. What was done was to stow them aft, as far from the compass as possible, and to stow them in pairs, face to face, with a keeper plate in between, thus reducing the magnetic field. Just before an expedition, the canoes would be fully loaded with all their gear and they would then be 'swung' for compass deviation.

It will be noted that this matter of attacks with limpets did not involve the use of the frogman's rig of swim-fins, watertight suit and underwater breathing apparatus. This equipment had not yet been evolved, but the instructions that led to its development were given by Hasler to Jock Stewart before he left Southsea, and, as a result of the tests and studies that Stewart and others made, the equipment that was to become so well known was evolved during the next few months. The frogman's suit does not come into our story, but, as it was an outcome and corollary of it, an outline of how it was developed is given in Appendix C.

8. A BAD FLOP

Into these new activities of submarine and limpet mine No. 1 Section plunged as soon as they arrived on 31 October. The faithful Stewart came also, either then or a little later. So did Storeman Drew, and Marine Todd to act as MOA to the officers. They were all in high spirits, chattering like schoolboys, looking around with interest at scenery new to all of them except Mackinnon and Ewart, whose homes were in Glasgow. They looked approvingly upon the pretty Scottish lassies, too, but had no time to do more than look, for Hasler met them at Gourock and whisked them away. Their new Mk II Cockles, incorporating all improvements, came also. The next day they had them out for the first time and made their first practice in limpet attacks.

The submarine detailed for them, *Tuna*, was unfortunately not yet available, but Ionides arranged for P339 and P223 to be at their service for trials and training in 'hoisting-out': they practised first, however, from the davits of the Dutch ship *Jan van Gelder* to get over teething troubles. They used the same ship also as a target for dummy limpet attacks. To simulate the tide that would be found running up and down the Gironde Estuary, the *Jan van Gelder* would keep about one knot of way on while the canoes manoeuvred in and placed their mines, so that every man became well versed in the craft of holding on with the magnetic holdfast and placing the limpet the necessary six feet below the waterline.

Extract from Hasler's diary:

4th November, 1942. A.m., preparing boats, and stores. 1100, hoist out. 1330, over to 'Jan van Gelder'. Hoist out on quarter davit. 1430–1700, practise daylight hoisting-out fully loaded and limpet attacks against 'Jan' under way, representing tidal stream. 1900–2100, repeating in the dark in Inchmarnock area with southerly breeze and lop. Good value. Eliminating teething troubles with slip-hook and slings. 2330, return to 'Forth'.

In spite of the chill northern November, they resumed their swimming. On 3 November all canoes left in formation for a long day's trip, fully loaded, arriving back after six and a half hours 'very exhausted'. A few days later all ranks embarked in the submarine P339 (Lieutenant-Commander Wingfield), practised hoisting-out in a heavy squall, and had their first experience of diving and action trials in a submarine.

The curtain was nearly ready to go up on the drama, but before that could take place there must be a rehearsal. It had already been planned that this rehearsal should be over a course that resembled the Gironde Estuary and its approach as nearly as possible, and the only one in Britain was the Thames. An exercise had accordingly been planned under the code-name of 'Blanket', the course to be from Margate to Deptford, a distance of approximately 70 miles, which was about the same distance as they were expected to have to paddle in the operation. The Commander-in-Chief, Nore Command, had given authority and all our coastwise defences over the route had been warned that the exercise was taking place. Any boats seen were to be challenged, and on answering with the code-word were to be allowed to proceed. This meant, of course, that all the defences were alerted, and the task of No. 1 Section was to get through unobserved. It was a stiff test, especially as the course prescribed required that, on reaching the Isle of Sheppey, the canoes must proceed by the narrow waters of the Swale, which lies between Sheppey and the mainland, emerging into the crowded Medway and passing back again into the open sea past the coastal forts of Sheerness and the boom at the harbour mouth.

Hasler and Stewart left Glasgow on 7 November, and after calling to see Neville in London and the staff of C-in-C Nore at Chatham, went on to Margate. Here the crews were briefed in the evening, and Hasler and Mackinnon worked until midnight on tide-tables for each boat. The next night they paddled out to sea from Margate under ideal conditions of misty weather and a flat calm.

Almost from the start this vital exercise was a complete failure. Navigation was terribly bad. Mackinnon, for instance, proceeding independently out of the Swale on a course of north, ran aground in fog among mud-flats and marsh grass. By the time he had twisted and turned in the dark to get clear he had quite lost his sense of direction. Now, the P8 grid compass then had a grid that could easily be read 180 degrees wrong, and that was what Mac did. When he looked at his compass and saw that the line of the grid was in sympathy with north, he followed it faithfully for half an hour, until, coming to a railway bridge under which he had already passed that night, he realized that he was heading south. By this feat he qualified for what Hasler's Party called the 'Reciprocal Club', an organization dedicated to those who were 180 degrees out in their bearings!

Corporal Sheard did even worse, losing formation altogether and finishing up miles outside the exercise area. Instead of going up the Thames Estuary, he went down it. His excuse was that he was following Hasler at a distance, until he saw Hasler's canoe get up and fly away. He then realized that he had been chasing a seagull.

Five nights after leaving Margate they arrived at Blackwall, somewhat short of their objective, and abandoned the exercise, completely exhausted. Every canoe had been spotted and challenged at least twice. And they had not stood up to the physical strain.

It was a bad augury. Much depressed, Hasler went to COHQ the next day to take part in a post-mortem on the exercise. At lunch-time he was drinking a glass of beer and eating a sandwich in the all-ranks canteen which Mountbatten had caused to be opened inside COHQ, when Lord Louis himself came in. Seeing Hasler, Mountbatten went over and said:

'Well, how did the rehearsal go?' No doubt he already knew perfectly well that it had gone badly.

'I'm afraid it was a complete failure, sir.'

Once again the famous Mountbatten smile. 'Splendid! In that case you must have learnt a great deal, and you'll be able to avoid making the same mistakes on the operation.'

The war-time sandwich tasted better after that totally unexpected reply, and that night Hasler and Mackinnon, though both 'very weary', went off to enjoy themselves at a Wrens' party.

A day back at Portsmouth, and a day at the SOE development centre at Welwyn, to discuss time delays on the limpets, and Hasler, together with Mackinnon, was back in London for a very significant duty at a special department of the War Office. From those practitioners of mystery and imagination they received secret instruction in what was known as the No. 3 Code. This was a means by which, if taken prisoner, a man might communicate a simple message back to Military Intelligence. In this briefing they made acquaintance with an officer in a special position, whom we shall ourselves meet again; this was Major R. G. Sillars, a well-known Clyde yachtsman and the father of D. R. G. Sillars, a Royal Marine officer who later became one of Hasler's best friends.

In spite of this very significant briefing, Mackinnon still knew nothing about the 'Frankton' affair. What his private speculations may have been we can never know, but the secrecy of the operation was extremely well maintained throughout and he, no doubt, supposed that this briefing was merely part of the normal training of an officer engaged in the kind of operation he would sometime have to undertake.

About this time Britain and all the free world were uplifted by the news of the Anglo-American landings under Eisenhower in French North Africa. On the hinge of fate the door of freedom was swinging more widely open. Our victorious Eighth Army under Montgomery was driving Rommel remorselessly back against the wall. In Russia the German advance had been halted. To our country had come the first of the great victories. Throughout the land the hearts of men and women were lighter and their hopes in the ascendant.

9. GOODBYE

When Hasler and Mackinnon arrived back in the Clyde they found that all the cabin accommodation in HMS *Forth* was occupied and the whole detachment was accordingly put in what was called a 'hotel ship' – the *Al Rawdah*, moored close by. It was 19 November and only ten days remained to them for all that they had to do.

To maintain fitness they went on forced marches over the hills of Bute, practising on the way with the pistol and the silent Sten gun. They were exercised in the use of the fighting knife according to the technique of the Fairbairn system as taught in Commando units. They carried out navigational exercises by day and by night. Most emphasis, however, was placed on practice with the limpet, both in its tactical use against the *Jan van Gelder* and in fusing it. Fusing was reduced to a drill, each operation done according to word of command, until every man could do it faultlessly in the dark.

Compass work also was given special attention, with the help of the Navigating Officer of HMS *Forth*. All canoes were fully loaded with their complete operational equipment and 'swung' to determine compass deviation, and the error was then taken out as far as possible by means of the compass corrector mounted underneath.

However, it was not all work. Feeling himself played out and stale from the unremitting pressure and sensing that the men were the same, Hasler decided that they all needed a 'run around town'. He therefore ordered shore leave for one night only, and they were all the better for it. His own method of relief, and Stewart's, was to go for a hill-climb on Bute. This relaxation was premeditated. Entirely unplanned, however, was an incident in the *Al Rawdah* which is briefly recorded in the diary as:

Number 1

Magnetic holdfast
One No. 69 grenade
Bailer and sponge
Paddle handgrip
Placing-rod
4 limpets
1 spanner
Half No. 2's spare clothes

Number 2
Box of small gear
Matches
Cooker
Placing-rod
4 limpets
Half No. 2's spare clothes

Number 3
Rations
Water-cans

Number 4
Camouflage net
50-ft codline
Repair bag
Navigating gear
Paddle handgrip
Sounding reel
Torch
Benzedrine
One No. 69 grenade

Number 5
No. 1's spare clothes
2 fuse boxes
2 cups
Soap
4 escape boxes

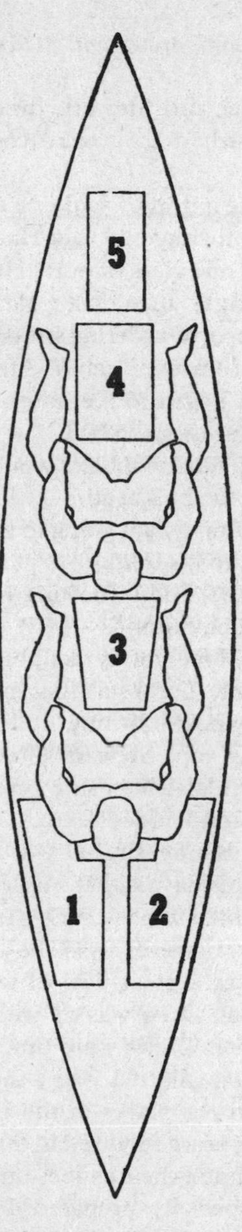

Figure 2. How the cargoes were stowed for the attack.

Evening – drinking in *Al Rawdah* with Poles. Disastrous results.

Hasler and Stewart, tired after their hill-climb, had finished dinner when they were casually joined by a couple of Polish officers.

'Have a drink?' said one of the Poles.

'No, thank you,' said Hasler. 'Must get to bed early tonight.'

'Just one glass of port? Help you to sleep.'

'All right, then, just a glass of port.'

Instead of ordering mess port, the Poles brought up a special bottle from their cabin. After having drunk it, both Hasler and Stewart began to feel most peculiar. At last Stewart said, 'Now I really must go to bed.'

He got up, wobbled, wondered what was the matter and leaned against the bulkhead.

'I definitely am going to bed,' he said again. Somehow he made his way to his bunk.

Marine Todd, meeting him at his cabin, said: 'My word, sir, you do look funny.'

'Yes, I feel funny, too; but I definitely am going to bed.'

Marine Todd saw that he did so.

Early next morning, still feeling as though he had swallowed a spinning top, Stewart somehow made his way out on parade. Sergeant Wallace came up to him, saluted, reported the parade correct, and added:

'Excuse me, sir, but you've got your face covered in chalk.'

To this day neither Hasler nor Stewart knows what could have been added to pack such a mighty punch in a glass of Polish port.

This, however, was the only 'let-up'. In addition to training, there was a great deal of work to do on stores and equipment. Storeman Drew was up with them, helping to check, make good and issue. Crews were practised in sorting all operational stores into their allotted bags, sewing up the bags, stowing them in their proper places in the canoes and learning to reach for and find any store required in the dark under the cockpit covers. They also painted their canoes and their canoe suits with a camouflage paint specially prepared for use on rubber. Each canoe, for purposes of recognition, had been named after a fish – *Catfish,*

Coalfish, etc. – and these names were painted in small letters on their bows.

One of the last things that No. 1 Section did was to sew their badges on to their clothing. Every officer and man carried the shoulder title ROYAL MARINES and the shoulder flash of Combined Operations with its triple union of anchor, rifle and wings. Rank badges of crown, stars or chevrons were also carried by all officers and NCOs. For Hasler's Party were going on their adventure as soldiers doing a soldier's task against the enemy, not as fifth columnists or civilian saboteurs.

The garment on which these badges were sewn was the man's specially camouflaged waterproof Cockle Suit of mottled olive green, with an elastic skirting that fitted over the top of the canoe's cockpit cover. On his legs he wore long woollen pants, sea-boots, stockings, battle-dress trousers. His feet were in gym shoes, over which he wore thigh-length waders of the same material as his jacket, with very light soles. On his upper parts he wore woollen vest, shirt, roll-neck sweater and blue scarf. Over these, and underneath the Cockle jacket was an inflatable life-jacket. On his hands were two pairs of gloves – a silk pair and a dark blue woollen pair over them. On his head was a dark blue Balaclava cap, over which he could pull the small hood of his Cockle jacket, either to keep out the wet, or, for the purposes of camouflage, to break the outline of his head and shoulders. For equipment he carried on him a .45 Colt automatic pistol, a fighting knife worn on his right leg, a clasp-knife and a 'bird-call' whistle that simulated the cry of a seagull and that was used to summon help or establish contact when out of sight. In addition there were two silent Sten guns for the little flotilla and these were assigned to the canoes of Hasler and Mackinnon.

A list of the stores carried in the canoes, astonishing in its variety and quantity for such small craft, is given in Appendix D.

L'Estrange came up from London with all the paper work–air photos of the Gironde Estuary, which would help them to select the best places for their hides each day; the latest hydrographical and topographical information; the most complete intelligence on the enemy's defences on land and at sea; and a complete set of sectional charts of the estuary for each canoe, on which were

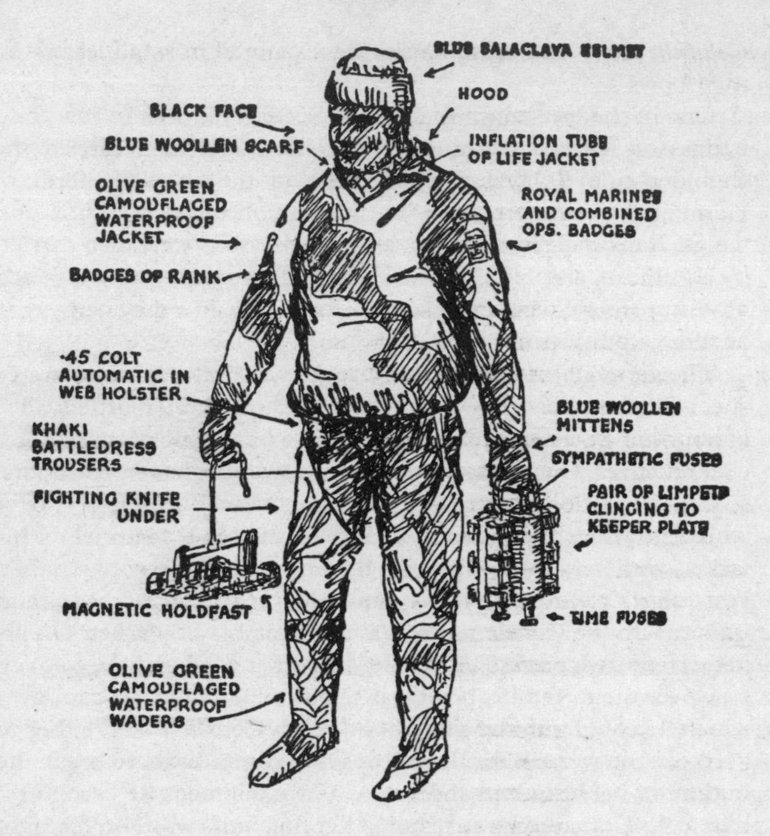

Figure 3. A 'limpeteer', as equipped for the raid.

marked, in addition to other information, the areas on the river banks that were believed to be safe and unsafe for lying-up at night.

All these L'Estrange communicated to Hasler only. So also did he brief him, by word of mouth only, with the very secret 'escape instructions', telling him where to make for, what to do about dress, how to behave in order to escape suspicion, and providing him with French money for everyone in the party. All these things we shall deal with later on. From L'Estrange Hasler learnt also that Mountbatten had written to Air Marshal N. H. Bottomley, asking him to arrange for the suspension of aerial mining in the

Gironde area, both for the safety of the submarine and also that the enemy's coastal watchers should not be aroused.

A few days before they sailed Hasler made his number with Dick Raikes, the commander of the *Tuna*. Raikes was about his own age and the meeting was the beginning of an entirely happy relationship between men who had so much in common in their outlook towards their task.

What, amid all these swirls and eddies of activity, were Hasler's men thinking? The waters of life were obviously being stirred by some strange force, a sharp wind was blowing from some unknown quarter and a breath of mystery and adventure filled the air. The barometer was set clearly at 'exciting'. From the very nature of the preparations, and the intensity with which they were pursued, it might have been guessed that something of import was afoot, but no enlightenment was shed, nor did they expect any. Mackinnon was fired by a new ardour; Laver felt a new quiet intensity of purpose; Sergeant Wallace and Mills tossed into the pool of gossip their squibs of wit. But the security throughout was amazingly good, and if there was any speculation about Norway in their lively young minds Wallace was there to suppress it and to uphold the official explanation that they were about to leave on a long exercise.

They were all advised to tell their families so and to say that they must not be expected home for some little time. Most of them did so. Mackinnon and Marine Ewart, whose homes were in Glasgow itself, paid their last visits to their families some time during the stay in the Clyde, but said no word. Marine Mills wrote to his mother in Kettering to say that he was in a ship, 'but cannot tell you any more, and if I don't come back for some time, don't worry.' He also warned them, however, that he did not expect to come back at all. This letter, and Ewart's, and no doubt others, were in fact written in the submarine and brought back in her. Marine Conway, who had expected to have leave about then, wrote to say that leave was 'temporarily stopped', that he could not tell where he was going and that they would learn about it later.

Robert Ewart, however, though he had said nothing when he went home, clearly had a premonition of death, for just before sailing he wrote his parents and brothers a touching and affectionate letter from which we will allow ourselves to read only a few sentences.

> I'm enjoying every minute of it [he wrote]. I hope that what we have done helps to end the mess we are in and make a decent and better world. . . . I've a feeling I'll be like a bad penny, so please don't upset yourself about my safety. . . . I can't thank you enough for all you have done for me but will take it with me wherever I go, so trusting we meet again I'll say good-bye to you all, thanking God for a Mother and Dad giving me the courage as you have done. . . .

He wrote also to Heather Powell, and she cried a little, though his letter said nothing of his fears, but told only of his feelings for her and his hopes for the day of his return. For her part, however, Heather had an even stronger premonition. We have seen her forebodings on the day the men left Southsea, and when she got Ewart's final letter she was more than ever convinced, and as we take up this pathetic little story again, we shall see how this persisting premonition led her slowly to an early grave. Her little diary during these weeks is full of entries: 'Letter from Bob', 'Wrote to Bob', and the like. She had bought him a cigarette case for his approaching twenty-first birthday, but an NCO advised her not to send it. 'Wait till he gets back,' he said, but he was never to receive it.

From these and other letters, it is touching to see on what fond terms they all lived with their parents and family. These youngsters of Hasler's all came from the humblest homes, but no toughness of training, no rigours of life could loosen the tenderness of their ties with Mum and Dad. They were proud of themselves and wanted their families to be proud too. None of them knew what lay before them, but each in these last days felt the strong bonds of the simple affections for home.

The last day came. On the morning of 30 November Hasler and No. 1 Section embarked in the *Tuna*. The canoes, folded flat, were taken with extreme care down the submarine's forward torpedo hatch. The stores followed, sewn up in their cargo bags. Finally the men themselves came aboard and went below. L'Estrange and

Jock Stewart, the only two in the secret, were there quietly to say goodbye and good luck.

As *Tuna* moved slowly from the side of HMS *Forth* the Marines, following big ship tradition, turned out as smartly as conditions allowed, stood rigidly at ease in single rank on the after casing until the coxswain's pipe shrilled from the bridge, and Hasler called them all to attention as the submarine saluted her depot ship. It is on such occasions as these, when every man's heart is filled with his private thoughts and with his pride in the part that he is playing, that the inner meaning of ceremonial and the ancient usages is felt and apprehended by every man who takes part.

Presently the pipe sounded Carry On, and the 'Royals' were dismissed and sent below. Most of them, save for a brief hour that night, would never see the sky again until the time came to launch their canoes.

Silently Stewart and L'Estrange watched the submarine, slowly at first, make her way down the Firth of Clyde and diminish in the distance.

PART TWO

THE WEAPON STRIKES

10. THE MEN WHO SAILED

Now all ranks were safely 'locked up'. Let us take a closer look at the men of No. 1 Section.

The senior NCO was Sergeant Samuel Wallace, who, as we have seen, was a Regular who had nearly completed his twelve years' service. He came from Dublin, was unmarried, was tall, dark, good-looking, of a fine physique, hardy and in the prime of fit manhood. He had the bearing of a professional soldier and in matters of drill, weapon training and the general round of military life and behaviour he had the efficiency and the instructional ability that one would expect from one so bred and trained. But his importance lay far more in his personal qualities and influence. 'Sailor' Wallace had an engaging Irish personality, a buoyant cheerfulness and a sense of humour that made him the first to laugh at himself when he got a ducking. He had a very strong formative influence on the temper and spirit of the men, who looked up to him with both respect and affection. When things were difficult for them, when they were harassed or exhausted or browned off, it was Wallace's example of cheerful willingness and his ready good humour that got them into the right spirit. In performance, he had the defects of his qualities, for his keenness and his fund of energy led him to be impulsive in his eagerness and sometimes apt to move and act without thinking. To this, if not to the natural chances and perils of the raid, may conceivably have been due the misfortune of his untimely end, but through this veil shines the fact that, in the hour of trial in the hands of a barbarous enemy, Sailor Wallace and his No. 2, Robert Ewart, stood firm and defiant in loyalty to their comrades, who, but for their heroic fidelity, must themselves have been put in greatest peril.

Wallace was No. 1 of *Coalfish*. His No. 2, and partner in his gallantry, we have already met. Ewart was a broad, six-foot young Scot of a simple nature who had a strong affection for his parents and his three brothers. As a boy, he had lived with them first at Scone and then at Alloa before they moved to Glasgow, where in due time, not caring for the farm work that his father had previously been following, he found employment in a textile factory. In his free time he liked most to go out with his father and brothers playing snooker or else to spend the evening talking to his mother. He was very keen on the Boys' Brigade and had won many prizes. When the war broke out he was offered employment in a munition factory, but refused it, preferring to join the Royal Marines. Posted first to the Orkney Islands, he found life far too dull, and when the summons came for volunteers for the RMBPD he came forward eagerly. In the unit he was regarded with that special kind of affection that one gives to the trier who is often doing the wrong thing but taking the laughter or the reprimand all in good part.

Corporal A. F. Laver, who was No. 1 of *Crayfish*, was a finely built young man, broad and square-rigged, fair-haired, round-faced, thoroughly dependable. He was a young Regular, having joined the Corps shortly before the war, and prior to joining the RMBPD had served in HMS *Rodney* and been present at the sinking of the *Bismarck* the year before. He was a quiet sort, had plenty of brains and thought things out. He was one of the very few who took little part in the convivial evenings of ale and song. But he was far from being stolid and possessed imagination, initiative and a fine fighting spirit. He was one of the better ones at navigation and seamanship, was a keen swimmer, boxer and runner, of splendid physique and stamina. Because of his quiet demeanour, he did not stand out in the training period, but the operation was to show that he had all, or very nearly all, the qualities of a daring raider. Laver came from Barnet, and was an exceedingly gallant young fellow. It was he who did a 34-mile paddle one night with Jock Stewart.

Marine W. H. Mills was Laver's No. 2 and an excellent foil to him in every way. For whereas Laver was quiet and reserved, Mills was full of fun and high spirits. Everyone liked him and he kept them all amused. He was of a stocky figure, with crisp, brown waved hair, clean, smart and well turned out, and kept himself extremely fit, being a good swimmer and footballer. Better educated than most, he came from Kettering, where he went to the parish church school and afterwards was employed at the Kettering Sports and Rubber Stores, and he had served in Civil Defence before joining the Corps. 'Bill,' says Mr Edward Collett, an older man who was a great friend of the family, 'was a boy of an extremely lovable character, full of life and always ready to do someone a good turn.' Mills was a fortnight short of his twenty-first birthday when they all sailed, and, like Ewart, left behind a sweetheart he was never to marry.

No. 1 of *Conger* was Corporal C. G. Sheard, a little chap, a terrier and as tough as one. He was a real, broad-spoken 'Janner' from Devonshire, with a ready wit, and was the life and soul of a party. Besides these qualities, he had plenty of initiative and a good power of command as an NCO, with a keen driving force and the will to go on. He was, however, one of those to whom navigation problems came hard, as we have seen from the incident of the seagull, about which he used to tell a good story against himself.

Sheard's No. 2 in *Conger* was Marine David Moffat. He came from Halifax, Yorkshire, but of a family that had come from Belfast, where he had been born. He was a big fellow with a great mop of dark, wavy hair. He was strong and a great trier, and, like many of the others, had a lively sense of humour and fun. At 'White Heather' he used to don a parson's collar and a mock solemnity, playing the part to the life. He could take a quiet rise out of a junior NCO, too, even if it cost him a 'double' to Eastney Barracks and back. Moffat was the particular friend of Fisher, who also had a Northern Ireland origin.

Cachalot was commanded by Marine W. A. Ellery, the only man without rank to be a No. 1. A Londoner, Ellery was a broad-shouldered, husky fellow, with black hair. As we have seen, he was a particularly good surface swimmer – quite the best in the unit. His No. 2, Marine Eric Fisher, the friend of David Moffat, was a fine type of young man, a little older than the others, stout of build, rubicund of face, full of keenness and with plenty of guts.

He came from West Bromwich, where he was a painter's machine-minder. Fisher came to the unit as a non-swimmer, and never became more than a very moderate one (under Mackinnon's rough-and-ready methods of: 'Over the side, Fisher'), but he never funked a job that obviously carried the risk of drowning. After the frogman's kit had been developed, he became a perfectly competent swimmer underwater. He was to take part, nearly two years later, in the brilliant little raid against Leros. He would have been an asset to any unit and was a very good influence on his younger comrades.

With Hasler in *Catfish* was Marine W. E. Sparks. Known as Ned to his messmates, he was a curly-haired, rather slightly built, wiry Cockney, with the typical Cockney qualities and an infectious laugh. When all was going well he was always grumbling under his breath – 'making disparaging comments on the situation in an audible undertone', as Hasler described it. But when the sky was black he became, Cockney-wise, full of cheerfulness, cracking pert little jokes. In a tight corner there is no better companion than your Cockney. Sparks had plenty of fighting spirit and was always cool and competent. He was very fit, had good sense and was an excellent foil for Hasler, who only too often had cause to be depressed.

Marine James Conway was No. 2 to Mackinnon in *Cuttlefish.* Twenty years old, he was a fresh-complexioned young man of about five feet ten inches and strongly built. His home was at Stockport in Cheshire. He was a keen swimmer and cyclist and was often seen cycling in the countryside. His real love, however, was horses. He was a milk roundsman of the Co-operative Wholesale Society, and used to talk to his horse as though it was his best friend, spending hours with it after working hours. Jim Conway had an elder brother in the 'Royals', and when his own turn came to join up he realized a boyish ambition in securing entry to the same Corps. His letters home were full of how happy he was. He was rather a quiet fellow, but quick-witted and liked by everyone, and was an excellent No. 2 to Mackinnon.

As 'twelfth', or in sober fact, thirteenth man, the little expedition also carried Marine Norman Colley, who came from

Pontefract. Like many twelfth men, he was not to be called upon and was destined to sit in the pavilion.

*

Such were the men who, together with Hasler and Mackinnon, assembled below in the submarine that cold autumn day – a collection of very ordinary young men: the coal-merchant's clerk, the milk roundsman, the factory worker, the ship hand, with the Regular Service officer and sergeant; yet united now in a common will and purpose. They were in great spirits. Cramped though their quarters were, it was a new experience for them, and at first they enjoyed the adventure and the novelty of it all. While the submarine was steaming on the surface the men could smoke and the air was fresh. The marines were not required to keep any watches and the naval officers and ratings of the submarine were kindness itself, as the Royal Navy always is to its guests, giving up their own bunks and mess spaces to make room for the 'Royals'. 'Jack' and 'Joe' were on the best of terms.

11. THE NEWS IS BROKEN

As soon as the hatches were closed and the ship under way, Hasler called his men together. He had out a blackboard, and in the little area allotted to them in the forward torpedo space, the men squatted down among the folded canoes and stores, rapt with attention, wondering what was in the wind. Hasler told them at once.

'This time,' he said, 'it is the real thing. I haven't been able to tell you before, but we have now started to carry out an actual operation against the enemy. We are going to do the sort of job that we have been training for these past four months, and I have chosen you chaps because I feel confident you can do it.'

So their half-guesses had been right. The men sat silent and motionless, their feelings a blend of excitement and a little anxiety. Suddenly, without warning, they were to be called upon for the great test. No longer were they in the nets; they were to face the bowling in the open field. There had been no embarkation leave for them, no goodbyes to mothers and sweethearts. This was it. In the cramped and crowded little deck the atmosphere was tense with excitement and anticipation.

A little at a time Hasler unfolded the general outlines of the job they were to be called upon to do. He drew a map of the Gironde Estuary on the blackboard. They were to be dropped from the submarine, he told them, in the dark, some 10 miles to the southward of the headland called Pointe de Grave, on which there was a lighthouse, at the entrance to the estuary. There they would have to pass between the headland and the small island of Cordouan. Then they would have to follow the coast on their starboard hand, making a gradual change of course of about 140 degrees to enter the Gironde itself.

From there they would have to paddle up another 60 miles before they reached Bordeaux, moving, of course, at night only, and lying up during the day in concealment on the river banks. They had been given air photographs to help them to choose the most likely lying-up places in advance, and these they would study later, together with the tide-tables and all other information that they had. They knew already that many of the islands in the estuary and many parts of the river banks were thickly covered in reeds and that they would have to negotiate a lot of soft mud when launching the canoes at low water each night.

The tides in the estuary, he continued, were strong and they would be able to move only on the flood tide, as it flowed from the sea towards Bordeaux. So they would have to work out their timings for each night's voyage very carefully. The period of the second week of December had been decided upon because that was the monthly 'dark period' in which there was little or no moon; also it was the period when tidal effects were strongest.

Well, this, thought Hasler's Party as they squatted around, rapt with attention, is all right. It's just 'Blanket' over again. Tough, but we can do it. Just the job.

Then Hasler went on to tell them about the enemy dispositions. At the mouth of the estuary these were quite formidable. On the sea there were two armed trawlers on permanent patrol of the river mouth, six minesweepers and escort vessels, up to twelve torpedo boats and twelve 'R' boats. Other boats patrolled the estuary itself. Enemy U-boats might also be met approaching or leaving Le Verdon, a small town just inside the estuary.

On land there were batteries of heavy and medium guns at Royan and there was a radar spotting station in the vicinity of Soulac and others north of the Gironde. Besides all these, there was the danger of being spotted from the air, for the Germans had aerodromes at Bordeaux, Hourtain and Royan; up to five Focke-Wulfs were known to operate daily from Bordeaux and there was constant air movement to and from other stations.

Besides all these there was known to be a searchlight battery at Pte de la Négade, to which they would have to pass very close, and there were bound to be other searchlights in the vicinity of any coastal batteries. There were also various lighthouses. 'So you will all,' said Hasler, 'keep your eyes and ears well skinned and in daylight lie as low as possible.'

Their intention, continued Hasler, was to sink up to twelve merchant ships in the Bassens–Bordeaux area if possible, excluding tankers, which would be attacked only if there were not sufficient cargo ships; tankers were protected by so many compartments that it would take a great many limpets to sink them. The submarine would arrive in the Gironde area about the night of 5 December and would disembark the raiding party at approximately 9½ miles south-west of Pte de la Négade. Having made their way up the Gironde, they would attack the enemy ships at high-water slack with limpets, and then withdraw on the ebb tide as far as possible.

Hasler paused. Then, as is often done at such briefings, he asked:

'Any questions so far?'

Sergeant Wallace, voicing the question that was no doubt uppermost in most minds, said:

'Yes, sir – how do we get back?'

'I am coming to that next,' Hasler answered.

'We must appreciate that it will be quite impossible for the submarine to wait or come back for us. It will be at least eight days before we can get back, and she has her operational patrol to do. In any case our navigation isn't anything like good enough to pick her up at a given spot some miles out to sea at night. Added to that, once the ships blow up in Bordeaux, the whole region will be alerted. Every ship, aeroplane and battery will be looking for us. Search parties will be combing the river banks and the coastline. Above all, they will be expecting a ship to take us off and will be on the look-out for it.

'For that reason, it has been decided that we must make our withdrawal overland. So, as I have said, after the attack we shall return down the estuary on the ebb tide as far as possible, each canoe independently. Get as far as possible from Bordeaux until dawn or the tide makes it necessary to land. Then, at low-water slack, crews will land on the east bank, scuttle their boats and all their equipment in deep water, go ashore with their escape gear and escape overland via Spain to the U.K.'

This was completely startling. If the men could have gasped, some of them certainly would have done so. 'The more we heard,' says Eric Fisher, 'the more we were surprised.' Up till now the plan, daring and difficult though it was, had followed a normal pattern. They were all eager to get at the enemy. But the prospect of being left in hostile territory and of having to make good their escape as fugitives among a strange people over several hundred miles was something that they had not expected. To some of them it came as an added spice of adventure and excitement, but it is not to be wondered at that to a few it was disturbing. They looked at each other with embarrassed grins.

Hasler continued:

'I will tell you later how it is to be done. You have each got a bag of escape gear, and we shall put ourselves in the hands of a French escape organization. But each canoe *must* withdraw separately, and even if two or more are accidentally together it is essential that they should split up before landing. So after you land you will travel only in pairs, each pair on its own. But before I go on, if there is anyone who feels that this operation is too much for him, I want him to say so now. No one will think any the worse of him.'

He paused for a moment and looked at the men and saw them turning to each other and grinning. He could almost hear them saying: 'Not likely; I'm going to be in on this'. For after the first startlement, every man felt that the escape added fresh spice to the expedition, which now became a tingling adventure.

'After all,' said Hasler with a grin, 'it's a good deal less dangerous than a bayonet charge!'

That eased the tension a little and then someone asked: 'How are we going to manage the language, sir?'

'Well, we shall have to try to swot up a few phrases before we start,' Hasler answered. Then he raised a laugh by adding: 'As a matter of fact, I shall be at a greater disadvantage than you, because what little French I speak, I speak with a German accent!'

He went on:

'Before we hoist out of the submarine, the Captain will be asked to give us a last-minute estimate of the magnetic bearing and distance of the headland which you will see on the chart, 2¼ miles NNE of Pte de la Négade. This course will be set on your compass grids.

'We shall keep on this course until one mile off-shore, after which all boats will follow the shore, which we should be able to see, as far as the point that I have marked 'X' one mile due north of Pte de Grave at the entrance of the estuary. Here I will decide which side of the estuary is to be taken for the first lying-up place. If we pass Pt X by two hours before high water Brest we will make for the east bank, if later, the west bank.

'Our forces will be organized in two Divisions. That way we shall be less conspicuous and it will be easier to find lying-up places. Also, if one party is spotted, there is still another to carry on the raid. So "A" Division will be *Catfish, Crayfish* and *Conger*. "B" Division will be *Cuttlefish, Coalfish* and *Cachalot*. We shall proceed in formation and while both Divisions are together "A" Division will lead in arrowhead, followed by "B" in arrowhead. Boats must keep out of the buoyed channel in the Gironde, to avoid being seen by other traffic, but they must not move close along shore except in the upper reaches where the river narrows and there are a lot of islands. Keep at least half a mile off-shore wherever you can.

'You will be issued with sectional charts, on which all areas within half a mile of known enemy positions will be coloured red, and those within the same distance of any known habitations yellow, and areas believed safe green. But you must bear in mind that our information may not be entirely up-to-date and that unplotted German batteries and defensive positions may be well camouflaged and invisible at close range. In addition, there are enemy coast watchers who are likely to have powerful glasses, and it is therefore essential for all ranks to keep right under cover in daylight, without movement. You may stretch your legs after dark whenever you get the opportunity. There must at all times be a concealed sentry on duty at each group of canoes.

'Our last lying-up place, which will be as near to the target area as possible, will be treated as an advance base. Here you will complete the fusing of all limpets, restow your cargo bags as I shall show you later, fold your breakwaters and stow your compasses below, so that the luminous markings will not be visible to a sentry looking down at you.'

He then allotted target areas as follows:

TARGET AREA	'A' DIVISION	'B' DIVISION
Bordeaux, west bank	*Catfish* (Major Hasler and Marine Sparks)	*Cuttlefish* (Lt Mackinnon and Marine Conway)
Bordeaux, east bank	*Crayfish* (Cpl Laver and Marine Mills)	*Coalfish* (Sgt Wallace and Marine Ewart)
Bassens, N. & S. quays	*Conger* (Cpl Sheard and Marine Moffat)	*Cachalot* (Marine Ellery and Marine Fisher)

The primary task of each canoe was to put two limpets on each of the four largest cargo ships in its area, five feet below the waterline. 'A' Division boats were to place them on the upstream end of each ship, one limpet just past amidships and the other midway between there and the upstream end of the ship. 'B' Division was to do the like on the downstream portion of the ship.

The reason for this dispersion of effort was to ensure that if the two Divisions arrived at the target area at different times, which was to be expected, the whole target area would be covered and every ship receive proper treatment.

Those were the primary objectives. Secondary objectives that Hasler ordered, in default of the above targets presenting themselves, were tankers and smaller vessels.

'That,' said Hasler, 'is our mission and that is how we are going to carry it out. But on a party like this all sorts of things can happen, and I want you all to be quite clear how you are to act in an emergency. The overall consideration is the success of our expedition and nothing must be done to prevent us, or some of us, from getting through. You may all have to act on your own initiative, and each man may have to try to get through entirely on his own. Any boat that gets separated from the rest must go on alone.

'Should the submarine be surprised on the surface while we are hoisting-out, the forehatch will be closed and the submarine will have to dive. Any crew then on deck will inflate their life-jackets, get in their boats and proceed with the operation independently.

'If any boat gets into difficulties and gives the SOS, only the boats of its own Division will go to its help. Any canoe that gets swamped and cannot be bailed out will be scuttled and the crew left to swim for it with their No. 5 bags, unless it appears safe to try to get the boat and crew ashore.'

It was to be a bare week before that order would have to be carried out.

'You must also be quite clear,' Hasler continued, 'how you are to act if you are approached by a hostile craft. The first necessity is evasive action. If you are so close that you are certain to be spotted, get into the 'lowest position' and stop paddling. If the enemy boat should come right alongside, you will throw your hand-grenades and endeavour to capture the boat by boarding.

'But never take offensive action unless compelled. Your job is to get through. If you are hailed or fired at from the shore, again adopt the lowest position and let the tide carry you clear. You will *never* on any account shoot back. When on land, if you are approached by German soldiers, remain concealed; but if you are discovered, then kill silently with your knives, conceal the bodies and get away as soon as it is dark.

'You are very likely to come across some French people. Here also remain concealed as long as possible, but if discovered, try to explain that you are English and instruct them to tell no one they have seen you.

'Any crew unable to reach their objective will scuttle or conceal their boat, go to the nearest safe lying-up place, and, four days after leaving the submarine, but not before, make their escape to Spain as I have already told you. I will explain to you later what the escape drill is.

'One final point. In case you should have the bad luck to be taken prisoner, there is a secret system by which you may be able to send a message back to England giving useful information. Mr Mackinnon will brief you all in how to work this system and we will practise it together several times before we leave the submarine.'

For the time being Hasler finished there. It had been a long session and there was plenty for everyone to think about! Unlike some raid leaders, Hasler's policy was to try to imagine every conceivable difficulty or disaster, describe it and tell the men what to do if it happened. The argument against this practice was, of course, that you might frighten them too much with a list of hideous possibilities. With good, intelligent men, however, he thought that this notion was quite outweighed in the scales by the fact that they would know exactly how to react to every eventuality. He knew his own men well enough to be confident that they would respond with the proper spirit and that they would feel that the plan was a complete and competent one. Everything had been thought out. He sensed as he spoke that one or two of them looked rather long-faced, but he knew that they would quickly recover their faith and that when they talked among themselves there would be little heard of any depressing conjecture.

In this he was entirely right. When they got together there was an excited buzz of voices, each man according to his character. They had, after all, to get used to the idea not only that this was a difficult operation, but also that it was one from which the chances of a safe return were not high.

There are no better words to describe the scene and the atmosphere than those of Marine Fisher, one of the few survivors. 'The morale,' he says, 'was really something and had to be seen to be believed. We all had tremendous faith in the Major and would have followed him anywhere. Of course, occasionally, someone might raise a query about the escape plan, but old "Stripey" Wallace at once had a few words to say, as he always did on such occasions, and everything was all right again. We were going to have a smack at Jerry and he wouldn't know what had hit him. Everyone was in fine shape and rarin' to go.'

12. LAUNCHED

That night they had a final rehearsal of hoisting out the canoes from the *Tuna* herself, and had cause to be well satisfied. The operation was completed in the excellent time of 31 minutes. Then followed, for the rest of this week's voyage in the submarine, a period of intensive work. The orders for the operations were gone over again and again, with question and answer to test every man's familiarity with them. Every man must be fully prepared to see the job through on his own if necessary. They were also exercised repeatedly in the No. 3 Code that Mackinnon taught them. An attempt was made to teach the men a few simple French phrases, but it was uphill work and probably most of them put their faith in sign language. The air photos and new intelligence that L'Estrange had brought up were closely studied, interpreted and passed round to each man in turn, so that the men might know what features to look for by day or night. Detailed time-tables of the first night's passage and of the night of the attack were worked out and Mac, who was on fire with enthusiasm, gave a lecture on the coastal features they were likely to see at the lying-up places.

The boats' gear, with all the cargo bags, was taken out, minutely inspected and restored, and the escape instructions given. We shall leave these until we come to Chapter 17.

For the first two days, as *Tuna* proceeded down the Irish Sea and the Bristol Channel, most of the men were very sick. There was a Force 4 wind and the submarine rolled. On the afternoon of the third day, having reached waters where enemy surface ships or aircraft might be encountered, she dived for two and a half hours, and thereafter, for the rest of the passage, she was dived all day but came to the surface at night.

Hasler and Mackinnon slept in curtained-off bunks, given up to them by Raikes and one of his officers, along the side of the main fore-and-aft gangway. Wallace was looked after in the Petty Officers' Mess. The men slept on the deck among the stores in the forward torpedo space. The marines were, to all intents and purposes, confined below for the whole week's passage, and even when the seasickness wore off, suffered badly from claustrophobia, exacerbated by the limited sanitary facilities. The air got very foul and they all got sleepy and headachy. Such living conditions was extremely trying for all these tremendously fit young men, who for the past four months had been constantly occupied in the most strenuous physical exertions. It was not an atmosphere for stimulating their faculties or their ardour for the task in front of them, but as they gradually got used to the conditions, they became eager to get going, counting the time until the fateful sixth of December.

Meanwhile, to observe the life and the handling of the submarine was to the marines a fascinating object lesson. 'Dick Raikes,' says Hasler, 'remains for me the very best type of British naval officer.' Though not a big man physically, his personality dominated every inch of his ship. Seldom raising his voice, never losing either his temper or his self-possession, he had only one standard – perfection. If any officer or man fell short of this while on duty, he could be certain that Raikes would materialize, as if by magic, would take in at a glance the full extent of the mistake, put it right, explain dispassionately exactly what had gone wrong and whose fault it was and probably repeat the evolution two or three times to make sure that it was understood.

He never took to his bunk, and when he needed rest merely lay full length on the narrow settee of the wardroom with his eyes closed, resting to conserve his energy, but never quite asleep, as everyone in the submarine knew. The captain of a submarine has perhaps a bigger personal responsibility than any other person one can name, because everything hinges on him to an extraordinary extent, particularly when coming up to periscope depth in daylight, when his eye is to the periscope and no one else has any idea what is going on on the surface.

Watching Dick Raikes handling his submarine in enemy waters

was an object lesson in leadership and efficiency. All orders and reports were made in a low conversational tone, speaking rapidly and without a single unnecessary word. For example, he would be dozing on a seat in the corner of the wardroom while his officer of the watch handled the ship. If it was night and the submarine was surfaced, he would be wearing dark-red goggles even though the ship was on dim red lighting itself. Then the quiet words 'Captain in the control room' or 'Captain on the bridge' would be passed by the officer of the watch and relayed by the messenger, and instantaneously Raikes would be awake and out of the wardroom.

When he was in the control room every man kept his eyes on his face, and many of his orders were given by signalling with one finger, without any words. It was naval discipline of the best, differing from Army discipline in that far more executive action and control is concentrated on the commander, and far less of it delegated to juniors. In *Tuna* it worked to perfection.

*

December the sixth arrived. All the morning *Tuna*, approaching the French coast, was dived. About midday she began closing in. at 1.40 p.m. her periscope up, she picked up land. Down below, Hasler's marines, eager to get going, began their preparations for disembarking. They were in high spirits, cracking jokes. The sea was a flat calm, with a slight swell.

But there was a check. It was most important that Hasler should know exactly where he was before he started, so that, at night, he should be able to calculate the distance, time and course to Pte de Grave, where he had to make his turning movement into the Gironde Estuary. No one was more conscientiously resolved to set the expedition off on the right foot than the captain of the submarine. 'It was imperative,' Raikes said, 'to be dead accurate.' To obtain a correct fix of his position, he would need to take a number of bearings of points on the coast by means of his periscope.

He told Hasler, however, that he was not optimistic, and that he was specially worried by a minefield laid by the RAF, the charting of which he did not trust.

'We ought to be able to take a look at the land this afternoon,' he said, 'but last night's star sights were not good and I shall have to try to get a decent fix before we approach that infernal minefield. Unfortunately there is precious little shown on the chart that will help us.'

He found in fact that he was quite unable to identify any of these points with certainty on the featureless coast. The primary trouble had been that, on account of mist, he had not been able to obtain an 'astro-fix' – a series of readings from the stars – in the last hour of darkness before the submarine submerged that morning. This would have given him a sufficiently accurate location in the afternoon for identifying landward objects. Moreover, throughout the whole of this day he was pestered by a number of French fishing boats, whose presence he could not detect while submerged. So the order for 'Up periscope' became an anxious moment, and was frequently followed by a 'Down periscope'. In the calm, glassy sea a fisherman might easily have spotted the periscope three-quarters of a mile away, and it was known that many of the French boats carried German observers equipped with radio sets.

Late in the afternoon Raikes told Hasler that it was no good. They would have to wait till tomorrow. Sorely disappointed, Hasler went along to his marines, who were already half-prepared for launching, and said:

'I'm afraid it's off for tonight. The submarine can't approach the minefield until she has got a better fix.'

Mac's eager face fell a little. The men, in the manner that men have on such occasions, gave a half-facetious groan, but then cheered up when some wag said: 'Oh, well, decent breakfast tomorrow instead of compo rations!' Then they unpacked all over again.

That night *Tuna* surfaced as usual. Hasler came on the casing with Raikes. They saw a dead calm sea, a black moonless sky and a slight mist.

'Just exactly what we wanted,' said Hasler. 'Damned shame.'

'Terribly sorry,' answered Raikes. 'Hope we will be able to do something better tomorrow. We'll see if we can get a decent astro-fix before the morning.'

The next day was again an oily calm with a long Biscay swell. *Tuna*, having obtained a good astro-fix before daylight, put up her periscope, and, gradually creeping right inshore, began to take bearings. There was intense air activity with Messerschmitt 110s and 109s, JU 88s and Dornier 18s. But the enemy was not Raikes's only peril. The mines laid by our own aircraft were in a most unfortunate position and although Raikes had a trace showing where they should be, he knew that it was not to be relied upon.

He said to Hasler:

'I don't think these mines could possibly have been laid in a more embarrassing position. They interfere with every possible line of action I can take. Even if the things have been properly plotted on the trace, it's going to need extreme accuracy in navigation.'

'If I'm reading your trace right,' observed Hasler, 'those mines are right in the spot I'm asking you to disembark me.'

'You are dead right. It is going to be very tricky.'

In spite of the peril from underwater, however, and of the peril from the air, Raikes worked his way step by step northwards along the coast, taking bearings the whole morning. He was never, indeed, able to identify anything on the coast properly, but just crept north, with his fingers crossed, until at length he was able to see in the distance the white tower of the Cordouan lighthouse.

It was an extremely risky undertaking, coolly and skilfully carried out. At last, at 1.45 p.m., Raikes was able to say to Hasler:

'It's all right now. I've got a very nice fix. I should be able to put you off tonight if these damned patrol boats keep out of the way, and if we don't get blown up by one of those RAF mines.'

'Grand!' said Hasler. 'I'm most grateful. Where will you be able to put me off?'

'Right where you asked – close to the RAF mines. The position will be here – 45° 22′ N-1° 14′ W – quite near where we originally planned.'

'That's wonderful.'

'There'll be a risk, though. These infernal mines mean that I shall have to surface four miles from the coast and only ten miles from the Boche radar station. We shall be lucky if they don't pick us up.'

'If we are quick about it, you should be all right.'

'You'll have to be. And there's another thing. I have been

watching one of those patrol trawlers that they've got over there. She's patrolling a line about 130 to 310 degrees, which means she is running nearly through our intended point for disembarking.'

Both Raikes and Hasler took these risks cheerfully, however, and Hasler, highly delighted, passed the news to Mac and the men. Then he went to sleep.

His diary entry for this day, written hurriedly just before they disembarked, is almost the only one written in pencil. It reads:

> *7th December*. A.m. 'Tuna' right inshore. Trying to obtain a fix. Succeeded about lunch-time. Self slept most of the morning and afternoon. 1700 (5 p.m.), final talk to troops. 1745, supper. All set for disembarking.

The evening approached. Carrying out the drill prescribed, the marines unfolded and built their boats one by one. They inflated the buoyancy bags. They put on part of their operational clothing. They loaded the bags, paddles, compasses. They greased the hatches that covered the hand-holds at each end of the deck, stowed the boats in the ready-for-use position, had a meal, completed their operational clothing and smeared their faces with black camouflage cream.

At about 7.30 p.m. the submarine surfaced. As always, Dick Raikes was first out on the bridge, long before the casing had broken surface, followed by the officer of the watch and the two seamen look-outs, all with their eyes fully adapted to night vision through having worn very dark red goggles for the last hour or so.

It was a very clear night, and an enemy patrol boat was in sight. It was extremely cold.

Hasler waited below, in the wardroom, fully dressed and camouflaged, tense with excitement that he was trying hard to conceal. There was an interminable wait – perhaps sixty seconds – while Raikes and his watchkeepers, each with a huge pair of Pattern 1900A binoculars glued to his eyes, searched the horizon all round.

'Object bearing Red Nine-O, sir, distant,' said the port look-out in a low voice.

'Right,' said Raikes, who was already looking at it. It was the enemy patrol trawler, perhaps two miles to seaward and lying between *Tuna* and the safety of the open sea. Raikes was unperturbed. He had been watching her all day, and had known that she would be there. His experience told him that the submarine would not be visible from the trawler at that range, lying as she was against the darkness of the land and the eastern sky.

'Major Hasler on the bridge' – it was Raikes's voice coming down the voice-pipe to the control room. No superfluous word is ever used in passing orders in a submarine. No '*Will* Major Hasler *please come . . .*'

Hasler swarmed up the conning-tower ladder, and stood by Raikes. He was annoyed to find he was breathless with excitement. This was the great moment.

The submarine lay stopped, rolling lazily in the glassy swell. Looking down from the bridge, the casing looked as long and narrow as a pencil.

'Beastly clear night,' said Raikes, referring to the unclouded sky and bright stars, 'but looks all right for your launching. We can see the patrol boat over there, but I don't think he'll see us. Do you want to start?'

Hasler did not answer at once, but moved across the bridge and stared out to the eastward, where a faint, thin shadow stretched along the horizon. France. It was not that there was any doubt about the answer, but just that it seemed right to pause for a few seconds before speaking the word.

'Yes.'

Raikes leant again to the voice-pipe:

'Up canoes.'

Instantly, down on that thin strip of casing the forehatch opened and the seamen hoisting party poured up with their gear, followed by the first of the canoes, manhandled by their own crews. At the foot of the hatch Mac stood to supervise. First the tackle for securing to the submarine's gun. Then the boats, Hasler's last, so as to be first on the hoist-out. Then followed the crews, their faces blackened, with their silent Sten gun and Nos. 1, 2 and 3 bags.

But not all the boats, for, as she went up the torpedo hatch, *Cachalot* fouled the sharp corner of the hatch clamp and tore a long slit in her canvas side. Ellery called Hasler over to see the damage. One look was enough.

'I'm afraid you can't go,' Hasler said. 'Strike the boat below again. You will have to go back in the submarine.' Ellery looked glum and Fisher, her No. 2, the man whose gameness overcame his inability to swim, broke down and cried.

As the second canoe came up, Hasler turned to Raikes: 'Well, I'd better get along and look after my own canoe. Thanks for everything you've done on our behalf.'

Raikes turned and smiled: 'Well, the very best of luck to you all.'

'Thanks a lot. Goodbye.'

'Goodbye.'

Hasler went back down the ladder into the control room, then forward through the strangely deserted mess-decks into the forward torpedo space, in time to join Sparks and take one end of his own canoe.

At this last minute a sudden anger inflamed Hasler: for he discovered that the naval ratings in their generosity had been loading his men with chocolates and other delicacies, which they were even now trying to stow about their persons. He did not blame the sailors, but, passionately single-minded as he was, he inwardly blamed his own men for accepting even an ounce of extra weight and for disturbing the finer details of his plans. Nevertheless, he said nothing. It was hardly the moment for dwelling on a minor lapse of discipline.

Then he and Sparks got into *Catfish*, the deck hands hoisted her up on the tackle, the gun, with its girder attached, swung out, and in a moment the canoe was lifting to the Biscay swell.

At that moment the German searchlights suddenly blazed out all along the coast, and the patrolling trawler began to close on the submarine. The German radar had plotted them, and the German naval commander in Royan had ordered the searchlights to show out and sweep.

But *Tuna* was safely beyond searchlight range and the deck hands of the submarine, under Lieutenant 'Johnny' Bull, went on deftly hoisting out one canoe after another. Fisher, Colley and Ellery wished 'good luck' to their departing comrades, and to David Moffat, whom he was never to see again, Fisher said: 'Hurry up back and I'll have a pint waiting for you at the Granada.' In thirty-five minutes they were all water-borne in formation, 'B' Division astern of 'A', and each in arrowhead, but with one barb of 'B' Division sadly missing.

At twenty-two minutes past eight, under a sky filled with stars, with the German searchlights playing, the patrol boat closing in on them, in a heavy swell and a freezing air, the ship's company of the *Tuna*, in the words of her captain, 'waved *au revoir* to a magnificent bunch of black-faced villains with whom it had been a real pleasure to work', and withdrew to the south and west.

Two days later, Cyril Horton, back at COHQ in London, heard the news that *Tuna* had sent the signal: 'Operation Frankton completed 2100/7' (9 p.m., Dec. 7). He knew that meant only that the submarine had successfully disembarked her Cockles and that Hasler had started on the last and most perilous lap.

That evening he went out into Whitehall and bought an evening newspaper. He turned to the Stop Press and there read the news of an official radio announcement by the German High Command, which said:

> On December 8 a small British sabotage squad was engaged at the mouth of the Gironde River and finished off in combat.

His heart sank.

13. A NIGHT OF DISASTERS

Away into the night. The five frail Cockles rode easily on the swing and swell of the Biscay sea. No sound but the rustling of the bow wave and the drip of water from the paddles. It was extremely cold and the spray from No. 1's paddle, upflung from its backward thrust, flicked into the face of No. 2 and stung his eyes. Heavily loaded, the canoes rode low in the water. About twenty yards about, the crews could see each other clearly as they made away on a course of 35 degrees, to take them between Pte de Grave and the island of Cordouan. Right at the start Hasler discovered, in spite of all their care, that his own compass was 20 degrees out, but fortunately the North Star was clearly visible and he was able to correct his readings accordingly. He also found that the canoe was leaking slightly, so that Sparks had to bail out every hour.

After the first hour's paddling Hasler, by placing the palm of his hand on top of his head, gave the order to close and they 'rafted up', hanging on to each other's gunwales as they made whispered remarks to each other. It had been a perfect passage so far and all the crews were in tremendous spirits, and all reported, 'Everything fine, sir.' Hasler was not sure about Sergeant Wallace, however; at some time he was heard being sick.

Then, after a rest, on again, all paddling strongly. Half an hour before midnight they found the ground swell to be building up into steep rollers. Hasler took soundings and confirmed that they must be passing over the sandbank known as the Banc des Olives. It was fortunate that they had kept out to sea, for if they had been further inshore the rollers over the sandbank would have been dangerous for these light craft.

The force of the flood tide was now being felt and Hasler

therefore altered course a little farther to the eastward to follow the line of the coast, now clearly visible about a mile and a half away. Then came the first augury of danger.

In the quiet of the night there came to their ears the sound of a roaring ahead of them, faint at first but waxing louder. As they approached nearer it had the sound as of surf breaking. They were all perplexed and Hasler began to worry. He checked his navigation and could find no mistake. The coast was to starboard, but the breakers were ahead. Meanwhile the flood tide that was carrying them along gained fierce momentum, reaching four knots. Presently Hasler could actually see the white froth of the breakers, and then he knew. They were approaching a tide-race, that fierce tumbling of water that tears over rocks or sandbank as the tide flows. His mind went back to tide-races at Start Point and St Alban's Head. His men had never encountered this hazard, and he realized that it was going to be a terrifying experience for them in the middle of the night. Nothing in the chart or in the sailing directions had led them to expect this obstacle.

Hasler therefore gave the order to close and explained to them quietly what they had to face. 'All you have to do,' he said, 'is to carry out your normal rough-water drill. When you have got through, raft up again.'

Accordingly they secured their cockpit covers right to their bodies, braced themselves and put their canoes head-on into the tide-race. They felt the canoes tremble beneath them as they drove into the surge, as if the craft themselves knew that nothing but the strong arms above could save them from the violent ravishment of the sea. Then, their bows lifting and dropping, the waves breaking over them, their paddles flailing to keep head-on, the men fought their way through, every nerve and muscle straining to preserve their body balance.

At length, in the calm water beyond, Hasler turned about and watched the others come up, soaked, chilled to the marrow, buffeted, but game and steady. Laver and Mills came in *Crayfish*, Sheard and Moffat in *Conger*, Mackinnon and Conway in *Cuttlefish*. But not Sergeant Wallace and Ewart.

They peered through the night on all sides, but there was no sign of *Coalfish*. Hasler ordered them all about to search, and

Sparks, behind him, sounded his seagull call. No answering cry came over the water, though they tried again and yet again. Hasler knew that Wallace, if he had kept formation, must come through on the left rear. Even if they had capsized, the canoe itself, kept afloat by its buoyancy bags, would have been carried through the tide-race, and the men, in their life-jackets, should also have been able to keep afloat and struggle through. But no object broke the outlines of the racing white horses, and no head bobbed upon the surf. No shout came to their ears nor any sound of seagull crying.

The tide was running so fast that they were unable to paddle against it. They were being swept away from the tide-race, stern first. Time was pressing and their orders that one man's peril must not prejudice the operation must be obeyed. With heavy hearts, they turned about and resumed their course. From the original six canoes, they were now reduced to four. Throughout the rest of the operation Hasler always held on to the hope that Wallace and Ewart, finding themselves separated from the rest, may have turned inshore in the hope of finding quieter water and, in accordance with orders, been able to proceed on the operation alone. What exactly happened, save their fate and their devotion, was never known.

The remaining crews paddled on, moving very fast. The outline of the lighthouse on Pte de Grave became visible, a landmark that was doubly welcome – first because it marked the entrance to the estuary, and secondly because the light was not burning and the darkness was undisturbed. Nor was there any light burning on the island of Cordouan. But at this very moment they heard with anxiety the same roaring noise once more ahead of them – but nearer, clearer, deadlier than before. It was a second tide-race. They braced themselves for the ordeal, cockpit covers drawn tight up, bodies tensed to keep balance. Then they went into the swirling waters.

It was worse than before. The racing waves, five feet high and at a slight angle to their intended course, threw them about like matches. In the roaring there came a sudden cry and splash. *Conger* had capsized and Sheard and Moffat were in the water. They clung on to their canoe, however, and came through the tide-race gasping with the December cold of it and coughing up sea water.

On Hasler's order the remaining canoes rafted up. They examined *Conger* to see if she could be refloated, attempting to bail her out, but it was no use. The waves were washing into her cockpit. Moreover, the fierce tide was carrying them on with tremendous speed as they were swept into the narrows between the mainland and Cordouan island. Worse still, the great revolving light of the Pte de Grave lighthouse, of 25,000 candlepower, suddenly lit up at full brilliance right on top of them. It was already two o'clock in the morning and the night was more than half spent. Hasler was faced with a terribly difficult decision. The only way of bailing out the swamped canoe would be to beach it, but the only beach available was alive with enemy defences; to take the canoe in there would be madness. Nor could they dawdle a moment longer bunched together under the beam of the lighthouse. There was, however, just a chance that Sheard and Moffat could land unobserved and make their way inland. He turned to Sparks behind him.

'Try to scuttle her,' he said in a low voice. 'Corporal Sheard, hang on to the stern of my boat. Moffat, hang on to Mr Mackinnon's. We will tow you as far in to the beach as we can. Then you must swim ashore and try to escape overland.'

Sparks, obeying, took out his clasp-knife and did what he could; there was a chance that, fully loaded as she was with 300 lb of gear, the canoe might go to the bottom.

No one knew better than Hasler what the decision meant. The loss of yet another canoe was bad enough, but worse still was that, in trying to tow the two young men towards the defended beach they were deliberately taking the rest of the canoes into danger. Furthermore, even if the men got ashore alive, they would be half-dead from cold and in no condition to avoid capture; and if they were captured the whole operation would be compromised. Worse, in fact, was to happen.

They were now entering upon the most delicate and difficult phase of the mission, when everything was poised on the knife-edge of chance and a single error of judgment, a single indiscretion or a single mishap might bring destruction upon them. Now reduced to three, the Cockles were brilliantly illuminated by the revolving beams of the light as they were carried through the

Lieutenant-Colonel Hasler in a replica Eskimo kayak at Portsmouth Harbour after the War.

Types of canoe. *Left to right:* the Cockle Mark I, the Mark II as used in the raid, two rigid types, and a very early prototype of the Mark III.

Sergeant Wallace

Lieutenant Mackinnon

A 'Sleeping Beauty' piloted by Hasler, trimmed down at full speed, and about to submerge.

Lieutenant Pritchard-Gordon and Marine Lambert demonstrate how the Cockle Mark II could move over dry land – a valuable launching method if the sea was rough.

Pritchard-Gordon and Lambert in a Cockle Mark II following a canoe of another unit. Note the stylish paddling with 'feathered' paddles.

A rigid type of canoe is carried up the espalanade wall at Southsea during comparative trials.

At Southsea a Cockle Mark II follows canoes of another unit.

Cockle Mark I being passed through the forward torpedo hatch of a submarine.

Marine Robert Ewart

Marine Eric Fisher

Marine James Conway

Marine W. H. Mills

Lieutenant-Colonel Hasler *(left)* and ex-Corporal W. E. Sparks, DSM, visiting Bordeaux after the War.

Hasler in Spanish civilian clothes at Barcelona.

Corporal A. F. Laver, an early photograph.

At the première of the Warwick film production, *Cockleshell Heroes*, HRH the Duke of Edinburgh, Captain-General of the Royal Marines, talks to W. E. Sparks. With them is Mrs Sparks, and beyond her Mrs Hasler, mother of Lieutenant-Colonel Hasler.

narrow passage between the mainland and Cordouan. The dead weight of the two men in tow was a terrible drag, and their speed was reduced to one knot as they struggled to make for the shore. It seemed impossible that they had not been observed and they expected at any moment to hear the shock of a gun and a shell bursting among them or to see the bows of a gunboat bearing down. Then, as they reached the middle of the passage they heard for yet a third time the dreaded roaring ahead of them.

At each previous tide-race they had lost a canoe. This time they would have to go through with two passengers struggling to hold on to their sterns in the swirling waters and under the cold, revealing stare of the lighthouse. But no one wondered whose turn it would be next and they braced themselves for a third time, tense but determined and unafraid. For Sheard and Moffat, pierced by the ice-cold sea, it was a terrible experience, but they made no murmur of complaint.

Mercifully, this third tide-race was less violent than the others, and the whole party came through unscathed and apparently still unseen by any watching eyes ashore. They were still in the full beam of the light, but steadily, keeping in good formation, they were carried at last by the tide round the Pte de Grave and into the Gironde. It was now somewhere about three o'clock in the morning, and after six and a half hours' paddling, they were getting tired. The condition of the two marines in the water was an unhappy one. They had been immersed now for an hour and were already far gone with cold and exhaustion. Hasler's thoughts turned to their first lying-up place.

He wanted, if possible, to make the NE bank for two reasons – first, because, if the wind were anywhere from NW through north to SE, there was less danger from discovery by dogs (always one of their chief anxieties), and, secondly, because there was less danger of their being silhouetted against the rising sun as they came ashore at dawn. Such were the kinds of points that had to be pondered over beforehand. There was, however, no safe 'green' area on the NE bank before St Seurin, and to reach it before daylight was now out of the question. Therefore it would have to be the SW bank.

First, however, they would have to clear the dangerous area

of the port of Le Verdon. Time was running out. Hasler's and Mackinnon's boats, labouring desperately under the dead weight of the men they were towing, were increasingly difficult to handle in the swift impulse of the tide. They could not possibly afford to spend many more minutes on the rescue attempt. Suddenly Hasler saw, nearly a mile ahead of him, the dim outline of the pier of Le Verdon with a blue light burning at the head of it, and saw, too, that the tide was sweeping them inevitably right into it. Across the thrust of that tide no human strength could have driven the overweighed canoes far enough out to avoid the mole. With a heavy heart, Hasler decided that he must abandon Sheard and Moffat immediately. Once more, humanity and the call of comradeship must not be allowed to put their purpose in hazard. Though exhausted, both men still had their life-jackets fully inflated. The tide would carry them very close to the pier; perhaps they would succeed in landing unobserved and making their escape. But, indeed, there was now no choice.

Approaching the shore as near as they dared, Hasler once more gave the signal to raft up. Then he leaned over the side and said to Sheard:

'I am sorry, but we have got to leave you here. You must swim for it. It is no distance. I am terribly sorry.'

Sheard, grey and trembling violently from the cold, gasped out:

'That's all right, sir. I understand. Thanks for bringing us so far.'

They all shook hands, their sodden wool gloves meeting in an awkward clasp, and Laver whipped out a small flask of rum and stuffed it inside Sheard's life-jacket. Hasler felt a slight shock at this discovery that his men were carrying rum without his permission – another gift from the men of the submarine – but this was no time for comment. As the two unfortunate men dropped off, he said: 'God bless you both.'

Tight-lipped, Hasler and all that was left of his companions turned their canoes to the north and, paddling hard across the current, made for the open channel to avoid the jetty. At once they were confronted by yet another predicament. They could now see, a few hundred yards beyond Le Verdon jetty, the outlines of three or four ships of the 'Chasseur' type, similar to small destroyers, anchored in line ahead. They were, in fact, drawn up ready for inspection by the German admiral the very next morning. Through this dangerous defile, with the Chasseurs to port and the jetty to starboard, on both of which there were almost certain to be armed sentries, they would have to pass; for the tide was far too strong for them to attempt a detour.

Again Hasler gave the signal to close and whispered to Laver and Mackinnon.

'We shall have to go through one at a time,' he said. 'Single paddle, lowest position. I shall go first. Corporal, you will follow when you see that I have passed the line of ships. Mac, you will follow when *Crayfish* is through; I shall wait for you both in the clear water beyond.'

'Very good sir.'

'Take it quietly.'

'Yes, sir.'

Crouching low, faces nearly down to the cockpit cover, Hasler and Sparks went away and began to drift through, the single

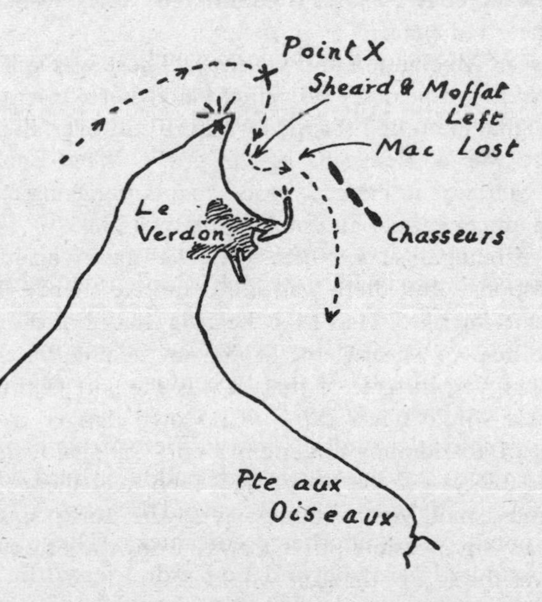

Figure 4. Map of Pte de Grave and Le Verdon.

paddles moving gently and without sound. Halfway through the defile a signal lamp on one of the ships began to call, winking in the direction of the jetty. To Hasler and Sparks it was like the beam of a searchlight and it seemed certain that they must be observed. They braced themselves for the lash of a rifle-shot that they felt must come; but there was none and they floated on to the safe pool of darkness beyond.

Turning and holding the head of the canoe into the current, Hasler and Sparks saw the dark shape of *Crayfish*, like a log on the tide, coming safely through and presently Laver and Mills joined them. Together they waited for Mackinnon and Conway and at that moment the signal lamp began to wink again. There was no sign yet of *Cuttlefish*. Sparks began to work his frozen fingers. Then on the still air they thought they heard a faint shout, repeated several times. Then silence again. What could it mean? The four waiting men listened anxiously and wondered: Was it a German sentry? Was it Moffat and Sheard? Was it Mac? Not until long afterwards was it to be known that Moffat's body was washed up on the beach at Les Sables d'Olonne, 70 miles away. Sheard was never heard of again.

And what of Mackinnon and Conway? There was still no sign at all of *Cuttlefish*, nor of any movement anywhere. It was bitterly cold. The signal lamp had stopped winking and over all the dark waters there was a silence as of the grave. What could have happened? Mac was in perfectly good shape, behaving as a first-class young officer should and making no mistake.

They gave their gull's cry. No answer. They gave it again, straining for a response, but there was still complete silence. Hasler's mind was working hard. Had Mac, hearing that faint shout, gone back to the help of Sheard and Moffat in their distress? It was against orders, yet, in spite of that, it was the sort of thing Mac might do. He would never think of his own danger and hated the thought of abandoning anyone in peril. Or, again, there was another possibility – if the shout had been a challenge from a German sentry, had Mac turned away to the north or south in order to draw any possible pursuit away from the other canoes? That also was the sort of thing he would do.

No answer came to their questionings.

Ah, well, they would have to leave him, too. The boy had guts and intelligence and Conway was a faithful No. 2. Unless some unexplainable disaster had befallen them, there beyond the range of the dark shroud that closed their vision, Hasler knew that Mac could be trusted to go forward on his own. No shot, no alarm had been heard. But it was a bitter moment. What trick the night had played was never known and not until these lines were written was it learnt that *Cuttlefish* was not yet lost but had gone on gamely alone.

Perplexed but undismayed, now, within but a few hours reduced to a mere two canoes, the little remnant of Hasler's Party turned away. They had no time to waste and must search for their first hiding-place. Proceeding on a course of 196 degrees, they picked up the south-west bank again and followed it. At about 6.30 a.m., creeping close in, they made their first attempt to land, but found themselves obstructed by a line of half-submerged stakes planted in a shingle bank some two hundred yards from the shore. Over these stakes the ground swell was breaking, making them dangerous to negotiate in the dark.

This was exasperating, for the day would soon be breaking. For nearly another hour the two canoes kept probing along the shore without finding any possible landing, and it was only as dawn was rising that they found a small sandy promontory called the Pte aux Oiseaux. Hasler stepped ashore in the grey light to make a quick and stealthy reconnaissance for about a hundred yards in each direction, as he always did. Then he signalled them in. Painfully, with stiff, cramped and exhausted limbs, the other three climbed out of their canoes, and then altogether they dragged and carried them up the beach and on to dry land, hiding them as best they could in some thin, low scrub a little above high-water mark and covering everything with their small camouflage nets. The place was chosen in desperation and it nearly led them into a desperate situation.

They were all very weary, soaked to the skin and chilled to the bone, very hungry and longing to relax from the tension of keeping so long on the *qui vive*. They had been paddling for eleven hours, had covered the equivalent of 26 land miles, had had no food except biscuits or sweets eaten at the hourly rests, and had undergone, on their very first night, an ordeal that would have shattered any men of lesser courage and physical stamina. They had been severely buffeted by angry seas. They had experienced, for the first time, that stretching of all the faculties that is keenly felt when the eyes and ears of an enemy are known or believed to be watching and listening beyond the dark. In a few short hours their little force of six canoes had been

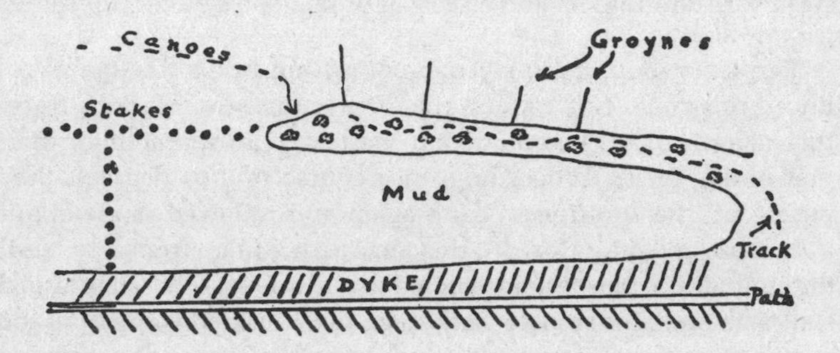

Figure 5. Plan of the 'hide' at Pte aux Oiseaux.

reduced to two. Six of their comrades were missing and at least two were likely by now to be prisoners or worse. Yet they felt the subdued elation of a job well done. They had escaped the perils of the sea and had come safely past the lights, ships and batteries of the enemy and had set foot on enemy-occupied soil. It is unlikely that any of them but Hasler were familiar with *Henry V*, but they might well that morning have exclaimed: 'We few, we happy few, we band of brothers. . . .'

But other thoughts than these occupied their tired minds. They began to get out their compact rations for a meal before sleep, but they had no sooner settled than their eyes and ears were pricked by a new danger.

Their 'hide' was close to a small creek and a little up the creek lay the hamlet of St Vivien. As day broke they heard the chugging of motors and, looking out from their scrub, saw the van of a small fleet of boats – motorboats, sailing craft and pulling craft – emerge from the creek to their right and make out into the river. About thirty came out in all. There was no cause for alarm until presently they saw some of the boats turn back towards the shore and make directly for the spot where they were hiding.

Almost at the same moment they heard the chatter of women's voices and a few moments later several women, carrying some utensils, emerged round the bend of a faint path that had led through the scrub to their right rear. Hasler's men kept very low, wondering what on earth was happening. The women stopped only about fifteen yards from them and almost at the same time the men came ashore, beaching their boats on the sandy mud. They were French fishermen. They greeted each other and the women began to make fires, while the men sat around. Hasler then realized what must have happened. The little creek dried out at low water and the fishermen therefore had to come out before the ebb. The early start had meant going without breakfast, so, now that the boats were safely out of the creek, the women had come to cook for them on the beach.

There were about a dozen men, the same number of women and a few children. Very soon it was evident that they had seen Hasler's men, though they pretended not to have done so. They were looking into the bushes out of the corners of their eyes and making remarks to each other out of the corners of their mouths.

Hasler thought hard. He reasoned that, if he did not disclose himself, it was almost certain that the French people would make some report to the police of suspicious characters in hiding. If, on the other hand, he disclosed himself as British, and their friends, there was just a chance that they would say nothing in answer to his appeal. There was a risk either way and he decided the lesser risk was to disclose themselves.

Ordering his men to keep him covered, he stepped forward, a tall, strong strangely clad Viking figure, with flowing red moustache, unshaven, strained with fatigue, his face streaked with the remains of camouflage grease, but somehow commanding. He went up to the fishermen and in his halting schoolboy French, repeating sentences that he had rehearsed, said:

'Good morning. We are English soldiers, your friends. We ask you not to tell anyone that you have seen us here.'

They did not answer him at first, but spoke among themselves.

'How do we know that they are English?' said one.

'For my part,' said another, 'I think that they are Germans. How could there be any English soldiers here?'

Someone else said: 'Whoever they are, it is safest that we mind our own business.'

Hasler saw clearly that they were frightened. Their instinct, as cautious French countrymen, was to have nothing to do with the affair. They had been living among the fears and suspicions of German occupation and Vichy rule, and their first care was to keep out of trouble. Finally one of them said to Hasler:

'We make no promises, monsieur. We will talk about it, but we make no promises.'

With that he had to be content and he withdrew to the bushes, where his three companions had all this time remained. They watched the Frenchmen finish their meal, get up, some to return to their boats, and others to wander about on the beach, apparently searching for shellfish; but not before one of them, perhaps an old soldier himself and understanding their wants, had walked over and given them some bread, for which they were very thankful. Then the women went away and they were alone.

After some food, they slept in turn, Hasler taking the first watch. He told Sparks that he would rouse him in an hour's time to take over, but it was four hours before Hasler did so. He was very anxious, for he apprehended that, whether it was Englishmen or Germans whom they had seen hiding, the Frenchmen could come to no harm if they reported having seen suspicious characters. It was their safest course and he was quite expecting to see a squad of steel helmets coming through the bushes at any moment. Even now he could hear men at work beyond the dyke that lay behind them. To these speculations were added his anxieties about their missing comrades – not only anxiety for their own sake, but anxiety about the difficulty that the little remnant of the expedition might experience in reaching their target, if any of the lost men, alive or drowned, had fallen into German hands. If so, then the whole of the defences must surely have been alerted and by water, land and air a search for them would very soon be taking place.

He was not to know that, *Tuna* having been picked up by radar and Wallace and Ewart having been captured, the Germans had in fact already ordered an alert and that before long they were to issue their lying announcement that on this day, 8 December, 'a small British sabotage squad was engaged at the mouth of the Gironde River and finished off in combat.' Not until now has it become known that the further progress of Hasler and his companions could scarcely have been possible if it had not been for the steadfast courage of Wallace and Ewart under a brutal inquisition, in which the German security police failed to extort from them a single word in betrayal of their comrades.

Late in the afternoon, while resting, Hasler was roused by the sentry on watch, and was not at all reassured when he saw approaching no steel helmets, but two of the French women who had been there before.

They stopped about twenty yards away, obviously wanting to talk but afraid to come any closer. Hasler thought it best to engage them in friendly conversation, so he crept out alone. One of the women was young and attractive and Hasler reflected how France, with so many of her army imprisoned in Germany, had been denuded of young men for two and a half years.

The women stayed for half an hour. The elder of them told Hasler that her husband was a prisoner in Germany. Then he fell for one of the oldest tricks in the world. She said something casually in German, and Hasler, whose German was better than his French, replied unguardedly: 'Ja.'

'So you are German!' she said.

Hasler laughed rather sheepishly and answered: 'Oh, no, I learnt German at school as well as French, only I am much worse at French.'

He didn't think she fully believed him, but they went on talking in French. She told him again about her husband and she told him also, to his greater concern, that the men they could hear on the other side of the dyke were German soldiers, employed on some new defence work. The talk ended non-committally and presently the two women went off. Perhaps one of them had been disappointed.

Save for these encounters, Hasler's little party of four, when they were not sleeping, looked and listened over a strange landscape. From behind the dyke came the sounds of pick and shovel, overhead the black-cross aircraft fled to and fro upon their missions. In the channel of the Gironde a few ships came and went. It was a drear, flat December landscape of grey skies and leafless trees. Between them and the shipping channel, as the tide ebbed swiftly, lay an ever-widening stretch of sandy mud, which they would presently have to negotiate. Yet it was a landscape of rich associations. From these shores had come Queen Eleanor, consort of our Henry II and mother of Richard Lionheart. In these waters the little ships of Richard himself and later of Richard II also had sailed long ago, here the American forces had steamed in the First World War, and here the argosies of Bordeaux carried to the countries of the world many

a beaker full of the warm South,
Full of the true, the blushful Hippocrene

For behind them lay the famous vineyards of Medoc, their harvest now all gathered in, from which, in due time, those same argosies would bring to our own shores their glowing vintages.

14. TWO ALONE

The Second Night (8/9 December)

No steel helmets came. Throughout this day the four marines lay resting, but getting very little sleep; nor did they on any other day, for the weather was very cold, they had no blankets and they had to remain almost without movement through all the hours of daylight. By unloading all the cargo bags, it was possible to sleep quite tolerably in the canoes themselves – one man with his feet in the bows and the other's in the stern, each mans' head level with the other's chest. This was the best means they had of sheltering from the wind and the rain. They washed and shaved nearly every day. They were able to urinate into their bailing bowls while afloat by night, but excretion was impossible, and by day, with restricted movement, very difficult.

For men who had to undergo such a trial of endurance, the food supplied was far from satisfactory. It was of the 'compact rations' type, which were still in the experimental stage; nor indeed have the people who order such matters yet found the right answer to this difficult problem. Every man had three waxed cardboard cartons for a day, each carton constituting what was considered to be a complete meal and each including a small tin of mixed tea-leaves, powdered milk and sugar, which by throwing into boiling water gave a ready-made mug of tea of tolerable palatability. In addition each man had a small tin of cheese and another of a meat mixture resembling Spam; also biscuits, sweets, cigarettes, chewing gum and 'lifeboat' fuzee matches. The food was unpalatable and lacked bulk. In fact no man ever ate the whole of his day's ration, the left-overs being carefully saved for the escape. One item was a block of compressed oatmeal, which could be made into porridge if it were possible to cook, otherwise it could be chewed as a hard-cake, and exceedingly hard it was.

During the long hours of paddling at night, their only sustenance was biscuits, sweets and water. They also had their benzedrine tablets for moments of exhaustion, which they took sparingly. Drinking water is always a serious problem on such expeditions, because of its bulk and weight, and the ration of five half-gallon cans that each canoe carried was a serious impediment, in the early stages, adding nearly 30 lb of weight to the already overloaded canoes.

Each canoe also carried a small dixie as a cooking pot and tablets of compressed methylated spirit as fuel. Cooking, however, often had to be forgone, though it was usually found possible to brew the tea with the inconspicuous flame of the solid spirit. These were all that the men had to live on for the whole expedition and for the start of the escape, except for the scrap of bread the fishermen gave them this first day.

Before the start of the second night's passage, Hasler's Party, squatting in the scrub at Pte aux Oiseaux, inspected their canoes and equipment, cleaned and oiled their weapons and destroyed all the air photos used on the expedition thus far. Sparks found that the small leak in *Catfish* which had bothered them all night had been due to a small rent in the canvas side, no doubt caused by the same projection as had ruled *Cachalot* out of the contest. This rent he made good with the small box of repair kit that each canoe carried. Then, while they cautiously brewed tea, Hasler gave them their orders for the night. It was to be another very hard trek, for they had to make up for the time and distance lost as a result of the first night's disasters. He intended tonight to get over to the other bank for the reasons stated already, and they would have only six hours of fair tide; that is to say, a tide flowing in the direction they desired, which, of course, in their passage up to Bordeaux, was the flood tide. In that time he wanted to make a good 20–25 miles.

As the sun was setting, they were the victims of one of those hallucinations of men under strain that are laughable in retrospect but serious enough at the time. One of them pointed to the dyke beyond which the Germans had been working and said:

'Look, Jerries!'

They all turned and saw the dim shapes of at least fifty men, advancing towards them in open order down the face of the dyke. The marines, keeping low, drew their pistols and felt for their fighting knives and Hasler himself took up his silent Sten. This was only what they had been expecting and Mills murmured: 'So the French have given us away after all.'

They watched the formation advance slowly in the twilight, and prepared for the fight that they saw coming. After a moment or two, however, the enemy halted, and remained so. Puzzled, Hasler put up his glasses, laughed and said:

'You can stand easy. They're not Jerries – just the same line of stakes that we have been looking at all day!'

Mills said: 'Cor, sir, but they were moving.'

'Just our imagination, Mills. Shows we are a bit on edge. We must shake it off.'

Corporal Laver said in his quiet way: 'Glad we didn't have to shake *them* off, sir. Bit too many for us, they'd have been.'

'That's true,' said Hasler grinning. 'Now, better get some more sleep while you can. We can't start for some hours yet.'

It was impossible to start their second night's passage until 11.30, when the flood stream began to run, but first they had to negotiate a difficult obstacle, where their training again stood them in good stead. As this was low-water springs, the ebbing tide had gone out three-quarters of a mile, and to get to the river the canoes had to traverse this bleak expanse of sandy mud. It was not, however, the deep, thick ooze of Chichester Harbour, the sand giving it an element of firmness. Instead of pushing their canoes over it, they dragged them by their painters, squelching ankle deep, the suck and slap as they dragged their feet out at each step sounding to their ears like pistol shots. Fully loaded, the boats were a hard pull for two men and they arrived at the water's edge sweating freely, but thankful for the wise planning of Goatley and Hasler that had given the canoes their flat bottoms and strong construction.

Getting the boats clear of the shore in the dark proved to be another difficulty, for there were large areas of outlying sandbanks beyond the low-water mark, and over these the Atlantic swell penetrating the estuary was breaking in small fast rollers, which had to be met by the canoes head-on. By skilful watermanship, however, Hasler led the way through into the open channel. The dotted line on the chart on pages xii and xiii shows their northward course before they finally turned upstream.

Navigation was easy, as the port-hand buoys of the shipping channel were all showing a flashing blue light and all they had to do for most of the passage was to keep parallel with them and about two hundred yards outside the channel itself – they did not, of course, want to meet any shipping. The weather was flat calm with no clouds.

Hasler set a hot pace to get on as far as he could and they all welcomed the call for effort, for the weather had turned even more bitterly cold than before. It has to be very cold indeed for seawater to freeze, but tonight the spray that broke over the Cockles was freezing on the cockpit covers. The drip from their paddles, running round the shafts, soaked through their gloves, numbing their hands and forming flakes and globules of ice on the gloves themselves. The spray splashing up on to No. 2's face was like the lash of a whip. Some or all of them took a tablet of benzedrine during the night. When they stopped for each hour's rest, Sparks and Mills, the two No. 2s, would crack some bawdy jest about the weather as they nibbled their biscuits or chocolate, while Hasler, with dim red torch, would show Laver where they were on the chart and tell him what he intended to do in the next hour.

This night they made an extremely good passage and the only incident occurred when, crossing the shipping channel, as they had to do to reach what we must now call the east bank of the estuary, they were nearly run down by a convoy of six or seven large ships, which came upon them quite unexpectedly from astern. A burst of hard paddling took them just clear, but they were so close that, as the wash of the leading ship rocked the canoes, they could see the reflection of her port light glinting red on the wave as it swept along their gunwales. 'More targets for us, sir,' said Sparks.

Six hours of hard paddling nearly exhausted the tide and the night. They exhausted the men, too, who, in spite of the exercise were chilled to the bone, their hands senseless with almost frozen water. They picked up the east bank just north of the tiny Portes de Calonge and followed it about a mile offshore until the approach of daylight made it necessary to find their 'hide' for the next day. Hasler, who had extraordinarily keen night vision, coming close in, saw that on this side there were many hedges, running down at right-angles to the river. He edged along the bank until he saw the outline of a double hedge. Here there was no shelving beach, the water running right up to a low, almost perpendicular bank. He stepped ashore straight into a field, made his usual reconnaissance and called the boats in.

They found themselves in an almost perfect hide in a dry ditch between two hedges. They had covered 25 land miles in the six hours (as against 26 in the eleven hours of the first night), and were almost exhausted as on the first night. As day broke they brewed some tea and then slept fitfully by turns under the lustreless grey marble of the winter sky. They were awakened very early by a German plane flying so low that they clearly saw the pilot in the cockpit, and thereafter there was constant activity in the air. Otherwise the day passed without incident, except for a herd of cows that were driven down into their field; but no drover appeared.

The only other cause of nervousness was a farmhouse about two hundred yards away beyond their twin hedges, but no one from it came towards them. During the day, in order to lighten their loads, they abandoned and buried in the ditch a few stores that they were no longer likely to need, together with the Sten gun, which Hasler considered an unnecessary weight. As they looked out over the widening mud and the moving water, it meant nothing to these marines that on the bank immediately opposite lay the vineyards from which came the delicate clarets of St Estephe, but Hasler cast wistful eyes a few miles upstream towards the great floating dock at Pauillac; he could see a ship lying in it. What a target, if they had had the means to attack it!

The raiders had nearly, in terms of distance, made good the delay that the first night's disasters had occasioned and Hasler, taking stock that day, was not dissatisfied. He was impressed by the excellent performance put up by Corporal Laver, that quiet man who had not shone very brilliantly in training but who now showed splendid qualities of steadiness, endurance and competence in the handling of his craft. He had caused no moment of anxiety. Of those they had left behind, he still hoped that Wallace and particularly Mackinnon were pursuing their objective independently. He knew of nothing that might have brought Mac to grief. He was sure the boy would have pressed on and perhaps was even now lying up somewhere not far away. We know now, after more than thirteen years, that his hopes were being so far amply fulfilled. Of Wallace and Ewart, Hasler was less sure. Left to themselves while still out to sea, they would have been faced with a severe test and he was afraid, both for the safety of the expedition and for their own sakes, that they may have been taken prisoner. He need not have feared, for *Coalfish*'s crew were even then proving their devoted loyalty.

Planning for the third night's passage, Hasler realized that, if they waited for complete darkness, they would have only three hours of fair tide before high water, as the flood began in the afternoon. The hide being so good, he therefore decided to take the slight risk of an early start. They were going to have a very difficult passage this next night, negotiating the many islands that lay farther up in the estuary. There was also a complication of the tides. The three hours of flood they would have at the start would be followed, of course, by six hours of ebb, and in those six hours they must find a night hide, after which there would be another three hours of the next flood before daybreak. The place he had decided to make for as his night hide was an unnamed island which they christened, hopefully, 'Desert Island'.

At evening twilight the weather was still flat calm, with no cloud and with visibility still unfortunately too good. The west yet glimmered with some streaks of day as the raiders, having made all shipshape, emerged from their hide, stiff and shivering and eager for exercise, and carried the canoes down to the river.

In doing so they were silhouetted against the sunset, and Hasler, keeping a look-out behind them, was alarmed to see a Frenchman coming towards them from the farm. He followed them to the bank and stood watching these queerly clad 'black-faced villains', no doubt wondering what on earth they could be doing with their strange craft in this quiet backwater of a remote countryside. As he said nothing, Hasler, uneasy about him, turned to him and repeated his little set-piece, saying that they were English and asking him to say nothing.

This fellow was not like the fishermen, however. He was a jovial sort and quite without inhibitions. He grinned broadly and said:

'*Eh bien, alors*, come up to the house and have a drink, all of you.'

This took Hasler quite by surprise. He replied, thank you, no; they must get along.

The Frenchman was clearly disappointed and said:

'Come now, it is a cold night. Whatever strange thing it is you have to do, a drink will be good for you.'

Very embarrassed, Hasler in his halting French declined again. The genial farmer was looking a little hurt, so Hasler did his best to make it easy. 'Perhaps after the war,' he said.

'Well, then, the next time you are passing,' the farmer replied, 'don't forget to come in. Good luck. I will say nothing, you may be sure.'

His seeming good nature did not allay their anxiety, and they were relieved at last to fend off and dip their paddles once more into the darkening waters. Even if his *bonhomie* were genuine, the dangerous fact remained that, as they moved away upstream, someone had actually watched them canoeing.

The Third Night (9/10 December)

They made good progress, but on reaching the restricted waters of the archipelago of islands were obliged to paddle close to the banks. Uncomfortably conscious of the noise of the dripping paddles so close to the shore, they longed for wind or rain to blanket the sound. It was still only early evening and on shore there were plenty of people about; they could hear and see the sights and sounds of normal life along the roads and in the villages as they passed. Abreast of the first island, they were startled by the sudden throb of a motorboat starting up by the next island ahead of them. They darted into a thicket of tall reeds on the water's edge and watched a motor-launch go by, within a hundred yards. She carried no lights, a fact that roused the men's suspicion. Was she a patrol boat that had been lying in wait for them?

When she was safely past, they pulled out again and in due time reached Desert Island, immediately opposite the famous vineyards of St Julien. By now they could feel the thrust of the ebbing tide bearing against them and they could make no headway. The banks of Desert Island were covered with a dense thicket of immense reeds, seven feet high, almost impenetrable and growing out of vertical banks of thick, oozy mud. At the first attempt the raiders were taken aback by a tremendous rustle and clatter as they tried to penetrate the reeds. After many attempts, however, at 8.45 p.m. they found a little opening where they got ashore into a small clearing and hauled up the boats before the tide fell.

Here they lay up for some hours and got some sleep. At 2 a.m. next morning (10 December), they roused up to catch the first of the flood but found the tide still ebbing and had to wait another three-quarters of an hour. To get launched, however, proved a difficult and filthy business. There was a six-foot mud cliff to

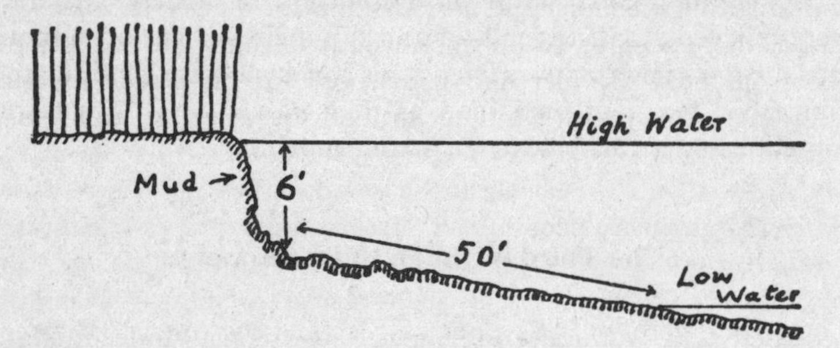

Figure 6. Section of typical mud cliff topped with very tall reeds, as at Desert Island, Ile de Cazeau and withdrawal point.

negotiate and then fifty feet of soft mud beach. Two men slithered first from the top of the cliff, and then, thigh-deep in icy mud, took the canoes as they were lowered from the top by the other two. Together they then pushed their boats over the soft ooze of the beach according to the drill that they had so fortunately learnt, arriving at the water's edge plastered with mud and wet through up to the waist. It was not only a dirty operation but also very noisy, and to their ears it seemed that the sounds of their squelching must have awakened everyone for miles about.

Pushing off, they then crossed the shipping channel again, without mishap, and entered the narrow, shallow passage between the west bank and the Ile Verte. Through these dangerous few miles, with the banks close to them on either side, they slunk with the greatest caution, using single paddle, and keeping right in close to the island, the banks of which, like those of Desert Island, were thickly forested with reeds.

By 6.30 a.m. they were approaching the southern end of the Ile de Cazeau, and began to look for a hide on the island. The west bank of the river was studded thickly with houses and farms and they clung close to the island, at times brushing the foliage and reeds with which it was clad. Towards the southern end all was dense undergrowth, looking pretty wild and uninhabited. In all this growth it was impossible for them to get in. Time was pressing and daybreak would be upon them very soon.

At length, near the southern tip of the island, Hasler saw the outlines of a small pier and although this meant that the place was used, there seemed to be thick woods beyond. He led the two boats in near the pier and got ashore for his reconnaissance. Finding a small path winding through the wood, he followed it cautiously for a little way keeping to the trees. After about fifty yards there was a clearing in the wood and in the centre of it a large rectangular object bulked. Hasler edged towards it cautiously, and found it to be a high wall, built of sandbags. Obviously, therefore, a military work. Its shape suggested an anti-aircraft gun position. The Admiralty Intelligence reports had, indeed, shown that anti-aircraft guns were believed to have been mounted on this island.

The value of reconnaissance again proved, he crept back along the path with extreme care to the point where the two boats were lying side by side. The situation was tense. Morning was at odds with night. Day was already breaking and at any moment they would be in clear view of the houses densely lining the mainland bank.

But, contrary to some accounts, Hasler got quietly back into his canoe, dipped his paddle and moved on upstream. In only a few hundred yards the island petered out in a fine point. He would just have to take pot-luck. Finally, in desperation, almost at the extreme tip of the island, at 7.30 a.m., with the dawn sky already bright on the port hand and sounds of traffic and movement already audible on the mainland, they pulled in to a field of long marshy grass. They carried the boats right into the middle of the grass, put up their camouflage nets and sat in the boats.

Here they had their most uncomfortable and anxious day. They were pinned down and had no sleep, except what they could get occasionally nodding in a half-recumbent position with no head rest. No cooking or smoking was possible and they could not relieve themselves. Their legs were still caked with mud and a thin cold rain came down, continuing most of the day. Only a thin fringe of trees separated them from the German gun site. During the morning some cattle came down from the north, paused on seeing the strange object in the middle of the grass, and formed a circle round the boats, staring curiously at them. At the same moment, reconnaissance aircraft came over, flying very low, searching the area. The marines, feeling like a bull's-eye in the middle of a target, sat rigidly still, extremely uncomfortable. After a little while the cattle moved on to the tip of the island, and on their return in the evening repeated their performance. At one time a man and a dog were moving among the trees not far away, but the dog never got their wind and the man never saw them. Their camouflage and their discipline of silence and immobility must have been extremely good.

Not until these lines were written was it known that Mackinnon and Conway spent that day on the self-same island – two or three miles from them on the east side.

They were now all feeling the strain, physically and nervously. In three nights they had paddled 60 miles. Through three days they had been able to make very little movement. They slept, when they could, cold and wet, and each evening when they crept stiffly from out their nets their movements were the stilted movements of numbed limbs. Frost formed on their wet clothing, so that, when they moved, it crackled like a starched shirt.

They had now left the Gironde behind them and were in the waters of the Garonne, in which lay Bordeaux itself, only some twelve miles away. Hasler had intended to make his attack on the enemy ships the coming night (10 December), but they had not got far enough up the river to enable this to be done with any chance of withdrawal afterwards. Having made a study of his charts and air photos, he therefore decided to make a short passage that night up to an advanced base within easy striking distance of his target. Unrested, but very glad to get away from a place of such acute discomfort and danger, the little party launched their boats again at 6.45 that evening, with the same difficulty that they had experienced before of steep and slippery mud banks.

The Last Night (10/11 December)

For the first time, conditions were ideal – a moderate southerly breeze, a cloudy sky with occasional rain. It was therefore much darker than on the previous night and the wind and the rain would deaden the sound of their paddling to anyone not very close. For the first two miles they kept up the centre of the river, then, changing to the silent single paddle, followed close along the reed-lined western bank.

Moving round a bend of the Garonne at about ten o'clock they saw, with a thrill of anticipation, what they had come so far to hunt – two fat ships moored at the quayside on the eastern bank. It was Bassens South, one of their two target areas. They paused for a moment to look, all fatigue forgotten. Yet the ships themselves gave them an immediate problem, for they were fully lit up and the raiders could hear the rattle of cranes as the stevedores worked at loading or unloading them. Very cautiously the hunters crept forward, clinging to the cover of the reeds.

Presently they could see, on their own bank, and immediately opposite the two ships, a small floating pontoon pier, at the end of which what appeared to be a coaling lighter was tied up. Unobserved, they glided up to the pier, then, ducking their heads, shot underneath it and beyond. A few yards beyond this, searching noiselessly, they found that little runnels of water penetrated the reed bed here and there. Choosing one of these, they slipped in among the reeds in a few inches of water, forcing the canoes in as far as possible. Here, side by side, in friendly fashion, they stopped at eleven o'clock that night, the men remaining in the canoes while the tide ebbed and allowed the canoes to settle on the mud.

There, for the rest of that night and all next day, they remained, not moving out of the canoes. But apart from immobility it was an ideal hide. The great rushes towered over their heads, nine feet high, and in the strong flat-bottomed boats they were able to stand up safe from observation. It was a relief to be able to do so and it gave them, also, the thrill of being able to gloat over two of their intended victims for the next night, immediately opposite them on the other bank. Both were good-sized cargo vessels (later to be identified as the ex-French *Alabama* and the German *Portland*) and should be easy meat for the hunters of the night.

Behind them, the waiting marines had no idea what was going on. The strip of reeds here was some five yards deep, but they knew from the air photos that it was densely housed almost right down to the river edge. They were, in fact, now right in the middle of what we should call a built-up area and during the day all the normal sights and sounds of human activity were abundantly evident all around them. On the two ships the winches rattled and groaned. On the land cars and lorries hummed and hooted. In the channel shipping went to and fro. Dogs barked in the distance, but not fortunately at them. Hidden away securely, Hasler and his companions smiled with a quiet satisfaction when they reflected that, among all this bustling activity around them, with the Germans just across the water, the Vichy police within hail, the shipping passing under their noses, the pontoon bridge at a stone's throw, there were none who dreamed that right in their midst, unseen and unsuspected, was this audacious little party, who on the next night were to shake the equanimity of the High Command to its foundations. It was nearly the end of the road and they tingled with anticipation.

Meanwhile the noise enabled them to talk freely in low tones and they could enjoy a smoke. It rained a little but, stretched out in the canoes, they managed to sleep.

During the day of the 11th, Hasler made his last plans for the attack that night. He had to ensure that the two canoes reached the beginning of the target area an hour or so before high water, so that they could drift along through the docks on the last of the flood tide, then, having reached the far end of the target area, turn round at high water and drift back with the first of the ebb. High water was at about midnight, and the ideal time for leaving their last hiding-place would have been 8.40 p.m.

Unfortunately, however, the sky was quite clear and the young moon was not due to set until 9.30. The danger of the canoes being seen when crossing the path of the moon was a very real one, and Hasler accordingly decided to delay the start until 9.10, as the best compromise between the two conflicting factors.

He decided that he himself in *Catfish* would work up the western bank of the main docks at Bordeaux, some three miles distant. To Corporal Laver he gave orders that *Crayfish* was to make along the eastern bank towards Bordeaux East Docks, but if he found no favourable targets there he was to return and attack the two ships at Bassens South that they had been looking at all day. He was to work independently, and each of them, after completion of his task, was to paddle back downstream on the ebb, as far as possible until stopped by the next flood tide or by the approach of day, and then make their separate escapes on the eastern bank, scuttling their canoes. Hasler still nourished the hope that, of those missing, Mackinnon at least would still get through.

During the day, they rearranged the stowage of the canoes, so as to have all the escape equipment in two bags. In the early evening they had their last meal in their beloved Cockles and immediately afterwards Hasler ordered them to get out their limpets and fuse them. It was a great moment. The gun was to be loaded for the battle. The prelude for action had begun at last. Finished was training, finished was the exhausting approach march, the moment had come to prepare to strike. Sparks was trembling with excitement.

For each pair of limpets there was a small tin containing two sets of ampoules – clear glass bulbs about the size of the top of a man's finger, each containing a liquid of a different colour. 'We will use the orange ampoules,' Hasler ordered, 'giving a nominal nine hours delay. In fact, as you know, they will run several hours longer in this temperature.'

Each man took a pair of limpets between his knees and unscrewed one of the fuse-caps, revealing a cavity inside. Taking an orange ampoule, he slipped it in, then replaced the fuse-cap and tightened it down. With the spike of his clasp knife, he scratched a cross on the outside of the fuse to show it was ready for starting. After doing the same for the second limpet, he turned the pair upside down, and fitted a soluble plug into each 'sympathetic fuse'.

Finally, he hooked the six-foot placing rod into each limpet in turn, to ensure that it would engage and disengage freely. To fuse all the sixteen limpets of the two boats took more than an hour. To ensure that nothing was forgotten, all four men worked in unison, Hasler ordering each separate operation and watching until it was completed.

Out of the corner of his eye, he was also watching the time, the moon and the weather. Before long both canoes were stowed and ready to go, the compasses hidden away so that their luminous dials should not be visible to a sentry standing above them in a ship. Faces were blackened. At nine o'clock Hasler gave the order: 'Start your time fuses.'

In accordance, they turned the thumb-screw of each fuse until a faint 'click' told that the glass of the ampoule had been broken, releasing the liquid acetone inside. The mines were now alive and nothing would stop them from going off in nine hours' time or a little more.

Light thickened, and the crow made wing to the rooky wood. The two crews shook hands and wished each other good luck. At 9.15 they slid the canoes quietly out through the reeds and mud, launched and set their separate courses for their last passage.

15. THE ATTACK

The weather was again hostile. No rain, no wind, no cloud. A flat calm lay on the waters of the Garonne and all the stars in the heavens looked down at them from a clear, frosty December sky. As *Catfish* stole out, her eight live limpets fizzing away quietly, Hasler was disconcerted to find that, unlike our own blacked-out ports, there were also a great many lights along the banks, including the lights of what appeared to be a factory. He therefore kept *Catfish* about two hundred yards off-shore for the greater part of his final approach.

After about ninety minutes' paddling, round a long bend of the Garonne the hunters saw at last their prey. In the distance, moored to the quays on the west bank, some of them brightly illuminated, was a long line of ships. How many, they could not yet count. Hasler and Sparks were filled with elation. Not stout Cortez, 'silent, upon a peak in Darien', could have been more moved. All fatigue, all distresses of the body, all stretching and pricking of the nerves and faculties were lightened, released and expunged. The hunter's stealth and cunning and fixed intensity of purpose had carried them at last to the end of the spoor and the quarry lay ready for the kill.

But cunning must still be their precept, for who, in that blaze of lights, could escape detection? Powerful cluster-lamps lit up the decks of several of the ships and the waters around, and lamp-posts were throwing a brilliant light across the entrance to a lock that they would have to pass to starboard before they could put their claws upon the prey. Coming to this lock entrance, *Catfish* swung in a wide arc, then wheeled in again, following the circumference of the lamp's rays.

There was not much time left. The tide was already almost at

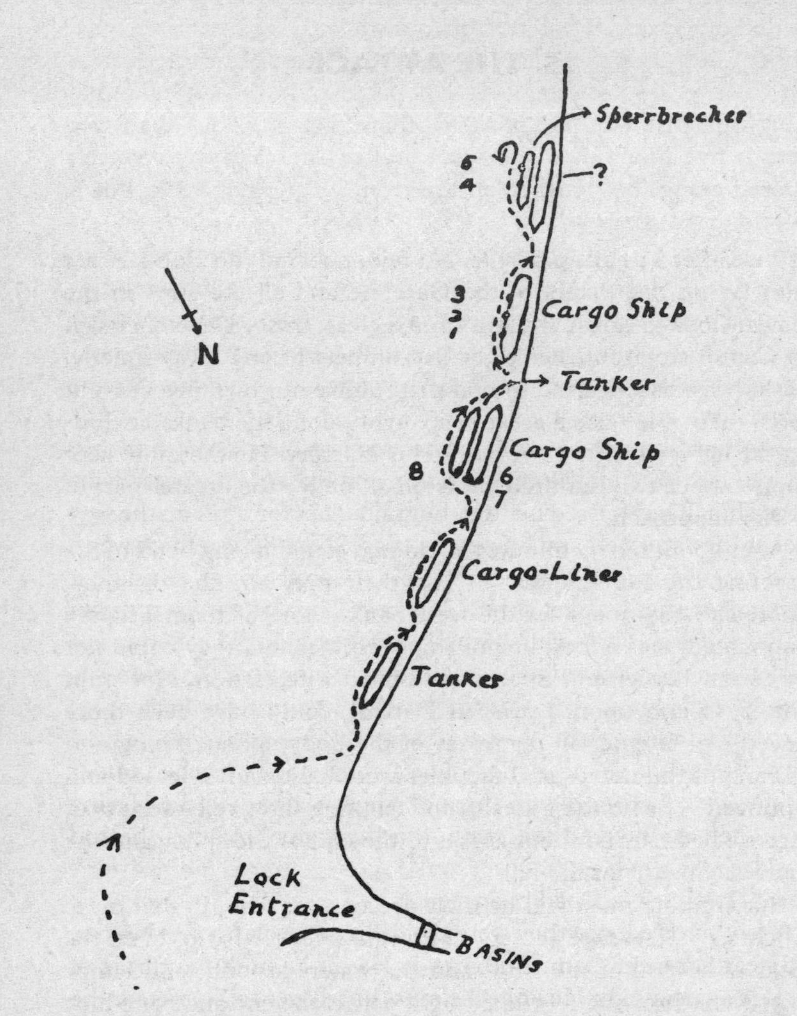

Figure 7. Hasler's targets at Bordeaux Docks. The black dots show the placing of the limpet mines, and the figures show the order in which they were placed.

high-water slack and would be turning against them soon. As they swung away from the lock entrance Hasler had the opportunity he wanted of viewing the ships from a distance, in order to see what types of ships they were; for, as we have seen earlier, once a canoe was close to the towering sides of a big ship, it was impossible to know what she was. He now saw that seven ships lay ready for them – five moored to the quay and two having other vessels moored alongside. Farther up the river lay another flock, but it was doubtful if the tide would allow them to get so far. Completing their deviation, Hasler and Sparks brought *Catfish* right up to the quay. Their camouflage hoods were up. From now on they must keep to the deep shadows within a yard of the quay wall or cling close to the waterline of each ship they came upon. They were in single paddles and must use all that they knew of the hunter's wit and cunning.

The first ship was a tanker. She was not their meat and they ignored her, creeping along her hull. Next to her was a passenger-cargo ship. They passed her too, but noted her for a kill on the way back if they still had any limpets to spare. Next in the flock was a good cargo ship, but a tanker that was moored alongside made it extremely difficult to get at her. The next ship was a perfect target – a large cargo ship with nothing moored alongside her – and Hasler eagerly prepared to begin putting in his claws. The tide was already beginning to ebb. Just past the bows of the ship he stowed his paddle. Behind him, Sparks, taking up the signal, clung to the ship's side with his magnetic holder, while Hasler reached under his cockpit cover for the first limpet. He attached it to the placing rod. Then he lowered the mine into the water as far as the rod would go, gently brought it up to the ship's side and felt the mine cling. The first blow had been struck.

A few yards on and they were amidships. No alarm yet. No one had heard or seen them. But already Hasler had felt the thrust of the tide against him. He knew he must hand over to Sparks, or the adverse tide would swing the bows of the canoe out and away from the ship's side. Stopping amidships, he therefore passed the placing rod back to his No. 2. Sparks understood at once and gave him the magnetic holder. The roles were reversed and it was now Sparks who dug in the claws. He did so again when Hasler stopped a third time near the ship's stern. That would be enough for this ship.

As they moved along each ship in turn, there was little that they could see except the towering rusty cliff of her side, studded with rivets and pimpled ironically with the real limpets from which their own took its name. From time to time they had to make their way past an outfall of water or sewage being discharged from a pipe several feet above their heads. Worst of their enemies were the cascades of the great condenser outfalls, forcing them out from the ships' sides and drenching them with spray. From the hum of the auxiliary engines they could locate the engine rooms, and from men's voices or a fragment of music the crew's quarters.

They came to the last ship in the group. They could not identify her nor get at her properly, for, moored alongside her, was a small German naval craft of the type known as a sperrbrecher, about the size of a frigate.

Lurking in the shadows, Hasler sized her up rapidly. She was not the kind of prey he was after – a gazelle among the big water-buck, a pigeon among the fat geese, a mackerel among the sharks. Further upstream he could see another plump herd, but he could never hope to reach them now against the tide. Downstream, on his way back, he knew that there was only one good quarry and that it was difficult to get at. He had five limpets left. He must go home with as full a bag as possible and little fish are sweet. As a German naval vessel, the sperrbrecher was anyhow fair game and a justifiable target, so he decided that she should have two limpets. With a few hard strokes *Catfish* was under her bows.

He stopped alongside the German's engine room and there Sparks fixed two limpets spaced several yards apart. Now they must turn to go back downstream, which meant that they must swing out and away into the stream from the ship's side in a wide loop. As they were in the middle of this risky movement, they heard a clang on the ship's deck and a torch shone down on them. A sentry had seen them. His shape was clearly outlined against the night sky as he looked over the rail.

There was only one thing to do. With a cautious drive of the paddles, they slid in right up to the ship's side and froze in the forward low position, hooded heads in their laps. 'I felt,' said Hasler, 'as though my back had been stripped naked.'

No shot, no clamour, but the torch still shining down on them from fifteen feet above. Bodies and paddles motionless, they allowed the canoe to drift gently with the tide along the waterline. The sentry, torch in hand, followed them down, iron-shod boots clanging on iron deck.

As *Catfish*, like an idle log, drifted down, the sperrbrecher seemed to the two marines to have the length of a battleship and that each clang of the sentry's boots was like the toll of a cracked bell. After an eternity of time, they reached the end of the ship's waterline, drifting in under the flare of her bows, where they were at least invisible from the deck. What now? Go on drifting into the open water beyond and under the glare of the lights? Quietly Hasler handed the magnetic holdfast back to Sparks and made the hold-on signal. With infinite care, Sparks 'rolled' the magnet onto the ship's side with a barely audible 'click', and the canoe clung motionless, moored by the stern with the ebb tide running past them to freedom.

When they stopped, the sentry above them stopped too. Presently his torch wandered over the surrounding water, then went out, but he was still there, shifting his feet occasionally. An age passed. No sound of the boots moving away. What was he doing? Waiting for them to show themselves again? Or had he decided they were a piece of driftwood and was taking a rest?

Well, they could not wait for ever. There was another fish to fry. Hasler signalled 'let go' and Sparks removed the holdfast. Without paddling, crouched in the lowest position, they drifted quietly out from under the bows, letting the tide carry them downstream. Once again the agony of waiting for a shot in the back. One minute, two minutes – at last they began to breathe again. They were out of the range of vision and no alarm had been raised. The whole incident was a triumph for those at SOE who had devised this camouflage technique and for the men who had now practised it so convincingly.

Moving quietly on downstream, they passed the ship they had already attacked and came to the awkwardly placed cargo ship, with the tanker moored alongside. Hasler wanted, of course, to distribute his limpets along the length of the merchantman, but the presence of the tanker prevented him from getting at her amidships, so he decided to attack stem and stern. They laid *Catfish* accordingly between the bows of merchantman and tanker and let her glide ahead until she was almost wedged in between them, with the tide now running strongly. Sparks, about to ship his paddle and get out the holder, saw Hasler in front of him suddenly spreadeagle his arms, one on the hull of each ship, as if trying to push them apart. Then he realized that the two ships, yawing slightly under the influence of the tide, were closing together and about to crush the Cockle between them. Sparks at once followed suit, and together, pressing with all their strength, they pushed the canoe backwards just in time. 'I felt,' said Hasler, 'like Atlas holding up the world.' Back-paddling hard against the tide, they rounded the bows of the tanker and drifted downstream to the stern.

Here they successfully pushed in between the two ships, planting two limpets on the stern end of the cargo ship, spaced as far apart as possible, and the last one on the stern of the tanker.

Their job was done. All their limpets had been successfully planted. The canoe, relieved of the weight of them, suddenly felt lively and unstable. Her crew also felt as though a great weight had been lifted off them. Hasler twisted round in his seat, gripped Sparks's free hand and shook it warmly. They were both smiling for the first time for many hours. Neither of them felt any worries about the dangers of the withdrawal; indeed a kind of quiet recklessness gripped them.

'I felt,' says Hasler, 'as though I owned the river and my respect for the enemy gave way to contempt. I took *Catfish* straight out into the middle of the river, where the tide was strongest, and we shot off downstream, paddling strongly in single paddles. We must have been visible and audible to both banks, if anyone had been looking, but we just didn't seem to care.'

None the less, there was still a great trial to be undergone. Up till now all had been carefully thought out and planned. They had been on the offensive. It was they who, in spite of the obstacles, had controlled events. Now there was no more planning. They would be at the mercy of events. They would have to live by their wits.

They were to be no longer soldiers on an organized expedition but refugees in a semi-hostile country. To reach safety, even by the shortest route, they would have to travel at least 800 miles, without transport, without means of subsistence and in the depths of winter.

No such thoughts, however, were in their minds as they made their way again down the Garonne. They thought only of their next purpose, which was to get as far down the estuary as the ebbing tide would carry them before daylight. So, making fast time, they paddled past their last hide, past the two ships at Bassens South that had been allotted as Laver's victims. Then, too early for safety, they changed to double paddles and really began to move, sweeping past the sleeping villages and the tall, silent reeds till they came almost back again to the scene of that disagreeable hide on the Ile de Cazeau and once more turned off the main channel to pass inside the islands. Here they stopped in midstream for a rest, drifting idly along with the tide in the utter stillness.

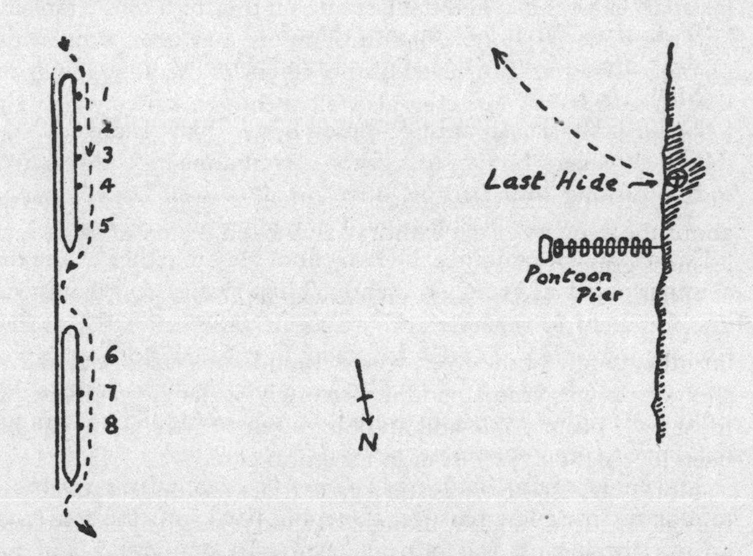

Figure 8. Laver's targets at Bassens South, and the last day's hide on the opposite bank of the Garonne.

Presently they heard a faint but familiar noise astern of them, rapidly getting louder. 'It sounded,' says Hasler, 'like a Mississippi stern-wheeler at full speed, but we knew what it was and we laughed aloud.' Turning *Catfish* round, they soon saw the shape of a canoe materialize out of the darkness, travelling fast in double paddles, 'with a bone in her teeth'. Suddenly the paddling stopped, and the oncoming canoe 'froze'. They had just spotted the stationary *Catfish*, but were not close enough to identify her. 'Good work, Laver,' thought Hasler. The cry of a very cautious seagull whispered over the water and Hasler, laughing aloud in the height of his spirits, sent back an answer that sounded like a seagull in the summit of intoxication.

Instantaneously, the other canoe 'unfroze' and paddled swiftly up. It was Corporal Laver. They rafted up together joyfully, Laver and Mills in great spirits.

'We went right down the east bank as far as we could, sir, like you said,' Laver whispered to Hasler, 'until the tide turned against us, and we found no targets at all. So we came back and attacked the two ships at Bassens South.'

'Well done. What did you give them?'

'Five limpets on the first ship, sir, and three on the second.'

'Meet any trouble?'

'None at all, sir. All went off much better than "Blanket".'

'Just as well for both of us. Anyhow, well done indeed you two. And' – turning round to his own No. 2 – 'well done, Sparks. You've all done wonderfully, and I'm really proud of you.'

For a few more minutes the two canoes lay together, while the men whispered and laughed silently. Then Hasler said that it was time for them to separate and withdraw independently, as laid down in the orders. Laver said: 'Couldn't we go along with you for a bit, sir? It would be nice to keep company as long as we could.' 'All right,' Hasler answered, 'if you would like to. But we shall have to separate before we land.'

So, united again, *Catfish* and *Crayfish* assumed their wonted stations for their last passage, sweeping back into the Gironde, through the narrow waters between the Ile de Cazeau and the mainland, driving the canoes as fast as they would go, for they wanted to put as much distance as possible between themselves and Bordeaux before the excitement began. As always the tide was the determining factor. Once the flood stream turned against them, they would be forced to land or be swept back upstream.

Hasler therefore turned away to starboard, crossed the shipping channel to the east bank and slipped past the sleeping town of Blaye. Here, lying opposite Blaye, they passed the big French liner *De Grasse*, at anchor and with no sign of life on board. Hasler knew, from his Intelligence briefing, that she was laid up for the duration of the war. One day she would set out once again on her familiar track to New York, and he wished her good luck.

A little north of Blaye the little party stopped and looked back. There, a few miles away, from the direction of the point where the Garonne and the Dordogne meet, a searchlight was sweeping the estuary; perhaps it was as well that they had avoided the main channel.

It was now six o'clock in the morning, only an hour and a half before dawn, and the flood tide had already begun to turn against them. But they had got far enough to be able to land in open country to the north of Blaye, with a clear escape route to the north-east. For five successive nights the two canoes had been at large in enemy waters, covering a total of 91 sea miles or 105 land miles, by canoe alone. Their Cockles had proved themselves.

For the last time, Hasler made the 'raft-up' signal. As Laver and Mills came alongside he said:

'Well, Corporal, this is where we have to separate. You are about a mile north of Blaye. Go straight ashore here and carry out your escape instructions. I shall land about a quarter of a mile further north.'

Laver looked at him steadily and said:

'Very good, sir. Best of luck to you.'

For him it was perhaps an even harder moment than the time, nine hours before, when they had separated for the attack. Now, a young fellow of twenty-two, without superior schooling, he would have to land in a completely strange and semi-hostile country, knowing nothing of the language, and use his own wits to get through, venturing into the unknown without guide or leader. It would have been a lot to ask of an officer, but Corporal Laver did not shrink from it.

'Goodbye, both of you,' said Hasler, 'and thank you for everything you've done. Keep on as you've been doing and we'll be meeting again in Pompey in a few weeks' time.'

Reaching across the gunwales, they shook hands all round, each with a 'Good luck!' for the other. But it was Sparks who struck the right note at the final moment.

'See you in the "Granada",' he said with his infectious smile. 'We'll keep a couple of pints for you!'

So it was with a quiet laugh that they pushed the canoes away from each other and paddled away on their separate courses. Just once Hasler looked back over his right shoulder at *Crayfish*, paddling strongly for the shore. She looked to him suddenly very small, very helpless, and he quickly looked away again. For a moment his heart was heavy, as it had been when he said goodbye to Sheard and Moffat, and it was with an effort that he forced himself to concentrate on the problem of landing.

It was the last they ever saw of the gallant Laver and Mills.

PART THREE

WHAT HAPPENED AFTERWARDS

16. RESULTS OF THE RAID

Back in COHQ no elation prevailed. The German radio announcement, though not taken at its face value without confirmation, caused anxiety but not great surprise. It was the inevitable business of COHQ to send men often upon their last voyages, and Mountbatten himself did not expect anyone to return from the Frankton expedition. It was asking a lot of anyone to penetrate 60 miles into the heart of enemy country along a well-used waterway, blow up enemy ships and make good one's escape by one's own wits. Yet when he asked a month or so later whether there were any survivors from 'Frankton' and was told 'None', Mountbatten glowered at Neville and said: 'I was persuaded, against my better judgment, to let Major Hasler go on the raid and now we have lost him.'

Nevertheless, in the report that he sent to the Prime Minister, in which he quoted the German broadcast, Mountbatten had not given up hope.

> It seems possible [he wrote] that the Germans may have only intercepted one section of the raiding party. The Commander of the party was Major H. G. Hasler RM, who would probably be with the leading section.
>
> The capture by the Germans of one section would not necessarily have compromised the other section, since no papers were carried other than charts.

For the purpose of getting some definite information, it was decided to send out an aerial photographic sortie, but not at once. The flight would arouse German suspicions and if any of our men were still alive and in hiding, search parties might be sent out. When the photographs were at length taken, they showed one good piece of news – that several ships had in fact been sunk or severely damaged. Some, at least, of Hasler's Party had therefore reached their objective and achieved their purpose. But of the men themselves all was still coldly silent, and on 25 January 1943, all were officially reported by Jock Stewart, on instructions, as 'Missing'.

The mothers of all the men who had set out on the expedition accordingly received immediate telegrams to this effect, and although this was to some extent a routine process, it caused acute distress to them all. Mrs Hasler, in particular, remembered that it was an exactly similar 'Missing' telegram that had presaged the news of the death of her husband in 1917.

It was not until towards the end of February that the sky lightened somewhat. At that time a coded message, sent from Switzerland by the Englishwoman known in the French escape circles as 'Marie-Claire', arrived at a secret office. It consisted of a continuous string of letters and the Intelligence staff were quite unable to decipher it, the only fact known being that it was from Hasler. It was not until years later that Ronnie Sillars, who, it will be remembered, had been present at the briefing of Hasler and Mackinnon in the No. 3 Code, told the story of how the problem was solved. Writing to Hasler, he said:

'It was an evening I shall always remember. Those of us who knew of the operation were tensely awaiting news of the raiders. Much sooner than we expected, your coded report arrived. Only night-duty staff were on, and there was no one in the decoding section who could make head or tail of it. That was understandable in view of the manner in which the letters were strung together. By great good luck, our extremely competent Wren, 2nd Officer Hamilton, was doing her homework in the office, and I suggested to her that she might have a go at your message on the assumption that you had superimposed No. 3 Code on a kind of bogus cipher, or the other way round. Marie Hamilton had both imagination and amazing skill as far as codes were concerned, and it wasn't long before there was a cloud of cigarette ash as she leapt to her feet, coughing, 'It's coming out – it's coming out!' When she got the hang of your method (which was excellent for that particular message, and made the code virtually unbreakable by any outsider, however expert), she quickly had the report decoded. She was just 'fey' that night. Shortly afterwards the decoded version was on its way to Combined Ops by special D.R.'

The message proved to be a very compressed report on the operation and from this epitome COHQ was able to reconstruct what had happened in broad outline. It was also evidence that Hasler, and Sparks, who was mentioned in the message, were so far safe and in French hands. These, however, were the only two of whom there was yet any news.

*

In spite of having been alerted through the location of the *Tuna* by radar and through the early capture of Wallace and Ewart, and no doubt other signs, the Germans remained entirely ignorant of the objective of Hasler's raid until after the explosions had taken place. This was due to the loyal and courageous silence that, under intense and brutal pressure, Wallace and Ewart maintained after capture. No doubt the Germans considered it fantastically impossible that canoeists would attempt to penetrate so far up the busy waters between well-populated shores. Many daring little raids were taking place along the shores of Europe by our uniformed forces, but they had been tip-and-run affairs, with objectives close to the shore and not requiring deep penetration.

The Germans were therefore taken completely by surprise when, on the morning of 12th, Hasler's and Laver's limpets went off one after another. With their timing mechanism and sympathetic fuses not yet perfected, the explosions were irregular and were exceedingly disconcerting thereby, for after repair crews had got to work on the first explosions, fresh ones were occurring. On Laver's main target, the ex-French ship *Alabama* at Bassens South, the explosions appear to have been spread over a period from 7 a.m. to 1 p.m., according to information from enemy documents after the war. None of *Catfish*'s limpets went off before 8.30 a.m., but all within half an hour. Such, at least, is what is said to have occurred, though we can by no means be sure of the exact details.

The dockyard fire and salvage squads were immediately summoned, and, according to one French report, contrived deliberately to add to the damage by excessive flooding with their hoses in putting out the fires. The stern of the *Dresden*, holed both in her outer plating and in her propeller-shaft tunnel, sank to the bottom. The *Tannenfels* listed over to an angle of 24 degrees, water pouring into her hold, and was soon sinking. The *Alabama* was holed by all five limpets. The *Portland* was badly holed also. There was much damage by fire. *Alabama*, *Tannenfels* and *Portland* were subsequently patched up with the aid of divers, pumped out and put into dry dock for extensive repairs. What happened to the sperrbrecher and the tanker is not certain, though it is known that one of the sperrbrecher's limpets fell off, perhaps under concussion from the others, and exploded on the river bed. So good was our naval intelligence that all this – a bare minimal estimate from the scanty sources available – was known to us in substance as early as 3 May.

To the Germans it was at the time a shock and a mystery. At Hitler's headquarters in Germany, as we know from a German naval captain there, the news of the 'heavy damage' was received with consternation. Hitler himself was extremely angry and demanded to know why these things were allowed to happen. In Bordeaux itself, the Germans first supposition was that we had somehow laid drifting underwater mines. These ships were much prized by the enemy and the objects of much congratulation; Admiral Bachmann, the German Commander-in-Chief of Western France, is said to have assured Hitler only a week before that in Bordeaux they were untouchable by an enemy. Among the civilians, according to a French officer who was there at the time, it was cynically said that the Italians, whose naval officers in the port were full of buck and swagger, had sunk the ships as revenge for the Germans' refusal of permission for their submarines to use the U-boat shelters. It was, the French said, 'the sort of thing the Italians would do'.

The truth did not begin to appear until a search revealed the remains of *Catfish* and *Crayfish* near Blaye on 12 December and an unexploded limpet on the hull of *Portland*. Sheard's *Conger* was found later near La Pallice, 50 miles north of the Gironde, not far from where Moffat's body was recovered. Mackinnon's *Cuttlefish* never seems to have been found.

Stringent measures were ordered at once by the Senior Naval

Officer, Inshore Squadron of Gascony (Captain Max Gebauer), to prevent the success of any such daring forays in the future. The area where *Tuna* had been located by radar was kept illuminated by searchlights and other areas swept. Guns of the coastal batteries stood to. Three searchlight batteries at Royan, St Georges and Le Verdon were to search 'at regular intervals'. Two vessels were to patrol the mouth of the estuary between Pte de Grave and Royan. Land patrols were to be carried out on both banks.

In addition, the Harbour Master of Bordeaux called for booms to be installed in defence of the Pauillac floating dock and at the stone bridge of Bordeaux itself; for the strengthening of patrols everywhere; for installations that could not be included in their rounds to be protected by barbed-wire entanglements; for additional lighting on ships and in harbour installations; for the crew of the guard vessel at the harbour entrance to be strengthened and its searchlight to sweep the shore at intervals; and for a patrol vessel to be provided to cover the whole harbour area, including Bassens.

It is not clear whether all these measures were put into effect, for there were shortages in men and in materials, but it is quite evident that the Germans, and no doubt the Vichy French also, were very angry and very anxious. There were 'rockets' flying and nervous sentries were reported to be shooting at floating driftwood.

The German naval authorities at once circulated information reports to both their own and Italian Commands, 'so that you may take suitable precautions in consequence', though they were still uncertain how it had all been done. 'It must be assumed,' said one of these documents, captured by us soon afterwards, 'that the enemy knows precisely our coastal and defence installations.'

17. THE ESCAPE

Escaper's Technique

The escape instructions that Hasler and his men had been given had two main purposes.

The first was to put them in touch with one or other of the secret organizations that the patriotic French had voluntarily built up to assist Allied soldiers, airmen or seamen who had escaped from German captivity or had been shot down from aircraft or had otherwise found themselves in French territory. By this time, as a result of the Anglo-American landings in French North Africa under Eisenhower, the whole of France had been occupied by the Germans, but the occupation had not yet been made everywhere effective and a 'line of demarcation' was still in force between the areas previously free and those that had been infested by the Germans ever since 1940, of which the Bordeaux region was one. Once across this demarcation line, escape was more easily effected, for the German military forces were more widely scattered and the only enemies of escapers were the French police and others who were collaborators or sympathizers with the Germans. But in the old occupied area it required a brave man or woman to help any escapers, for the hand of the German was heavy and without mercy. Within these areas the fever that they had spread among the population was fear.

The second main purpose of the escape instructions was to ensure that our men behaved in such a manner that, if captured, they would be entitled to be treated as prisoners of war, and not as spies, civilian 'saboteurs' or others outside the pale of protection. Those who are in uniform are of course entitled to such protection, whether armed or unarmed. It is also recognized by all decent nations that an escaping soldier does not lose his right to protection by wearing civilian clothes, provided he does not carry any weapons.

Obviously it is impossible for a uniformed escaper to get very far undetected, and the first instruction that the raiders had accordingly been given was to obtain civilian clothes as soon as they could and then to discard their uniform and arms. They were to obtain these clothes, however, by legitimate means, going to farms or other isolated houses, declaring themselves, asking for clothing and offering payment for it. The only military equipment they should retain were their identity discs, worn under their clothing round the neck.

Until they had obtained these disguises, the raiders were told, they must move furtively, by night, avoiding roads and public places. But after they had discarded their uniforms they should behave as normal French civilians would, travelling by the roads openly and by day, asking for food and shelter at isolated houses when necessary and offering payment for it. They would behave, in fact, in the very opposite manner to that which they would have to adopt while still in uniform – not stealing along hedges, nor climbing walls, nor doing anything else that might catch the eye of a policeman. They were to travel in parties of not more than two, for two is a natural sort of companionship and anything more than that number is liable to attract notice.

Even expressed in these simple terms, an experience of this sort was obviously full of dangers. Apart from any chance encounter or incidents, a serious risk was taken every time a man approached a house for food or shelter and a more serious risk still when he did so while still in uniform. An escaper had therefore not only to possess a great deal of shrewdness and cool nerve but also he had to have all the luck in the world.

All these points of guidance Hasler and his men had been taught. They had also been told, more specifically, that, in order to contact one of the French escape organizations, the place they should make for was the town of Ruffec.

This town, famous for its *foie gras aux truffes*, stands about 70 miles from Bordeaux and roughly north of it. From Blaye it is, in a straight line, about 70 miles north-east. All about is the land of

Angoulême, once a diadem of the English crown and famous today as the Cognac country, the town of Cognac itself being only some 30 miles away. The raiders were told that the French escape organization had been warned to expect them and would be on the look-out for them at the approaches to Ruffec. This direction of escape had been chosen as it was not on the route from Bordeaux to Spain – the direction in which the Germans and the Vichy police would be expected to search for them and where in fact they did search.

To help him in his escape every man had been given two of the famous 'escape boxes'. These were little plastic boxes, of about the size of a flat packet of fifty cigarettes, which included a few essential items to help the man find his way. There was the silk 'escape handkerchief' with a map of the country printed on it, some book-matches printed with the V-sign and the name of the English manufacturers, some malted milk tablets, and several luminous toy compasses about the size of a farthing. The reason for there being several of these compasses was that they were susceptible to wet. As a reserve for special emergencies, there was one compass fitted into the base of a collar stud and an extra-special one that was made in the form of a trouser-fly button, which could, however, be used only in a last resort, for it had to be cut off the trousers and balanced on a pin.

These escape boxes, together with the handkerchief and the V-sign book-matches, were pretty well known in large areas of France and other occupied countries and were a sure passport to all civilians of good faith and heart. If the men were caught by the Germans, they were also evidence of proper prisoner-of-war status. Hasler's marines were provided with double the supply usually issued to RAF aircrews. They were also given a pair of felt-soled boots to replace their gym shoes and thin-soled waders, which were unsuitable for a long march.

Into the Unknown

After parting from *Crayfish*, Hasler and Sparks paddled on hard against the young flood tide for another quarter of a mile. Then they turned inshore, still adopting the standard drill of the cautious single paddles. They were near the village of St Genés-de-Blaye. The shore seemed entirely deserted and they grounded on soft mud, climbing out stiffly after nine hours in the canoe, in which they had covered 26 miles that night.

Fifty yards away they could make out a mud cliff six feet high, crested with a solid wall of tall reeds. It was the sort of bank with which they had become only too familiar in the last five nights. What lay behind, they could have no idea and they therefore kept as quiet as possible, though the slap of their squelchings in the deep mud seemed to deride their efforts. They then unloaded the Nos. 4 and 5 bags, which contained spare clothes, boots and the escape equipment for each man. These they carried up to the top of the mud bank, together with a half-gallon can of water and the residue of their compact rations – about two days' supply, of which one and a half days was food saved up by not eating the full ration.

They then trudged back to the water's edge to the necessary task of scuttling their canoe. This they had already learnt from experience was not easy, but they did what they could by cutting up and exhausting both the buoyance air bags at bows and stern and slitting the canvas sides. The paddles were tucked in under the decks. Then, while Sparks guarded the beach, Hasler waded out up to his waist and let the canoe fill up with water. With the tide swirling past, the canoe lying almost submerged, halfway between sinking and floating, there was nothing that Hasler could do but push her out as far as possible and hope for the best. Now that this job was done, the most important thing was to get themselves away as soon as possible, and standing waist-deep in freezing water was not a very good start for an overland escape.

With a little pang, he pushed the faithful *Catfish* as hard as he could, and when he saw her for the last time she was being carried rapidly upstream with the tip of her cockpit just visible in the gloom. He felt a little sad at having to give her so ignominious a funeral after she had served him so well. Then he turned away, slowly squelched up the mud beach again and took up his bag.

To climb the slippery mud wall took him and Sparks a good ten minutes and to penetrate the great forests of reeds, cracking like pistol shots as they made their way through in the dark, was an eerie and startling experience. It was now about an hour before dawn, pitch dark. Emerging from the reeds, they came into what seemed to be an open field, but they had not walked many steps before they stumbled against a wire fence, three feet high and running through what appeared to be a line of bushes, forming a sort of hedge. They climbed it but in less than two yards came to another. Hasler thought: 'Ah, we are crossing a fenced cart-track.' They climbed that too, only to come to a third, and then a fourth.

Sparks said: 'Seems to have plenty of fences in this country, sir.'

Hasler laughed suddenly; the explanation had come to him.

'I know what it is – we are fighting our way through a ruddy vineyard! Let's walk *along* the rows instead.'

These vineyards everywhere, with their vines trained horizontally along wires, were a constant nuisance to them throughout this period of their escape. Like the rivers of Italy, they never seemed to run in the direction one wanted, and the constant zigzagging that they entailed not only cost the escapers a lot of time, but made direction-finding by compass so much the more difficult.

There was still no sign of life or habitation. They now got out one of their little escape compasses and found them crude but good enough for maintaining a general direction. They kept on an average heading of north-east, pausing now and then to let the tiny card of the compass with its luminous dot steady down in its quivering and stop sufficiently for them to take a reading. They were carrying their bags rather awkwardly under one arm, but they were both in good spirits and glad to be ashore. They had had enough canoeing for the time being. They were both very wet and muddy and Hasler had been drenched to the waist, but they found that mud, once it had dried on you, made a good insulation against cold. Walking soon made them warm, if not yet dry. The whole countryside was still fast asleep.

Thus, during this last hour of darkness, they followed a zigzag course, walking along hedges or tracks that ran roughly in the right direction, but occasionally making a detour when a farmhouse loomed up in front, for fear of barking dogs.

Going by these devious ways, they had made good only about a mile and a half when dawn began to break. They heard the first crow and in the copses the birds began to stir. It was time for all fugitives to go to ground. They were lucky to find at once a remote wood halfway between St Genés-de-Blaye and Fours, with enough undergrowth to give them some cover for the day. What a relief it was, they thought, not to have to drag up and conceal their heavy canoes, not to be pinned down motionless to the river bank, not to have to work out fresh sums of tides and times. For the first time, Hasler and Sparks felt free as birds, or as schoolboys enjoying the fun of camping. None of the constraints or fears of the fugitive oppressed them. They felt only an immense relief.

As light slowly welled up, they found a little stream – just what they had been hoping for – and they settled down about twenty yards from it, so that they could go down to wash and drink. They were too tired to want to sleep at once. They looked at each other, the major and the private, and saw each other filthy, haggard and with the remains of black camouflage cream streaked down their faces. For a moment, in the words of the great admiral, Robert Blake, they 'beheld one another face to face', saying nothing, but with their hearts very full. Then Sparks asked:

'What time is it, sir?'

Hasler pulled out his faithful Government-issue pocket watch, inside its waterproof cover, which had served him so well, and answered:

'Half-past seven.'

'Any chance that we shall hear the limpets go off, sir?'

'Not a hope, I'm afraid. Remember the ones we exploded in Holy Loch? You could hardly hear them a mile away. We're twenty miles from Bordeaux now. They are just about due to go up any moment now.'

'It would have been nice to have heard them, sir, wouldn't it? To know they had really gone off. And I would have liked to have seen that sentry's face when they did!'

They set to collecting grass and bracken to make themselves some mattresses, then brewed tea with their solidified 'meth', ate a little compact ration breakfast, and then settled down at last to an utterly peaceful day, one sleeping while the other kept watch.

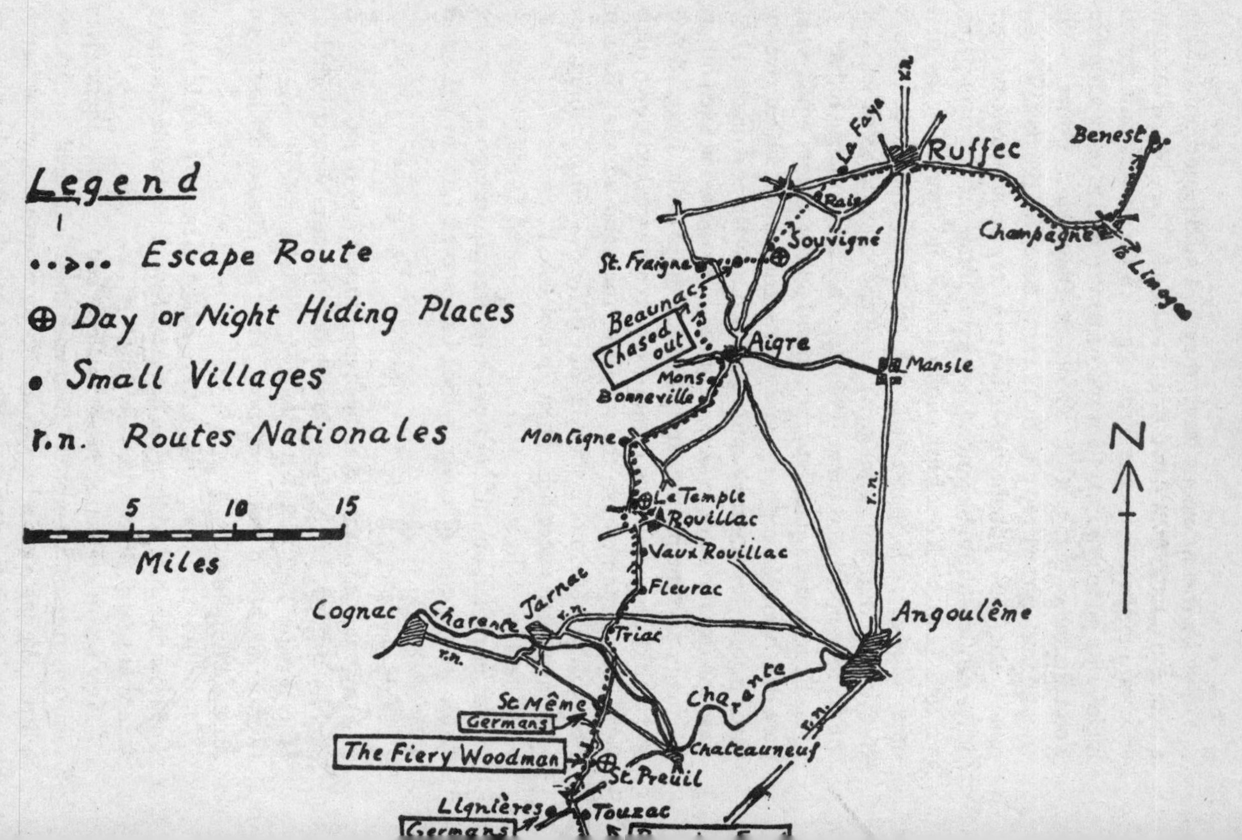
Legend
Escape Route
Day or Night Hiding Places
Small Villages
r.n. Routes Nationales
5
10
15
Miles
N
Ruffec
Benest
Champagne
to Limoges
Mansle
Angoulême
La Faye
Raix
Souvigné
Aigre
St. Fraigne
Beaunac
Chased out
Mons
Bonneville
Montigne
Le Temple
Rouillac
Vaux Rouillac
Fleurac
Triac
Charente
Chateauneuf
St. Preuil
Touzac
St. Même
Germans
The Fiery Woodman
Lignières
Germans
Jarnac
Cognac
r.n.

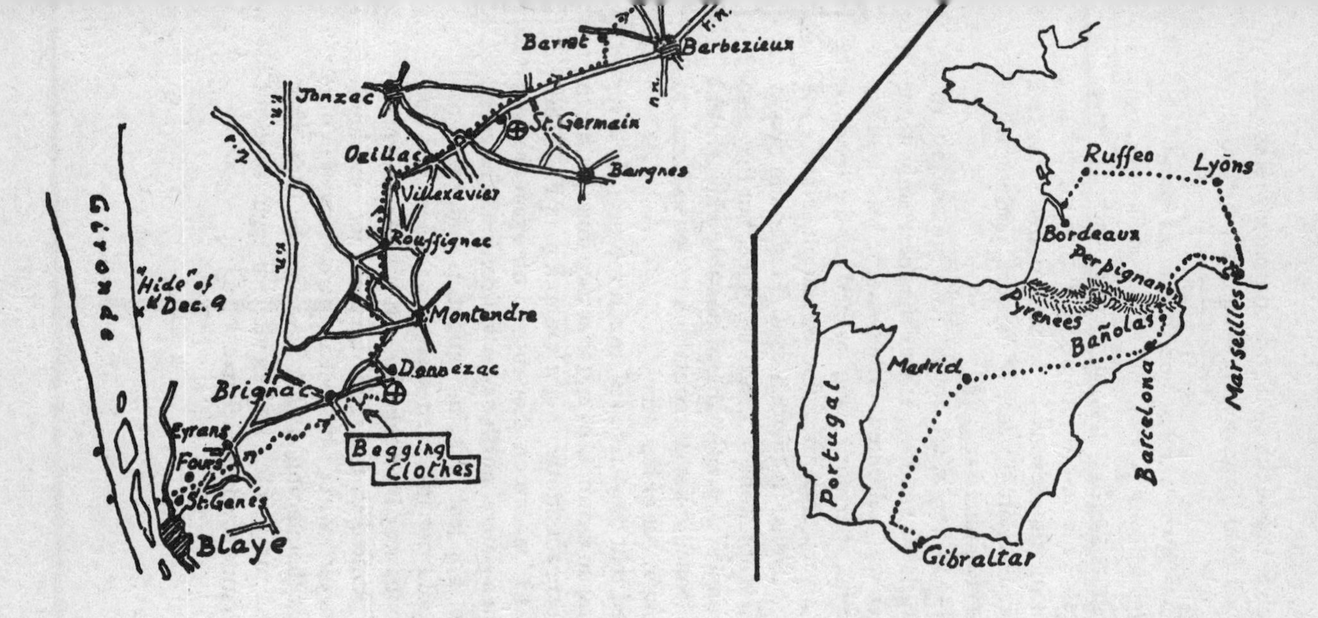

Figure 9. The escape route of Major Hasler and Marine Sparks.

They seemed no longer to feel the cold and, completely relaxed in mind and body, took back from nature what they had so prodigally expended.

Hasler, during his own watches, occupied his mind with concentrating on memorizing every detail of the whole operation from the moment they had left the submarine, with all dates, timing and distances. This he did repeatedly during the ensuing days, so that, when the time came, he would be able to write a complete and accurate report. In case of capture, nothing whatever of any sort was committed to paper.

During the afternoon they went down to the stream in turns and had the best wash for six days. It was the 'best' only in the sense that the water was unlimited. Otherwise, it was icy-cold, and on such occasions, after not having washed for several days, washing is always a very uncomfortable operation. Nature, no doubt, never really intended us to wash at all. Hasler and Sparks therefore limited their ablutions to hands and face, but they also shaved, in order to appear as presentable as possible when knocking at doors. They looked quite disreputable enough as it was to frighten many a woman out of her wits.

Hasler considered that they were still much too near the river area to start knocking up farmhouses and that they must get much further inland. This meant another night's march in uniform. So, on this night of 12/13 December, they moved off again at seven o'clock, still going in a general north-easterly direction. The going was extremely slow. For fear of being caught in uniform in car headlamps, they could not use even secondary roads, and had to make their tortuous way by fields, footpaths and cart-tracks, few of which ever pointed in the right direction for very long. Everywhere the vineyard wires obstructed them. However, the little compasses kept them going, and at dawn on the 13th, after twelve hours on the move, they had made just eight miles of progress and were a mile south of Reignac.

The Frightened People

Hasler thought the time had now arrived when they should chance their luck at a farmhouse, and it seemed a good idea to do so early, while there were few people about.

As soon as the sun was up, therefore, he picked a small farmhouse and he and Sparks approached it across the fields. A small, wiry, elderly farmer was already working in the yard, in black beret and shirtsleeves, a 'Gauloise' dangling from his mouth.

He looked up and saw the two strange figures but did not take the slightest notice and went on working with his hoe. Hasler went right up to him and said:

'Good morning, monsieur. We are two English soldiers escaping from the Boches. Can you give us some old clothes?' The poverty of his French, Hasler hoped, was made up for by the intense sincerity of his manner!

The old fellow stopped working for a moment, glanced quickly at the two Englishmen without a trace of expression of any sort, and then shrugged his shoulders. How well Hasler and Sparks were to get to know that Gallic shrug! The farmer merely indicated the house with an inclination of his head, saying, 'You'll have to ask the missis,' and immediately started working again. One might have supposed that this kind of encounter was for him an everyday experience.

Madame, it seemed, not only controlled the purse and the cooking and the clothing, but was also responsible for making important decisions on policy, such as whether or not to help two scarecrows who claimed to be English but who might equally well be German *agents provocateurs*. Throughout the next few days they were to find that this was nearly always the case. It was madame who made the decisions.

This madame, the escapers found when they had gone to the kitchen door and knocked, was stout, middle-aged, dynamic, and their knock clearly interrupted her in the midst of frenzied domestic activity. Steam and the smells of aromatic cooking wafted out past her as she opened the door. Oh, that tempting smell of cooking! How they were tempted to ask for a good square meal of hot food! They thought of the famous advertisement but put temptation aside. Clothes were the essentials, all else must wait.

Once more the little formula from Hasler: *'Bonjour, madame,'* etc.

Surprise and indignation leapt into the good woman's face.

'Impossible! You can't be English. I can't possibly help you!' – followed by a torrent of speech which to Hasler meant less than a tumbling of angry waters.

He tried to look hurt and disappointed and to reassure her that they were genuine. No doubt, he thought, she is really terribly worried for her own skin and the safety of her family; perhaps all the indignation and disbelief and spate of words is only a façade to conceal it.

She disappeared back into the house, but did not shut the door. Hasler and Sparks stood there, wondering what she was up to. The farmer, a few yards away, was still going on with his work, his back turned to them, but yet watching. A few minutes later Madame returned, bearing in her arms two old, battered and exceedingly dirty objects – a black beret and a cloth cap. She looked round furtively and thrust the garments at them. She was no longer indignant, but terribly worried. Perhaps she thought: 'Even if they are Germans, surely just an old cap and beret would not be a very serious matter.'

Aloud to them she said: 'They are very old, but we have no good clothes left. It is the war. Now go away, please, and do not tell anyone you have been here.'

Hasler thanked her profusely, and with real sincerity, for he knew well that these good people were risking their lives by giving such help. God knows, he said to Sparks, our story must sound pretty thin and unlikely. They turned away from the house and called out 'Thank you, monsieur' to the back of the old farmer, who didn't take the slightest notice of them.

They trudged away again across the fields, tired after their all-night work, commenting to each other that it was not going to be all that easy to acquire their wardrobe. And suppose the taciturn old farmer, to cover himself, went and spilled the beans to the police? Or merely gossiped with neighbours? This sort of speculation was to nag them all the time.

However, there was nothing for it but to go on trying till they got what they wanted. They accordingly called at another farm and again Hasler found himself trying to persuade a reluctant madame. The second one, however, was dry and mean-looking – a real 'sour puss'.

'We have nothing,' she said firmly. 'We cannot help you.'

Hasler pressed her with persuasion, but she stood firm. 'No, I cannot,' she repeated. 'Try the farm over the hill yonder.'

Disappointed again, they made off in the direction that she had shown. They were still in uniform, in broad daylight. They had not yet broken their fast and were a little dejected, feeling, as Hasler said, that a beret and a cloth cap were hardly sufficient camouflage to see them through France – particularly as he himself took an outsize in hats.

With no confidence, they knocked at the kitchen door of the third farm and madame appeared. Ah, this one, they thought, looks kind and brave. To their opening gambit she answered with a long, thoughtful look. Then she said quietly: 'I will see,' and disappeared. There was a long, long wait and the escapers began to feel nervous. But at last she came back and their spirits leapt, for she carried in her arms a bundle of clothes, which turned out to be two pairs of trousers and a jacket. The trousers were torn and patched and thin and the jacket almost in shreds, but they were just what the men wanted. 'Bless you,' thought both of them. Hasler plucked up courage to ask her for something else, nearly as important as the clothes. They badly needed something in which to carry their cargo bags, with their load of food, water and spare heavy clothing for sleeping out. He had no idea what was the French for 'sack' but there came to his mind the term *cul de sac* (which many of us so wrongly use), so he chanced his arm and asked for '*un sac, pour porter nos choses*,' and lo! it worked. She trotted back and brought out a sack with a hole in it and into this they stuffed their cargo bags. Hasler thanked her fervently and she smiled and said: 'Good luck'. The most pleasant moment they had had for many a day.

The most important thing now was to turn themselves into civilians, however inadequate the materials. They hurried off to the nearest copse and spent an hour effecting the transformation. First, they discarded their weapons – .45 Colt pistol and fighting knife – and buried them. Then off came the uniform trousers and canoeing jackets with their badges and these were buried too. They felt sad at discarding their warm trousers for the old, threadbare ones, but it had to be done. Luckily, they still had their warm Service underwear to withstand the December chill, and for the bitter nights they put their gloves, sea-boot stockings and Balaclavas into the sack. They left the copse with Sparks wearing civilian cap, jacket, blue naval sweater, trousers and felt-soled Commando boots, and with Hasler in the same but with the beret and wearing no jacket. They took turns at carrying the sack over their shoulders. Hasler's great, sandy, 'handlebar' moustache would have been quite out of keeping and he therefore trained it to droop over his mouth in the 'walrus' fashion so common among French peasants and far more convincing than shaving it off. They had a good look at each other and had a good laugh, but decided that they sufficiently looked the part of poor but respectable yokels.

Though they had been marching all night, and trudging about all the forenoon in search of clothes, Hasler decided that they must forgo sleep and press on. So they headed north-east again, still moving across country at first, as there were no roads leading in the desired direction. Arriving at the little village of Brignac, however, they felt sufficiently confident and inconspicuous to enter it – the first French village they had entered. Sparks looked about him with interest; it was all so different from what he had known – all so less solid than an English village, and with something of a brittle nature about it, yet somehow picturesque. No little cottage gardens with hedges and bushes, but cultivated almost to the doors for utilitarian crops. Away beyond stretched the chequerings of vineyards, now naked, with their long wire alleys, and the leafy groves of olives.

In Brignac they had some more luck and a couple of backdoor visits provided them with a second sack, so that they could divide their load, and a jacket large enough for Hasler's frame to get into. By now the short winter day was over and they did not relish the prospect of the long night out in the open in their thin new garments. They decided, however, not to 'crowd their luck' by begging for shelter, so once again they took to the woods, this time just south of Donnezac. Owing to their zigzagging between villages and farms in their search for clothes, they had advanced only four miles on their route towards Ruffec that day. But they were well content with their luck.

On mattresses of bracken, wearing all the clothes they had and covered with the sacks, they got little sleep that night and so had little temptation to lie abed. Cramped and chilled they rose early and were on the road by 6.30 – an hour before daylight – walking very fast to get warm. Now they began to use roads all the time, not hesitating to pass through villages. To avoid them would have involved endless détours across awkward country and would tend to arouse suspicion if they were seen. In their old clothes and each with a sack over his back, they were, after all, quite typical figures of the countryside.

Dead Beat

The special maps with which they had been supplied were, of course, much better than the smaller-scale standard silk escape maps, and their method of 'navigation' at this stage was simply to select roads leading in the nearest right direction, avoiding large towns and the main *routes nationales*, which were much used by the Germans, and also avoiding cart-tracks and cross-country routes as far as possible, as these might arouse suspicion if used by strangers. They passed through Donnezac while it was still dark, a few lights in the windows showing that the farm workers were only just astir.

It was getting light as they approached Montendre, where they turned left to avoid the town, and after a circuit of confusing secondary roads that led in all directions, they entered Rouffignac quite suddenly, misled by an error in the map. Rouffignac was the largest village so far – almost a small country town – and they realized for the first time that, quite apart from other dangers, the towns and villages were going to be difficult to navigate, because of the numerous turnings and the scarcity of signposts. Direction-finding in a strange town is always puzzling, and escapers cannot safely produce map and compass in public. However, they blundered their way through after several false moves and headed north along a glorified cart-track marked 'IC53', meaning *Chemin d'interêt commun No. 53*, and when Hasler explained what this meant, Sparks observed typically: 'Can't see that the common interest in it can amount to a hell of a lot.'

As they trudged along, Hasler worked out a 'drill' for this navigation of towns, and he and Sparks practised it during the day, as they passed through Villexavier and Ozillac. First, they would stop outside the town they were approaching, study the map and memorize all the roads leading out of it, together with the compass bearing of each and how it was likely to be sign-posted, if at all. In complicated cases they jotted this information down on a very small piece of paper, that could be folded up and concealed in the palm of the hand. They then put away the map and, sacks on backs, trudged confidently into the town, trying to give the impression that they were life-long inhabitants, never looking around them and gazed rather glumly down at the road. Periodically Hasler would address to Sparks some mock-French remark, accompanied by what he hoped looked like Gallic gestures and expressions. Sparks played up well, doing his part 'straight', without his natural Cockney humour, which was just as well, for otherwise Hasler was certain to have ruined the act by bursting out laughing.

When they reached a fork or crossing in a town and were at a loss which way to go, with no sun to give them a direction, they used to play a special act. They stopped and Hasler asked Sparks for a cigarette, at the same time feeling in his pockets for matches, escape compass and the folded paper with the notes they had made. By some awkward juggling, he then lit a match and cupped his hand so that the compass and paper lay face up but concealed from passers-by. He lit Sparks's cigarette and then took a long time lighting his own, lifting his face now and again to make some remarks to Sparks while he waited for the little compass needle to steady. Thus he made his decision which road to take, put away the props and off they went.

That day – 14 December – they had no contact at all with anyone and they covered 18 road miles. In spite of efforts to keep their minds on the humorous aspects of this strange new life, they were getting exceedingly tired, and hungry. Their food was almost gone. None the less, Hasler decided that they must spend one more night in the open, and, just as it was getting dark, they found a convenient wood near St Germain-de-Vibrac. Here, in their threadbare outer clothes, very hungry and spent, they lay down on the sodden ground and had another extremely uncomfortable night. It rained intermittently until dawn. Quite unable to get dry, they had little sleep and they found their strength and their morale at the lowest ebb. They would have been more wretched still if they had known that that day the gallant Laver and Mills had been captured a few miles away.

Shivering and miserable, they ate the last remnant of their compact rations at a cold dawn breakfast in the dripping wood. Much as they disliked them, it was with real regret that they chewed the last of the cardboardy biscuits and the last of the iron-hard oatmeal cake, and threw away the cartons. Today they would have to beg for food, difficult though they knew it would be, for food was rationed, and every contact with civilians was a new danger. They must also in future beg for shelter, as their strength was ebbing and they had not slept properly for eight days. They were also very dirty and foxy in clothes that were sodden alternately by rain and by sweat.

With the barometer of their spirits at its lowest, now mere vagrants, shelterless and foodless, they wearily pulled themselves together, stumbled through the dark and sodden wood and started off on the road again with stiff limbs, wet clothes chafing their skin and the sharp claws of hunger beginning to stretch out and grip their vital parts. Through St Ciers-Champagne they went, then, after four miles, made a détour to avoid Barbezieux, which was altogether too big and too police-ridden for two tramps in search of food. They began to warm up with the exercise, but were as wet as ever, for the rain did not stop. Hunger was beginning to get insistent, but they decided not to beg food before the afternoon, when they hoped that there would be something left over from midday meals. And so on through Barret, wearily following the winding secondary roads, their pace much slower now and the sacks heavy on their backs.

In the early afternoon they began to look out for friendly-looking people, trying to size up the nature of a man or a woman from a passing glance. In a small village a mile south of Touzac they picked on a fat man standing outside a garage with a small house attached. Fat men were generally good-natured. 'He looks,' said Sparks, 'as if his old woman feeds him all right.'

Hasler approached him and said:

'*Bonjour, monsieur*. We are two English soldiers who are escaping. Can you give us something to eat?'

The Frenchman looked round and they saw now that he had little pig's eyes, and they knew what his answer would be. He shrugged and said: 'Ask madame.' As usual.

They went round to the back door. Madame was as thin as he was fat and had a sour face. She bristled with indignation. 'Certainly not!' she said. 'I have nothing to give you. We have not enough for ourselves. Clear out!'

Bitterly they turned away, tramping right through the village of Touzac without attempting any more calls, in case the skinny shrew called up the police. They noticed that there was a telephone wire going to the garage; they must watch out for that in future and avoid houses that might have telephones.

Beyond the village there were two or three little modern houses near the road, very hideous. One of them had a chicken run at the back and a woman was out there feeding chickens. A good omen, thought the marines, even if she gives us only some of the chicken food she is throwing to the scraggy birds. They approached diffidently, standing outside the wire netting. They saw that she was plump, in her thirties, with a nice, plain, honest face. She looked maternal and kindly and Hasler said his piece.

She looked at them closely and saw two dejected, sodden figures with black pouches under their avid eyes. There was compassion in her face.

'Are you really English, monsieur?'

'Yes, indeed, madame.'

'And your friend?'

'English too, but he speaks no French.'

She turned to Sparks: 'You do not speak French, monsieur?'

Sparks rose to the occasion, smiled, rubbed his stomach and said very loudly and very slowly: 'VER-Y HUN-GRY.'

She understood the gesture if not the words, smiled at Hasler and said: 'Oh, he is hungry. Wait here.'

She went into the house and presently came back with half a loaf and a leg of chicken, and gave them to the men over the wire. They divided the food carefully and began to eat, slowly, savouring each mouthful. The chicken was delicious; the bread was stale, yet seemed even better than the chicken, for it gave them that quality of bulk that they had been missing after more than a week of concentrated foods. When they ate the kind woman stood and chatted to them.

'There are Germans in Lignières-Sonneville,' she warned them, and they were glad of the advice. They finished their food, spending an extra five minutes sucking every shred of nourishment from the chicken-bone. Then they took off their battered headgear, thanked her and said goodbye. With a smile, she wished them good luck and returned to her chickens.

The Fiery Woodman

They went on their way through the rain, avoiding Lignières, and they saw no Germans. Hasler found that the moisture from his saturated clothes had penetrated under the glass of his compass and he had to take out another. Going on through heavily wooded, leafless country, dripping with moisture, they came as it grew dark to the small village of St Preuil, having covered another 18 miles that day. As it was still raining, Hasler was doubly resolved to try to get shelter that night. He knocked at the first house they came to in the village. Madame here seemed sympathetic but very frightened. 'You cannot stay here,' she said. 'It is not safe – not safe for you, nor for us.'

Hasler pressed, begging her to tell them where they could get in out of the rain for the night; anywhere would do. Hesitating anxiously, she called back into the house and her call was answered by the emergence of a tall, gangling boy of about seventeen, who looked half-witted. The woman rattled off a quick-fire of instructions to the youth, then turned to the Englishmen and said: 'Go with him; he will find you a place.'

They followed the half-wit, who turned off the road and went down a squelching cart-track that led into the depths of the woods, now quite dark. The rain still fell without mercy. The vagrants wondered whether they were being led into a trap, but decided that small hope was better than none and after what seemed an eternity they came to a tiny, isolated, thatched house in the middle of the wood, with a dim light shining through the chinks of wooden shutters. Even in the gloom, they could see that the place was very decrepit. A dog started to bark, fiercely, drawing in its breath and snarling. The whole scene – the dark night, the pouring rain, the dense, enveloping wood, the angry animal, the shabby hovel, the half-wit youth – was charged with every element of sinister omen. In such places are men made away with, without trace; in such places treachery cheaply earns its living: in such places violence sharply closes all accounts.

The wanderers waited anxiously while the half-wit went up to the door and rapped. It was opened by a very small, wiry, fierce-looking man of about forty. His attitude was tigerish. His wife and numerous children were lined up behind him. The half-wit muttered something and the man, who was a woodcutter, then stood back from the door and sharply summoned them in. When they had done so, he bolted the door behind them.

Hasler and Sparks looked wonderingly around. They saw a large one-room dwelling, dimly lit. Nearest the door were a rough table and benches. Against a wall was a great iron cooking range with a roaring fire, and wood-smoke pouring from all the cracks, filling the whole room and making their eyes smart. Against other walls were huge, battered old cupboards and chests. An enormous bed filled the far end of the room and mattresses lay about elsewhere. The floor was of earth. The dog was still growling, and the wife and children quite still and watching suspiciously. Overall there was the indescribable, thick, hot smell blended of human bodies, garlic, dog, wood-smoke and food. To the stricken wanderers it smelt incredibly desirable.

Having shot the bolt, the woodcutter turned on them, fierce as an angry wasp. He was violently hostile. He glared up at Hasler's six feet of height and his shabby red moustache, his black beret and his sodden threadbare clothes, and he barked:

'Who are you?'

Hasler replied with his set piece but it only made the man more furious. 'Why do you come here?' he stormed. 'Who the devil told you to come to *me*?'

Hasler, prepared now for anything, indicated their guide, and the tiger turned on the youth and rent him with the same angry questions. The youth returned him soft answers, and the woodman swung round again on Hasler, looking as though he was likely to try to kill him.

'You are *not* English!' he stormed. 'It is not true! You cannot be. Where is the proof? Where is the proof? Where are you from!'

Hasler reached inside the collar of his sweater and pulled out his identity disc, and Sparks did the same. The woodman glared at them, but waved them away angrily.

'That means nothing! What have you been doing? Where did you escape from?'

Hasler, keeping quite cool and not ready now to take 'no' for an answer, replied. 'We can't tell you what we have been doing. That is still a secret. But it was a Commando raid.'

The word 'Commando' seemed to mean something to the woodman, but he still would not believe them. 'Where is the proof?' he barked. 'Show me some English things.'

They both pulled out their escape boxes, and he snatched them from their hands. He pulled out the silk escape maps, the V-sign matches, the escape compass, the sheets of British toilet paper. It seemed as though he recognized these items, but his demeanour did not alter, and he fired off the same questions over again. Then all of a sudden he swung round on Sparks and shot off a string of brusquc questions at him.

Sparks, imperturbable, grinned, pointed at himself and said: 'English – savvy?'

That simple, native action had a magic effect. Whereas it was possible to imagine that Hasler might be a German, it was quite impossible to take Sparks for anything but a chirpy Cockney Englishman. The tiger jumped to the door, bundled the half-wit outside, bolted the door again with a clang, bounded round again on his visitors and became as fiercely friendly as he had been hostile.

'Have you eaten? Tell me, have you eaten?'

Sparks, who had by now learnt the meaning of *manger*, said to

Hasler: 'Did he ask if we wanted something to eat, sir? Tell him I could eat a horse.'

'My friend says,' reported Hasler to the Frenchman, 'that he could eat a horse.'

'A horse? Good. I am not sure if we have horse, but we will see. *Alors*. . . .'

He swung round to his wife, uttered some crisp orders, and she ran smartly to the kitchen range. Hasler smiled inwardly. Here was one French household at least that was not ruled by the petticoat.

Now the bevy of children plucked up courage and came shyly forward, crowding round them, looking at the escape gear and saying '*Anglais*' to each other in wonder. Sparks made friends with them with his typical, sure, lower-deck manner that is always so engaging and persuasive, while Hasler talked to the little tiger of a woodman. He had already summed up that the Frenchman's first hostility had sprung from anger and alarm that he was being regarded as the local resistance centre – an idea that, if it spread, would surely lead him into handcuffs. Now that he was satisfied, there was nothing that he would not too fiercely do.

'You are going back to England?' he asked.

'Yes, so we hope,' replied Hasler.

The little human dynamo whirred into a fresh impulse of activity with a new idea that fired him, and he dashed all over the smoky, odorous room in a mad pantomime as he tried to explain it.

'Good! I tell you what you must do, then. You must go to the Air-Ah-Eff.' (How often they were to hear of the RAF in their sojourn in France!) 'And you must tell them to drop some weapons here! Drop them by parachute!' He tore round the room among the children, catching imaginary objects from the air.

'A pistol!' – Bang! Bang!

'Or better still, a rifle!' Takes aim across the table – Bang!

'Or a Tommy-gun.' Jumps round the room going rat-tat-tat!

'We will fight! We will kill plenty of Germans.'

Hasler gravely promised to tell the RAF when he got back. The woodman raised a clenched right fist on high.

'*Communiste, moi!*' he exclaimed with pride. 'Drop me a gun and I will kill Nazis for you. I kill them behind, the Russians in front. Soon the war will be over.'

What Hasler and Sparks were really interested in, however, was food. The pangs inside them only sharpened by the intensity of the smell that assailed their nostrils exasperatingly. They were swaying with fatigue, and here at last were all the things they longed for – warmth, hot food, human company and the release of tired limbs and strained muscles. To them in such extremity the mingled strong odours, which might have revolted them another time, spelt infinite ease. From the corners of their eyes they kept watching the preparations for a meal, fighting down their urgent impatience. The elder children were laying out crude wooden bowls and spoons on the table and two bottles of the red wine of the country. The smell of food became almost unbearable.

But at last they sat down and started the most wonderful of dinners – the first hot meal since they left the submarine and perhaps, they say, the meal that they have most enjoyed in their lives. There was a huge bowl of vegetable soup, followed by roast chicken and vegetables. The family pressed the lion's share on their visitors. Madame was proud of her dinner, proud of entertaining her guests, and, now that the veil was withdrawn, almost as fierce as her man. Wine flowed. Sparks said: 'Can't we stay here the rest of the war?'

With warmth, food, wine and fumes, the two Englishmen became terribly tired, fighting to keep awake, but their host was bounding with vitality. Another idea had come to him. He pointed to an old wireless set in the corner – possibly the only thing in the room that was not appropriate to the Middle Ages – and said:

'We have a radio, you see. We listen to the Bay-Bay-Say every day. Da-da-da-DA, da-da-da-DA. Every night there are messages for people in France. Now, when you get home *you* must send a message, so that we know you are safe. But it must be in code.' He thought for a moment, drumming the table. 'I have it! You must send: "The chicken is good." Just that. We shall be listening and we shall know it is from you to us.'

Hasler promised to do so, though he was more than half asleep on the bench. The Frenchman would have liked to go on talking all the night, but he saw how it was with them, and suddenly jumped up and packed them off to bed with the same insistent urgency. Against all their protests, he insisted on putting them into *the* bed, the huge old marital couch that would enfold a family. So they took off their outer clothes and climbed in together, the major and the private, both feeling dirty but blissfully happy. That the bed itself was not too clean did not worry them in the least. Thus, long before the family itself went to bed, they fell asleep as though dead – the first proper sleep since they had left the submarine nine nights ago.

The family was astir before dawn and the marines rose with them. They were pressed to stay longer but they had to get on. The escape organization at Ruffec would already be expecting them. Madame blew the embers of the fire with bellows and soon there was a fine blaze going again. The Englishmen asked for water to wash in, and were given a bowl each – hot. What luxury! They washed and shaved and then ate a good breakfast of coffee and bread. It was now full daylight and they wrenched themselves away. There were fervent farewells and thanks and reiterated promises to send a message by the BBC. Madame thrust into their sacks a parcel of bread and cold chicken, then they went quickly out of doors and up the muddy cart-track again. As they went, Hasler said to Sparks: 'If that is a typical French communist, I hope we meet plenty more of them.'

Friendless

Back through St Preuil and so on, by mid-morning, to the small country town of St Mème-les-Carrières. Here all seemed quiet and peaceful, but as they crossed the main road in the middle of the town they were alarmed to see a number of German soldiers. They were doing nothing in particular and looked as though they might be waiting to fall in for a parade. Hasler and Sparks turned down a side street leading out of the town and were just congratulating themselves on having successfully avoided the Germans, when a burly young Nazi private hurried out of a gate just ahead and came straight towards them. Hasler and Sparks put on their Gallic conversation act as they approached, but the German took no notice of them. He was anxiously straightening his belt and buttons as he hurried past. 'Obviously late for parade!' said Hasler. 'Looks like it, sir,' replied Sparks. 'Hope the silly —— gets put in his company commander's report!'

The incident helped to give them further confidence, and they soon realized that they were less likely to look suspicious to a German than to a Frenchman.

Down the hill, and before long they crossed the river Charente, hurrying away north-west by way of Rochefort and Triac – all thickly populated here – then by a secondary road to cross the *route nationale* at the tiny hamlet of Lantin. Here they stopped to rest their feet and to eat sparingly of the food given them by Madame Woodcutter, resolved to conserve it as long as possible, so that begging at houses should be reduced to a minimum. As often, they discussed Laver and Mills and wondered how they were getting on. Perhaps, they thought, they might be quite close, though probably not so far on. It was unlikely, thought Hasler, that the others could be ahead of them, for, although the mileage did not sound much, he and Sparks had been going pretty hard.

They went on again by quiet country roads, all the time wet through from the continual rain. A second compass seized up from the damp, and they got out a third. Occasionally they met a man or woman walking along the road and if it was open country, as opposed to town, they nodded and mumbled '*Jour, m'sieu*' or '*Jour, madame*'. They had been advised to do so in their briefing, since to ignore passers-by in the country might appear suspicious.

So on through more sleepy villages that looked as though they did not know what a great war was being fought, till, as darkness fell, they approached Le Temple, another tiny hamlet. Here, after having covered another 15 miles, they had the good luck to find a small disused hut beside a light railway. Thankful for any shelter from the rain, they went inside, their wet clothes steaming from the heat of their bodies, ate a little more of their bread and chicken and had a passable night, wet and blanketless on the hard floor.

They were now only 21 miles in a straight line from Ruffec and next morning they were up early, shivering in the dawn, to see with gloom that it was again raining steadily. Having eaten another morsel of their food, they went on again through drenched leafless woods, vineyards, olive groves and cultivated fields, and among incurious peasant people. They were getting so used to the rain that they hardly noticed it now, and, like an Irish labourer, began to think little of it, as long as they could keep warm. After eight miles of it, they stopped and ate the last of their food.

Ruffec, their goal, was not far off now and Hasler began to plan their approach to it. In order to avoid main roads, he decided to come in from the west. The easy route was through Aigre, but it was too large a town for their liking, so they turned away north by the side of a little stream meandering through marshy fields, splashed down a cart-track, crossed the stream by some stepping stones in the pelting rain and so on through woods and fields to St Fraigne, lying in a hollow between two hills.

Night approached, and after having eaten very sparingly for two days, they were obliged reluctantly to seek food again. They picked on the little village of Beaunac, as being too small to be likely to be infested with Germans or police. They had walked 15 miles that day and it was still raining hard.

They knocked at the first door in Beaunac, but the woman was hostile. 'No, not here,' she said. 'Go somewhere else.'

They tried the next house: '*Nous sommes deux soldats anglais*,' etc. Madame stared at the ragged figures with fear and hostility. 'Impossible,' she said and shut the door.

Wearily, they tried the third house. Again a refusal. Not a crust.

'Friendly little place,' said Sparks.

'They are all frightened really,' Hasler answered. 'Perhaps the Gestapo has been around here.'

They tried a fourth house, a small farmhouse with out-buildings. The woman looked warm-hearted but was too frightened to say anything. She called her husband, and up came a dour little man in waistcoat and shirtsleeves. As best he could, Hasler pressed him to give them something to eat – anything, a piece of old bread would do – and to let them lie for the night in one of his sheds. 'We shall be gone before dawn,' Hasler said.

The little farmer was good of heart, and decided to take the risk. 'Come with me,' he said. He led them in the half dark to a cattle shed at the back, and up a ladder to a hay loft. It was quite dark, but dry and warm. Exhausted and soaked to the skin, the two marines sank down on to the soft bed of hay, grateful for the promise of a night's rest. The farmer went away but presently came back with a light and half a loaf of bread. 'Do not move from here,' he said; 'it is dangerous in the village.'

He went away, taking the lamp. Hasler and Sparks ate all the bread, lay down and pulled some hay over their bodies. They heard some voices raised in the farmhouse, but were too tired to take notice and in a moment were asleep.

Almost at once. Hasler felt himself being roughly shaken. He roused himself with difficulty and the farmer turned to rouse Sparks, who awoke cursing. By the light of the farmer's lantern, Hasler saw that it was 11 p.m.; they had had three hours' sleep. The farmer spoke urgently. 'You must go at once. There are people in the village who do not want you here, and they have sent for the police. Hurry!'

His panic was infectious, and in less than two minutes Hasler and Sparks had collected their things and were down the ladder. Outside the rain was pouring down harder than ever. How it rained all those weary days! Dousing his lamp, the farmer led them to a cart-track pointing away from the village to the eastward, and said: 'This is your best way. Don't stop till you are well away from the village. I am sorry you have been driven out.'

Thanking him for his help, the two wanderers squelched off down the track, feeling very low and sore in spirit. Sparks gave vent to his feelings and Hasler said:

'Yes, it is a bit rough on us, but I don't think we can blame them. Something has happened to make them all frightened, and if we were caught there the whole village might suffer.'

He was specially anxious to avoid stirring up trouble as they approached Ruffec, and he had fears that if Laver and Mills were following they might walk into any trouble for which he had been responsible. He got out his compass – the third – and found that this also was now seized up with damp, so got out his fourth and last and headed across country in an easterly direction. For a quarter of a mile they were walking ankle-deep in water along a flooded track and Hasler reflected that at least this would save them from being tracked by dogs.

The last escape compass seized up. They were dead weary, stumbling as they walked through the wet fields, faint and half asleep. Nothing but rain, cold rain, sodden earth underfoot, empty bellies and no friends. They were almost dropping in their tracks, when emerging on to a small road south-east of Souvigné, they saw a haystack loom up in front of them. With their hands they tore a hole in the base of it and were immediately asleep.

It was, however, for but a few hours only and at dawn on 18 December they dragged themselves on to the road again, their stomachs empty and with little strength in their limbs. None the less they were buoyed up by the fact that it had at last stopped raining, and that now they had but nine miles to go to Ruffec. Hasler managed to dry out one of the little compasses sufficiently so that it could be made to revolve by tapping. He was wondering how they were to make contact with their unknown friends in Ruffec. There were eight roads leading into the town and their friends could not know on which day to expect them.

Passing through Raix, they struck the main road leading westward out of Ruffec at La Faye, with only three more miles to go. The sun was now trying to come through the leaden sky. As they approached Ruffec they abandoned some of their shyness and looked enquiringly and hopefully at the faces of every passer-by. No one, however, took the slightest interest in them, and by noon they were in the town itself. Though only a medium-sized sleepy country town, it seemed to them after their long loneliness like a roaring metropolis.

What to do now? After having paddled 105 miles, they had now walked just another 100 miles since Blaye, most of the time wet to the skin, with only one square meal. Famished and tired, they walked slowly right through the town from west to east along the main street, taking as long as possible to look into shop windows, and watching every passer-by for any sign of their longed-for shepherd. As a secondary object, in case they should find no friend and have to take a plunge by themselves, Hasler also looked in at the window of every *bistro* and small restaurant, to choose one that seemed to present the least danger. For food they must have soon.

Having traversed the town from west to east, they turned

wearily about and came right through again, passing close to a policeman on point duty, but still no one took the slightest notice of the two tramps. They had peered into hundreds of faces, without any sign. They were baffled, footsore and famished, and the position was getting desperate. Hasler had already noted one or two suitable *bistros* – small, cheap places used by workingmen, where they would perhaps be acceptable in their disreputable clothes. By now, besides their raggedness, they were also smelling pretty stale. But they must now take the plunge. 'Their stomachs were moving with the hunger within them.' They went back over the selected *bistros*, and at each one stood pretending to study the *menu* posted up in the window, but in fact looking through to see if the place was crowded and what sort of a person the *patronne* seemed to be.

In The Bistro

Eventually, Hasler elected for a little place with only two or three customers and several empty tables, presided over by a large generous-looking woman, who was doing the double duties of serving the few customers and officiating at the cash desk. They went in unobtrusively and sat down as far away from the other customers as they could. Madame came up for their orders. Hasler had already decided what it was to be – something easy to order and which needed no ration cards, for of course, they had none.

'*Du potage, s'il vous plaît, et du vin.*'

'*Pour les deux, monsieur?*'

'*Oui, madame.*'

'*Bien, messieurs.*'

Off she went. No trace of curiosity in her manner.

What was she thinking? Hasler knew that France was full of 'displaced persons' of all sorts and that foreigners did not attract the same notice as they might ordinarily have done. But he reflected as well that France was also full of Vichy spies and informers and that any face might be the mask of an enemy.

Presently the large woman came back with two rough earthenware bowls brimming with thick, fragrant soup, with plenty of vegetables and broken bread swimming in it, and with two glasses of rough red wine. Then she went back to her desk, absorbed in her accounts. Sparks said:

'Cor, this is good. I could eat a bucketful of this scran.'

'Don't eat too fast,' Hasler advised. 'We've got to wait till the other customers have gone.'

As they ate, Hasler was covertly watching the *patronne*. Was he really going to put their lives into her hands, or should he just pay the bill and walk out? What then? They had nowhere else to go, and she looked a good sort. He made his decision.

It was now nearly 2 p.m., but there were still two or three working men talking volubly at the other end of the room. Every now and then madame looked speculatively at them all, obviously wondering when they were all going to leave. The two Englishmen had finished their food but were still ravenous. He caught madame's eye. '*Encore du potage, s'il vous plait, madame, pour les deux.*'

'*Et du vin, monsieur?*'

'*Oui, madame.*'

When the second helpings came, they ate very slowly again. Surely the others wouldn't stay much longer? But they were in the middle of an animated discussion in some patois that Hasler could not understand and they seemed to be set for the rest of the day. Hasler was worried lest the *patronne*, waiting to close the place, might ask him and Sparks to leave first. Perhaps the others were old friends, or attached to the *ménage*? Quickly he made a new plan. Getting out pencil and paper, he wrote:

> We are escaping English soldiers. Do you know anyone who can help us?

Then he caught her eye and asked for the bill. She did not write one out but came over and named the sum. Hasler handed her a 500-franc note, with his message folded in it. She noticed it at once, but went back to her desk without sign or comment.

Very anxiously they watched her reading it at her desk.

No expression at all on her face. Not even a glance in their direction. But they saw her write something on the bottom of their note and get out their change. She brought the change over to them, laid it on their table and walked straight back to her desk without a word. They picked up their change and read her reply.

'Stay at your table until I have closed the restaurant.'

Hasler breathed again. Here was hope at least, if not actual deliverance. Presently he heard the good woman call out to customers in general that it was time to close, and the workmen at the other tables got up, still arguing garrulously. Madame got up, locked the door and beckoned the Englishmen to follow her into the kitchen. There they met her husband, the chef, who was still clearing up the dishes. They seemed amiable and unsuspicious, but asked:

'Whom were you told to contact in Ruffec?'

'We were given no name,' Hasler answered. 'We were told that friends of England would be on the look-out for us and would help us.'

'Why did you come in here?'

'Because we were very hungry and this looked a good place.'

The couple seemed to accept their story and spoke between themselves for a moment. Then madame said: 'You can stay here while we find someone to help you. Come with me.'

Right gladly they did go. She led them up into what seemed to be her best guest-room, clean and simple, with double bed ready made up with clean sheets.

'Here you are, messieurs. My husband will not be able to go out until the evening. In the meantime, you can go to bed and get some sleep.

Hasler looked down ruefully at himself.

'Thank you madame, but we are very dirty and we should soil your bed-linen.'

'You would like to wash? Wait a bit.'

In a few minutes they were overjoyed to see her come back with an old-fashioned hip-bath, towel and soap. Then, after another journey, a large bucket of hot water. Finally, going out of the room, she said:

'Leave your clothes by the door. I will wash them.'

Quite dazed with this sudden turn of fortune, they pulled off their filthy clothes, each in turn had a good wash, and then got naked into bed. Hasler could not help thinking: 'She is curiously unsuspicious. Supposing she really means all the time to give us away? Well, if she does, we have "had it" in a big way. Could hardly fight our way out stark naked.' Then he was asleep. Some time later he was instantly awake again as he heard movement at the door; but it was only their clothes being taken away. Then oblivion.

When they were awoken next, it was to find madame in the room, the blinds drawn and the light on.

'You have slept well, messieurs?'

They left her in no doubt, and then she asked if they would like something to eat. Sparks picked up *manger* at once with a broad grin and said:

'Cor, yes please. I could eat everything you've got in the house.'

'What does he say?' asked Madame.

Hasler interpreted and she said: 'Good. Wait a little.'

She came back presently with a large tray carrying more soup, plates of meat and vegetables and two glasses of *vin ordinaire*. They sat up naked in bed and ate, care cast aside. Madame treated them as important guests and Hasler felt embarrassed that he could do nothing but lie there and accept such hospitality. She told them that someone might come that evening who could help them and she brought them some clean underwear so that they could feel less embarrassed.

A little later they heard the tread of several male feet on the stairs. Hasler tensed. They would know now whether madame was genuine or whether she was playing them false. It was her husband who came in, accompanied by two other men, nondescript middle-class Frenchmen, who looked as though they might have been shopkeepers or perhaps local civil servants. They drew up chairs round the bed in which Hasler and Sparks were sitting up in their underclothes and started to cross-examine them. Unlike their host, these two visitors were taking no chances, and made Hasler give a full account of himself, as far as security allowed him. They looked at the remains of the escape gear, asked them questions about England, watched the Englishmen narrowly and tried to talk to Sparks with the few words of English that they knew. These men, thought Hasler, were obviously experienced resistance workers, and he was worried that their story might sound very thin and because, contrary to expectation, the Frenchmen had obviously not been expecting them. He told them about Laver and Mills also and asked them to help them when they came.

At last the Frenchmen seemed satisfied and told the Englishmen to be ready to leave the following afternoon. Then they left, in a very matter-of-fact kind of way. A great load was off Hasler's mind, to be replaced, however, by a new kind of anxiety. Hitherto they had been using their own wits at every turn and always retained the initiative. Now they were to become merely a parcel, handed on from one Frenchman to another, with no say in their own destiny, and no knowledge of where they were to be led and what precautions should be taken to escape capture. They would have to place their lives in the hands of people whom they knew nothing whatever about, knowing that the Germans were vigorously hunting the French escape organizations and might pick up Sparks and himself in the process. But there was nothing he could do about it, and meanwhile it was a blessedness to relax for the first time and to go to sleep again.

They awoke on 19 December refreshed in body and mind. The *patronne* brought them back their clothes, all clean and dry, together with one or two better garments. Dressed and fed again, they stuffed their few possessions back into their sacks and at two o'clock one of their interrogators of the day before returned and told them to follow him. Hasler and Sparks paid a cordial and fond farewell to their kind host and hostess, who refused to take their proffered payment (as had the few others who had helped them so far). Then they went out through the dining-room, climbed straight into the back of a waiting baker's van and the doors of it were shut on them at once.

Now they experienced for the first time the feeling of being a 'parcel'. They had no idea where they were going in the back of the windowless van, save that, after bumping over the cobbled streets of the town, they felt a smoother surface that told that they were in the country. After about twelve miles the van stopped, the doors were opened and the marines got out to find themselves in a wood on a country road. Their guide led them into the wood a little way, the van drove off and the three men settled down in the undergrowth. Their guide explained: 'We are just south-east of Benest, close to the "line of demarcation", and this line is still patrolled by German soldiers and police dogs, even though they have now occupied the whole of France. At twilight a guide will come here from the other side and will lead you across the line to your next house.'

He was taciturn, this Frenchman; he looked efficient and ruthless and Hasler was mighty glad he was on their side and not against them. Sparks said:

'Where are we going now, sir?'

'I don't know,' Hasler answered. 'And I don't want to ask him questions. We have just got to put ourselves in their hands from now on.'

He could see that, like himself, Sparks was worried by this new routine. There was a long wait before dusk, and their guide then got up and stood by the side of the road. Before long low voices were heard and their guide came back to them in the undergrowth with a young man who, as far as they could tell in the dark, looked like a farm worker.

No words were wasted. 'Come with me,' he said, and the marines got up and said goodbye to their efficient friend. Their new guide led them along a footpath through the wood they were in and then out in the dark across fields, stealing along close to the hedges. Every now and then he stopped for a long period, listening intently and motioning them to dead silence. Then on again at a silent jog-trot, the marines following. All was deathly quiet. No sound or sight of any human activity.

Monsieur Armand

After about a mile they could discern the outlines of an isolated house, one chink of light showing through shuttered windows. As they approached a dog barked and they could hear the noises of animals in outhouses. Therefore a farm. Their guide motioned them to stand behind a wall and when the had done so he went up to the door of the house and the farmer appeared. After a few words with him, their guide came back, shook hands and motioned them forward to where the farmer was standing, holding the door open. Hasler and Sparks entered a lighted kitchen and the door was locked behind them.

Their new host was tall, slim, intelligent-looking, in his early thirties. We will call him Monsieur Armand, his Christian name. His wife also was a quiet woman, of pleasant appearance, obviously hard-working and efficient. There were also one or two children. None of them had any English. Monsieur Armand asked them no questions and from now on the escapers found that they were accepted without any doubtings, being passed from one trusted operator to another. No more cross-examinations. No more suspicions and fears, though always, except as we shall see, great caution.

Monsieur Armand led them straight to their room, which was all ready for them, and where they were to spend nearly three weeks before making any further move to liberty. The room was on the ground floor, next to their host's living room, and with a connecting door to it. There was also a door giving direct on to a yard outside. The room was furnished in typical French middle-class style, with well-made but heavy, not very attractive furniture, reminiscent of Victorian English. There were a double bed, a table, two chairs, a washstand with china basin and ewer – all that they needed and all very clean.

Monsieur Armand gave them their instructions. They must remain in their room all the time and never go outside except to visit the privy. When they needed to do this, they must open the outside door, look carefully to right and left to make sure that there were no strangers in view, then they must cross the yard to the privy, which was a wooden outhouse at the end of a cattle shed. The door of their room was to be kept locked at all times and after dark the heavy curtains were to be drawn across it, for the door had glass panels.

Hasler and Sparks settled themselves in and after a very good dinner brought in by their hostess, Monsieur Armand visited them again, bringing some more respectable clothes. From now on they could pass as respectable citizens or shopkeepers instead of destitute tramps. He brought also a few books. 'We have only one or two in English,' he said, producing some battered popular novels of considerable age. Hasler wondered how many British soldiers or airmen had been in this room and read these same books, but he knew better than to ask, and never knew the answer. There were also a few French books, including a French edition of *The Swiss Family Robinson*, which was to give Hasler special joy. The stilted conversation between papa and mama and the children, which his brother had taught him to laugh at when he was ten years old, sounded even more entertainingly fatuous than in English. More valuable still was the day's French newspaper, which they were to see nearly every morning and which Hasler translated to Sparks. They news was, of course, all Vichy and German propaganda, but they could sometimes read behind the lines and guess what was going on. Real news was brought to them from time to time by their host after listening to the BBC. Thus they were able to learn how the Eighth Army, advancing 1200 miles since Alamein, had driven Rommel from his defensive position at Ageila and were pursuing him yet further on the road to Tripoli; and how the First Army were almost at the gates of Tunis but bogged down by rain. Slowly but surely the horizon of the Allies was beginning to lighten.

They were getting used now to sharing a double bed. The first morning, while they could hear their host busy about the farm, madame came in with the luxury of hot water for shaving and washing and later brought them a breakfast of coffee and a great loaf of home-made wholemeal bread – real food as compared with the French baker's white, emasculated stuff, which is all crust and no inside. There was also a little butter and jam, for which the refugees were doubly grateful, knowing that these things were rationed. Then out into the yard, enjoying for a moment the brief sniff of fresh air, before plunging into the horror of the privy, with its wooden box perched over an enormous and unspeakable cavity in the ground.

Afterwards, like hotel guests, an idle morning with nothing to do until Madame Armand brought them their luncheon, with which every day, there was a bottle of red wine and another of *vin rosé*; both of them preferred the rough, masculine strength of the red. On the first day their host looked in and told them that he had sent a message to 'Marie-Claire'.

'Marie-Claire?' asked Hasler wonderingly.

'Yes,' said Monsieur Armand. 'She is the one who will arrange your journey. It is not her real name, but she is English.'

This took them by surprise. It all sounds, thought Hasler, rather like the Scarlet Pimpernel, as indeed was the case. On about the third night Monsieur Armand came in again and said that unfortunately he had not been able to contact Marie-Claire and was not quite sure where she was. A few days later still he came in to say that Marie-Claire had had an accident and was in hospital. Perhaps that was why he and the others had had no warning of their coming. He would now try to contact her son, who seemed to be some distance away.

Hasler and Sparks could do nothing but wait and presently they slipped into an idle, dreary routine. They saw little of the family and, wisely, the children were kept away. After the first few carefree days, the effects of their fatigue, exposure and semi-starvation wore off and they grew very bored sitting together all day in the room. It was worse for Sparks, because he could not read the French books and newspapers, and because he was in any case an extrovert, a town-bred boy who liked to be surrounded by people and was not well equipped to amuse himself. Hasler, however, did not mind the solitude, for he was always busy with his own thoughts and had been used to amusing himself, as we have seen, since boyhood, but he was worried how to keep Sparks from getting too depressed. They were an ill-assorted pair for conversation, having hardly a personal interest in common. Sparks was longing to get back to the city streets, the cinemas, the pubs and the cheerful Cockney crowds; while Hasler dreamt of the wild West Country coastline, of stout-hearted little sailing vessels driving through heavy weather, of the freedoms of the quiet countryside and the companionship of a few close friends. Even that traditional common ground of all Englishmen, sport, was no help, for Hasler's interest in it was limited to that which he had taken part in himself. He loved running, swimming, fives; had to a lesser extent enjoyed rugger, hockey, boxing and tennis; and had tolerated cricket. He had, however, no interest in following the performances of others, particularly those of professionals, and never had any idea who was competing in Test Matches, Cup Finals or other battles of the popular sport heroes.

So they could not talk sport. Indeed, they could talk of little, so Hasler cast around for something to do with his hands, as of old, and found it in carving little human figures out of wood with a knife that he borrowed from Monsieur Armand. This he did for several hours every day. One of his little figures he gave to the Armand children, and another still sits on a corner of his mother's chimneypiece.

After about a week or ten days, Monsieur Armand came in to say that he had made contact with Marie-Claire's son, who was arranging to take them away as soon as he could. Meanwhile madame continued to look after them superbly and sometimes she made a special culinary effort and produced one of her own specialities of the house – some rich, garlicky dish of meat, perhaps simmered in red wine and swimming in butter and garnishings. Sparks did not enjoy those foreign tricks and sometimes went so far as to give his portion to his commanding officer – a red-letter day for Hasler! Sparks's tastes in food were completely English, and often he would say with longing: 'What wouldn't I give for a nice steak, eggs and chips!'

Christmas arrived, but it was like any other day, except that each member of the family came in to wish '*Joyeux Noel*', which the Englishmen reciprocated, and except also for an extra good midday meal. New Year's Day of 1943 came, and all exchanged greetings again. A day or so later Monsieur Armand came in with good news: he had heard from Marie-Claire's son, and he would be calling for them on the morning of 6 January. The last days dragged terribly. They would have been eighteen days in the one room, plus the privy, their horizon bounded by the cattle shed and that privy.

Monsieur Armand asked them, when they got back to England, to send him a message by the BBC. 'We are already sending one,' said Hasler, 'for some of our previous helpers. When you hear "*Le poulet est bon*", it will be for you too.'

This did not satisfy the host. 'No, it must be a message for us alone,' he said. He thought a minute and added: 'I know. Send as well: "The two chickens have arrived," and we shall know it is for us alone.'

Hasler promised, of course. How these good people all loved

the BBC French broadcasts! To receive a personal message on their radio was a great joy to them.*

Hasler raised the question of payment, and asked Monsieur Armand if he would take what they had left of their French money as some recompense of what he had done.

'No, thank you,' said the worthy Frenchman. 'We shall get paid by Marie-Claire. You will need your money later on.'

On 6 January they were up early and soon ready to leave. Sparks was in his usual good spirits again. They were both now plump, white-faced and soft after their idleness and hoped that there was not yet going to be too much walking or sleeping in the open again. At midday Marie-Claire's son, Marcel, arrived and was brought in to them by Monsieur Armand. He was a slender young man of about nineteen, good-looking, friendly and quietly well dressed. He spoke English with very little trace of accent, but not fluently.

'Good morning,' he said. 'I am sorry you have been kept waiting here so long, but my mother got knocked down by a bus! She did not get the message about you until after we had heard from Monsieur Armand that you had arrived. Now I am going to take you to Lyons, where she is waiting for you.'

Lyons! thought Hasler. Why, that is about 200 miles to the east, even further from the Spanish border than where they were now. He asked: 'Will you be able to get us through to Spain?'

'Yes,' Marcel replied, 'but it is difficult just now. The route we were using has been closed and we shall have to find another. You will be quite safe with us at Lyons till then.'

Hasler's heart sank a little; he had been counting on a swift journey straight to the frontier, and so home. He had not reckoned on a prospect of wandering indeterminately over half France.

'I have got three bicycles outside,' said Marcel. 'I hope you can both ride? They are not very good bicycles,' Marcel warned. 'We have no tyres in France now – they are all on the black market. We shall have to ride eleven miles to Roumazières and from there we shall get a night train to Lyons.'

* Hasler fulfilled his promise and both messages came through in due course.

While they lunched, which Hasler and Sparks did alone as usual, Sparks said: 'I don't go much on this train journey idea.'

'Nor do I,' replied Hasler. 'It's going to be very different from anything we've done so far. We've been trying to avoid crowds all the time, but from what I hear the escape organizations go on the opposite tack. It's rather like a criminal trying to hide from the police in England – the crowded towns are safer than the isolated villages, where a strange face is spotted at once. Anyhow, these people are the experts and they risk more than we do. So we must just string along.'

'Marie-Claire'

After luncheon Marcel came in to them and said: 'This is not going to be too easy, I'm afraid, because we haven't got you any identity cards yet. We've got plenty of blank forms here at the farm, but there's no camera to take your photographs, so they will have to wait until you get to Lyons. I shall have to get you on the train without passing the ticket collector somehow, because there is usually a policeman at the barrier inspecting identity cards. If anyone comes up and talks to you, pretend not to understand and say "Breton" in a guttural sort of way. You see, there are still peasants in Brittany who do not speak French!'

He spoke with a smile and his manner was of one who made light of a tricky situation. After fond farewells of their kind host and hostess, they went out and mounted the three decrepit bicycles, and Hasler reflected what a very efficient organization it was that had arranged all this.

They were soon out from the cart-track on to a secondary road, heading south through Alloue. Marcel, who seemed to know every road and track in the district, talked gaily in English as they went along. He told them who his mother was, an Englishwoman married to a Frenchman of position. She had a flat in Lyons, which was a good city for their purposes, as it had until recently been one of the main cities of unoccupied France and the Germans had not yet got a strong foothold in it.

It began to grow dark and as they were sweating up a hill Hasler asked: 'Won't we be pulled up for having no lights?' Marcel laughed heartily at the idea of such a thing happening in rural France.

Arriving at Roumazières, which was primarily a rail junction with marshalling yards, they discarded their bicycles, and after walking about casually were fortunate to find an unfenced portion of the railway track some fifty yards from the entrance to the passenger station. Marcel went in to buy the tickets, came back, and told them to saunter into the station from up the line and to watch for him to beckon to them from the train.

Feeling very conspicuous, but still unchallenged, they obeyed and all went well. On seeing his signal, they made for his coach, where he led them to a third-class compartment already half full of sleepy country people. Marcel was calm and pleased, and the two Englishmen, now wedged in between other travellers, tried to still the beating of their hearts.

There followed a long night journey in an incredibly stuffy carriage, with interminable stops, much shunting to and fro and with constant going and coming of passengers in the compartment. It was impossible to sleep and young Marcel was wide awake and cheerful all night, often leaning over and whispering remarks to them in English. In this he took an impish delight, knowing that it would alarm them.

Daylight came as they steamed into the great city of Lyons. Here Marcel was on his home ground and full of confidence. Composedly they surrendered their tickets at the barrier, and looking shabby and unshaven, walked into town. Marcel stopped at a newsagents to telephone his mother and then took them straight to her flat.

It was a memorable meeting, and one that neither of them was to forget. They found Marie-Claire to be a handsome woman of about forty-five, of medium height, greying hair, clear blue eyes and wearing a uniform with two rows of medal ribbons.

Hasler noted that she had two English decorations and that she wore them in front of her French ones, thus loudly proclaiming her nationality, as they were to find she did on all occasions. She looked, thought Hasler, like a typical English foxhunting woman – tough, jovial, fearless, rather unfeminine and with a touch of arrogance. It seemed strange that, having lived so long in France, she should have retained such strong characteristics of a peculiarly English caste. But then, if she had not, she could not have been Marie-Claire, nor accomplished her extraordinary work with such efficiency and such contempt for the risks. When she spoke French, even Hasler could tell that, although her idiom was no doubt perfect, her accent was scornfully English. She was a very brave woman.

She still had one leg in plaster when she met them at her flat and after welcoming them she started them off with a bath, shave and a good breakfast.

While they were eating she said: 'I'm so sorry you were stuck at the farm for so long. My route across the Pyrenees has folded up and I've got to try to open a new one. Meanwhile, we're going to accommodate you in a large house in the northern suburb – don't know the people myself, but they are friends of my son and he says they are all right. We've got only one rule for Englishmen in our care – NO GIRLS. From past experience, we know that once they meet a pretty girl, everything goes to hell. So we shall take care to keep them away from you.'

Sparks and Hasler looked at each other glumly.

'Now I'm going to take you along to a photographer's, so that we can fix you up with proper identity cards.'

Very soon they found themselves in a very crowded tram with the redoubtable Marie-Claire. She looked as conspicuous as a lighthouse in her uniform and with her imperious ways and English accent. They were separated from her in the crowded car and when they reached their destination she shouted across to them in English: 'Here we are.' The refugees crept out after her, trying to look as though they were not certain what she had said.

Their photographs taken – obviously part of a regular routine – they were supplied with identity cards, with fictitious French names, but in case of capture they still kept the identity discs round their necks. Marie-Claire told them that she was going across to Switzerland and if they wanted to get a message through to their headquarters she could send it from there.

Hasler thought a while and then asked: 'May I code it? It would be top-secret material.'

'Yes, anything you like, as long as it is fairly short.'

Hasler therefore sat down and thought hard. He did not, of course, know whether the submarine had returned to Britain safely or whether they themselves would do so, so he decided to give the whole story as briefly as possible and include any information likely to be of any use to COHQ for future raiding parties. He therefore first wrote out a very condensed message in clear, which ran as follows:

> COHQ. Tuna launched five cockles seven Dec. Cachalot torn in hatch. Pad hatches. In bad tide-race SW Pte de Grave Coalfish lost formation fate unknown. Conger capsized crew may have swum ashore. Cuttlefish lost formation nr Le Verdon fate unknown. Catfish Crayfish lay up in bushes Pte aux Oiseaux. Found by French but not betrayed. Ninth in hedges five miles north of Blaye. Tenth in field south end Cazeau. Eleventh in reeds thirty yds south of pontoons opp Bassens South. Attack eleventh. Catfish Bordeaux West three on cargo ship two on engines of sperrbrecher two on stern of cargo ship one on stern of small tanker. Crayfish Bassens South five on large cargo ship three on smaller liner. Back together same night. Separate and scuttle cockles one mile north of Blaye. Sparks with me. Fate of Crayfish crew unknown. Hasler.

He now proceeded to code this in the No. 3 Code, the only one he could do in his head. The first stage was to apply the code word to the message and produce a string of meaningless letters. The next was to convert these letters into innocent plain language, but he found to his horror that he had quite forgotten the method of doing this, even though he had been taught it only two months before he had practised it in the submarine. He consulted Sparks, but found that Sparks had forgotten, too. There was nothing for it but to send the first stage as it was and to hope that the quick brains at the other end would realize what had happened. As we have seen, it fell out as he hoped, thanks to Marie Hamilton and Sillars; only one passage foxed the Intelligence men, for the words 'Back together' came through as 'Back to get her'! This was the message, received in England on 23 February, on which the staff of COHQ wrote their 'reconstruction' of the raid, as related in Chapter 16.

During the afternoon Marie-Claire regaled them with stories of her war experiences. She was a very stimulating woman and obviously enjoyed playing a dangerous game. She had already been twice arrested by the Germans and released. In prison she behaved as arrogantly as elsewhere, and on the first occasion, when the warder brought her a bucket of water and ordered her to scrub out her cell, she refused point-blank. She was brought before the commandant and told him flatly: 'I won't take orders from that fellow. I am not accustomed to that sort of thing.' The Germans were at that time anxious to get 'chummy' with the French and the commandant was very polite. He showed her a copy of his standing orders and asked for her 'co-operation'. She said: 'Oh, well, in that case I will: but remember I don't take orders from that fellow.'

Her eccentricity and her commanding aristocratic manner enabled her to get away with a great deal. She told everyone, including the Germans, that she was utterly pro-British, and she did all but go about waving a Union Jack. It was a curious way, thought Hasler, of operating an underground movement.

After dark, Marcel took him and Sparks away to a large house in a northern suburb of Lyons, on the banks of the Saône, where it raced south over rock-strewn shallows. This was the beginning of a month's sojourn in Lyons, a month of constantly being moved from one place to another, lying low like criminals on the run, never allowed out and obliged always to keep quiet and unobserved. For five days Hasler, separated from Sparks, was in the luxury flat of another Englishwoman with a French husband. For another spell they were both in a big empty and unfurnished house. The tedium was trying and no progress towards freedom seemed to be made. Marie-Claire came back from Switzerland and told Hasler she had got off his message, but she also told him that she had not yet been able to open up a new escape route across the Pyrenees and was therefore handing them over to another and larger organization. This was another exasperating check and they felt now like parcels that had been wrongly addressed and sent back to the sorting office.

The Escaper's Club

A horsey-looking little Englishman, who strongly disapproved of Marie-Claire and her unsubtle methods, came and whisked them away and early in February they made yet another change. The little horsey man arrived, bringing with him a Monsieur F., a Parisian who spoke a little English and a most likeable character, quick-witted and full of fun. He had come, he said, to carry them off to Marseilles and that evening he took them away for another all-night train journey.

F. went to particular pains to search impishly for a third-class compartment in which there were two German soldiers, and with a grin plonked the British major down next to one of them. To embroider the jest, he addressed painfully audible remarks to Hasler in English from time to time, and Hasler, squirming in his seat, wished that the earth would open and swallow up the Germans.

Miraculously, the Germans did not seem to know what language was being spoken and the Englishmen heaved a sigh of relief when they saw the bright Mediterranean sunrise glow in Marseilles to the promise of a warm day. They walked openly through the town to a modern block of flats, and, having climbed several flights, were admitted by a small, fierce-looking little woman.

It was a medium-sized flat, well furnished in a middle-class manner, and Madame M. was a typical Marseillaise – small, slim, dark, volatile, emotional and generous. There were two RAF men in the flat already – the first fellow-escapers Hasler and Sparks had yet met. They had baled out of a bomber and had never been captured. The place was a regular 'transit camp' for escaping British Service men, and there was a large array of beds, couches and loose mattresses all over the flat. Madame M. warned them not to speak or laugh loudly, as other tenants beyond the walls were not to be trusted.

In the evening Monsieur M. arrived home – the exact male counterpart of his wife. He had some job in the docks and told the Englishmen with pride that he was a Communist and obviously regarded them as being the same, since they were allied to Russia.

He was a splendid type – a good family man, a hard worker and as brave as a lion. The flat was officially rented by someone else, who was an executive agent of an escape organization, the head of which was a man known as 'Pat'. This man of mystery, imagination and apparent wealth visited them on one occasion, and young Frenchmen who acted as guides for the escapers were in and out of the flat all the time, bringing fresh refugees with them.

The two RAF men soon left, to be succeeded by others, until at one time there were fully a dozen Britons all in this little flat. Hasler found it worrying to be in such a vulnerable focal point, but nice to have other people to gossip with, although it was sometimes difficult to explain that they could not tell the others what they had been doing. These others were all RAF men, some of whom had escaped from prisoner-of-war camps, others of whom had been obliged to bale out and had been looked after by the French.

Madame M. coped with all this superbly. She was out every morning at 5 a.m., coming home loaded with food, much of it from black-market sources, which was not very difficult in such a place as Marseilles. She cooked splendid Mediterranean dishes, full of garlic and olive oil, but not at all to Sparks's liking.

The days ran into weeks. They were again told that there had been a stoppage in their route to Spain but that work was going on hard to reopen it. Hasler could not help wishing that they would give him and Sparks a small boat and let them make their own way to Spain by sea; it would have been much easier and safer. About the third week they were joined by two interesting new people. One was Flying Officer Prince Werner de Merode, a young Belgian who was serving in the RAF, together with his flight-sergeant, Dawson, and the other was a French girl who was going to England to join the Free French. She was keen to learn English and teamed up with young Sparks, who, however, to Hasler's alarm, could not resist the temptation to teach her some quite remarkable phrases. De Merode was semi-incognito, not using his title, and he had, of course, been able to make his way freely through France without a guide.

The days dragged terribly, and they got very soft and flabby lounging about the flat all day and Hasler became worried. The crossing of the Pyrenees might turn out to be a considerable test of endurance, and, after his own special training, he shrank from the idea of being unfit for it. But there was no means at all of taking exercise. It was nearly a month before at last Hasler, de Merode, Sparks and Dawson were told to be ready to leave at short notice to cross the Pyrenees. They were each given a small canvas haversack and two pairs of the Basque rope-soled shoes that the French called *espadrilles* and the Spaniards *alpargatas*.

In the early hours of 1 March, under a young French guide, they at last took a train westwards along the famed Mediterranean coast, through a sleepy, sunny countryside now clothed in all the apparel and emblems of spring and with few signs that beyond the sparkling blue waters a bloody war was raging. Hasler thought of gallant, lonely Malta, out in the middle of that sea, of our still advancing Desert army beyond and of all the deadly business that was going on in the seas and in the air. He longed to get back and play his part again.

They left the train at old Perpignan, encrusted with history and rich in old associations of art and song, enfolded that warm spring afternoon in an atmosphere of siesta. Here, after an hour's wait in a garden, the refugees were bundled into a rickety van and squeezed in among a jumble of crates. They were now joined by a fifth companion – a tall, intellectual, cadaverous young Frenchman, carrying a rucksack and a bunch of books tied up with string.

They bounced off along a vile road, climbing gradually, able to see little save that the country was getting more and more barren as they climbed. The air grew chillier and Hasler began to wonder how, after more than two months of soft living and with absolutely no exercise at all, they would face the physical ordeal before them of crossing the mountains on foot. Their guide had told them that the chosen crossing place was one rugged enough to make it impossible for either the Germans or the Spaniards to maintain effective frontier guards there, but not so high as to give the escapers arduous snow conditions.

Ordeal in the Pyrenees

The van stopped at the corner of a deserted road at the foot of the Pyrenees beyond Ceret. Here two fresh guides were waiting – Basque mountaineers, swarthy, unshaven, tough, dressed in dark, dirty, warm clothes and wearing *espadrilles* and that headdress which our own armies were now taking from the Basque – the beret. It was getting dark as the two Basques and the five refugees started walking up a rough path, but after clambering for about two miles they arrived at an isolated hut, where they all crowded in, lit wood fires, ate some of the bread and sausage with which they had been provided and went to sleep on the earth floor. Gone were the luxuries of Lyons and Marseilles.

Up before dawn, they were on their way in the dark, still climbing by tough paths or going over virgin rocky ground. It was very cold and Hasler noticed with anxiety that, in their unfit state, he and Sparks, as he dreaded, were beginning to feel the onset of high-altitude distress, their strength draining away, their breath labouring and their mouths going dry with thirst. They felt as though dehydrated. As the sun rose, he could see away to the right the battlements of high, forbidding Pyrenean peaks covered in snow and was thankful they would not have to face them. The lower courses were bad enough. The strange French intellectual seemed fit and at home in these parts, keeping up with the guides and talking to them. De Merode, who had been talking to him, told Hasler that he thought the stranger was a left-wing intellectual wanted by the Germans. Apparently the books that he had would incriminate him if he were captured, and he carried them separately in that fashion so that he could discard them instantly.

De Merode and Dawson, who had been immobilized for only about a week, also seemed fit and kept up without difficulty, but Hasler and Sparks were soon in distress from the unaccustomed exercise and the rarefied air. They suffered not so much from muscular fatigue as from shortage of breath and terrible thirst. They panted and laboured and lagged behind, while the rest of the party exhorted them to keep up. No one in the party carried any water and their thirst could not be slaked. Hasler, however, had the remains of a bottle of wine in his haversack and he paused to share it with Sparks, but the cadaverous stranger strode back down the mountainside, snatched the bottle from them and threw it far below. Hasler was furious, but controlled himself. He was embarrassed and ashamed that the others should regard him and Sparks as soft, gutless creatures. They were far from being the men they had been three months before, when they could have gone up at the run, and it was only the peril of the alternative that drove them desperately on, their breath coming in gasps, their tongues dry and hard. The only liquid now possessed in the party was some very rough red wine that each of the Basque guides carried in the goatskin *bota* slung around him; like Arabs, these highlanders could keep going all day with practically nothing to drink.

Presently they came to a small stream. The others ignored it, but the two marines lay down and drank deep. The others tried to prevent them, urging them to come on, but the exhausted men knew that they must have water or succumb altogether. They drank a full quart each, their mouths down to the water, and after that they were able to go on again feeling a great deal easier, though still their breath laboured painfully, like that of a man half-stifled. They were climbing a steep slope of rock and barren soil, utterly deserted, a stark mountain wilderness bare of all animal or vegetable life, enfolded by a million years of solitude. Among these wild, forbidding crags no attempt had been made to defend or even mark the frontiers between France and Spain. Only some widely separated guard posts, where the few roads and paths crossed, attempted a slender surveillance over the bleak wastes of man-forsaken territory.

It grew colder yet as they went higher, and the air yet more rare. Distress of thirst seized the two marines again. The others were puzzled and angry at their inability to keep up, yet it was plain to see that, as they stopped every few yards, gasping for breath, they were now almost *in extremis*. It was to the credit of the others that they did not go on and leave the marines to die, as they would very soon have done. Only an inner strength and the will to cling to life drove Hasler and Sparks forward step by feeble step, as though staggering under an intolerable load that must at any moment crush the last gasp of breath from their lungs.

Then salvation. They reached the snow-line and the means for quenching thirst lay all around them. Hasler called to mind the ancient warning against eating snow, but the body was crying for liquid and would not be refused. He said to Sparks: 'Put the snow in your mouth and hold it there till it melts.' They both did so, and very soon began to feel better. Their pace improved a little. Their stops for breath became a little less frequent; not every few steps now, but at each twenty yards and then at fifty. For a mile or more they were continually melting and drinking snow in this way, and loving it. It was the turning point in their fortune, and before long they were able to keep up with the others.

At about midday the curious stranger said that they were now near the frontier and would soon be in Spain, but the Basque guides became indecisive, often stopping and arguing with each other which way to go. They became of less and less use. The sky was overcast and they could get no direction from the sun. No one had a compass, and Hasler cursed himself for having given away his escape compasses as souvenirs to helpers. They could now see no more than a mile in any direction, as they were following the courses of valleys, with crumpled and jagged hills all round and no clearly defined ridge visible anywhere to mark the summits. In these high valley courses the snow was only six inches deep and no serious barrier to progress, though here and there they floundered into deeper drifts. To Hasler and Sparks, snow was now their friend; cold and hunger were but childish trials. Throughout all the afternoon they wandered about the twisting gullies and all sense of direction was lost. The guides themselves were at sea, stopping frequently to argue and to drink wine from their goatskin flasks. The gaunt stranger, who spoke their language, joined in these arguments and presently he took the lead himself. Obviously he knew more about these parts than had appeared at first, as they were to recall later, and they were all glad to see someone competent taking charge of the party. The useless guides wandered along with the rest of them, arguing and muttering. After another hour or two of indecision, in which, according to the stranger, they had crossed into Spain and then back again in to France, they began to come down from the snow-line.

Night fell after a weary day. After twenty-four hours of marching, they had made good about ten miles, but to the marines at least it had been the physical equivalent of forty miles. They bivouacked in a shallow mountain cave, desperately cold, but in fairly good spirits, for tomorrow, they all hoped, would see them out of danger. They ate, however, very frugally of the bread and sausage with which they had been provided, not knowing when they might eat again.

Before dawn they were off again. With the sky still overcast, there was still some doubt about their direction, but gradually they found themselves to be going progressively downhill and knew that they must now be in Spain. They knew now that their objective was Barcelona, and that their first care must be to avoid being captured by the Spanish police, which would mean a long imprisonment under brutal conditions. Fortunately the Catalans, the inhabitants of North-East Spain, were strongly anti-Franco and therefore anti-police, and not likely to give them away.

Gradually the first signs of man's existence began to appear, though they still had no idea where they were heading, except that it was downhill. The guides were still quite lost. All day they walked thus. The sun passed its meridian, darkness came and still they stumbled on, their food now all gone. At length they struck a rough road and, following it for some way, came to a signpost ten feet high. No one had torch or match, but the stranger, borrowing de Merode's cigarette lighter, climbed on the back of one of the guides, and by its flickering gleam at length read out the names. They appeared to mean little, however, for there was again much argument before, dog-tired, they set off down one of the roads.

Presently the road began to peter out into cart-tracks and there were still no houses to be seen, but signs of cultivation around them told that there must be a farm not far away. The night was very still and cold and all were quite at a loss now. Then one of the guides threw back his head and with open throat gave a wonderful imitation of a watchdog disturbed by an intruder. He was immediately answered by faint barks from two different directions. He repeated his call and, on being answered again, made off towards the one that seemed nearest. They all followed him, across country, and as they went he stopped occasionally to bark again to get the right direction from the answering bark.

At about nine o'clock, all quite tired out now after walking since before dawn, they came upon a little farmhouse, firmly locked and shuttered and quite dark. Inside a dog barked furiously, but the inhabitants remained fast asleep, and it was not until after long and furious knocking – enough, one would have thought, to wake a city – that eventually an upper window opened and an angry voice spoke. There was a long cross-talk in Spanish with the guides, but eventually the farmer was persuaded, came down and admitted them and blew up the fire. His wife came down, too, and before long they were satisfying their ravenous hunger and slaking their thirst with wine so rough that it was like sandpaper to the mouth. Then they lay down where they could in that rough peasant living-room, and slept.

That was their last night as tramps. The next day they trudged on again until, some time in the afternoon, they came to a small hotel in the little country town of Banolas, where they found that they were expected and were made comfortable, but kept in concealment for fear of the police.

Old Spanish Customs

Barcelona, and its British consulate, was some sixty miles distant, and after a stay of three or four days immured in the little hotel, the five refugees – the Basque guides having returned – were told that a lorry was outside to take them there. They trooped out and climbed into the back of an ancient covered van loaded with an ostentatious cargo of WC china, reposing unashamed on large quantities of straw. They climbed in with rude jests and concealed themselves in the straw, having been warned that there was a police check-post ahead. Under the straw it was stuffy but comfortably warm and when the police stopped them nothing was to be seen but the evidence of modern hygiene.

At the consulate they were interviewed by a cynical young Englishman who doubted their identities but provided them with a complete outfit of clothes. They were of miserable Spanish manufacture, but were clean and the four Service refugees – the cadaverous stranger having mysteriously left them – threw away with joy their old garments, by now pretty offensive. Hasler learnt from the vice-consul that the consulate was being swamped by large numbers of men seeking sanctuary from France. A few were escaping British Service men, but the great majority were Frenchmen, who all made themselves out to be French Canadians and thus claimed the protection of the British consulate. Had they admitted to being French, the French consulate would have sent them straight back to France. The British consul therefore sheltered them in a special transit camp, from which they were sent on to Britain if proved genuine or to a Free French district in North Africa if not. Many were poor specimens, with no intention of joining in the fight, but merely anxious to get away from France.

There were, however, many exciting and amusing stories of genuine Service escapers, and not least of them Hasler enjoyed the story of the British private who arrived in Lisbon in uniform, having spent several months wandering through France and Spain without discarding his uniform and without having been picked up either by the Germans or the police. When he was interviewed at our embassy he was nervous and worried, because, as his first words to the embassy official disclosed, 'I'm afraid I've lost my rifle, sir.'

In Spain anyone of military age caught coming out of France by the police was imprisoned for a fixed period under odious conditions and then released with a special police pass. While in prison they were subjected to abominable overcrowding, to a starvation diet and to brutal and callous warders. The Spaniards were always a cruel people. Hasler met several Service escapers – mostly RAF – in Barcelona who had been so caught and treated. As a result they hated all Spain and all Spaniards. One of them drew a plan of a single berth cell in which he and eleven others were immured – two were in the narrow single bed, one underneath it, one on the WC, six carpeting the floor and the others taking turns to stand up. They existed like this all day and night.

The British vice-consul at Barcelona was therefore at pains to keep all his charges 'underground' until they could be got away. Sparks was so dealt with, but Hasler was luckier. Thanks to his bald pate, he looked above military age and the vice-consul was able to convince the police that he was a commercial traveller and he thus obtained a police pass, which enabled him to move in Barcelona at will. Together with other pass-holders – nearly all men who had endured a spell in the Spanish prisons before being released – he was put up in the second-class Hotel Victoria, with a little spending money.

A few days later Hasler was shocked to hear from the vice-consul that the gaunt Frenchman who had accompanied them on their trip across the Pyrenees was now believed to have been a Gestapo agent. Someone at least had betrayed part of the escape organization, and suspicion lay at his door. He had disappeared on arrival at Barcelona and had not sought refuge like the rest. It was an agonizing thought that their brave friends in France might now be in danger of their lives and that the safety of their wives and children might also be in jeopardy. 'It is they,' he said, 'who are the heroes of nearly all escapes.'

The vice-consul received orders that Hasler was to be sent home with the 'utmost priority', though his identity was still unwarranted (and, as he passed through the hands of various wide-awake security officers on his way home, it continued to be suspect until he was able to be vouched for at last by Cyril Horton and by 'dear Pat Elliot, best of all my Wren friends at COHQ'). In spite of this priority, he had to wait for over a fortnight before a car was available to take him, now the proud owner of a cardboard suitcase, to our embassy in Madrid. Sparks was left behind to come on at a lesser priority. In Madrid Hasler spent several days as the guest of the naval attaché, revelling in a gay round of parties and also revelling in an afternoon at the Prado, Madrid's famous art gallery, where he had the Velázquezes and the El Grecos almost to himself. From Madrid he embarked in an embassy car on the long drive to Gibraltar, pausing for a night at Seville, where he saw some Flamenco dancing but found his attention almost as much distracted, but less tastefully, by a party of German officials, who were dining at the next table. He found that hard to bear.

Lunch the next day at Jerez and a glass of Tio Pepé in its home town led him at long last in the afternoon of 1 April, after 1,400 miles of wandering, across the Gibraltar frontier back again on British soil.

When Field-Marshal Keitel, at the headquarters of the Wehrmacht, heard of the escape of Hasler and his companions, he was exceedingly angry with the Spanish government. A stiff diplomatic note was sent to Franco, complaining of the lax and inefficient watching of the Pyrenean frontier. Franco replied in effect: 'If you think it can be done better, do it yourself.'

In due course, on the recommendations of Lord Louis Mountbatten, Hasler was awarded the DSO and a brevet majority. Sparks received the Distinguished Service Medal. Laver and Mills were also recommended for the DSM, but, under that rule by which only the Victoria Cross and the George Cross can be awarded posthumously, their memories were rewarded by the oak leaves of Mention in Despatches and by that unvarnished record in the Casualty List which is itself a soldier's highest honour.

18. THE ABOMINABLE DEED

Meanwhile, back at Southsea, all was still in doubt and uncertainty. The German radio announcement (which was quite untrue) was reported in the Portsmouth papers as in those of London and when this was shown by Sergeant King to Jock Stewart, who was acting in command of the unit, Stewart gave orders that the matter was not to be discussed.

It was seen, too, at 'White Heather' guest house and added further to the fear of Heather Powell, though she had no grounds for connecting it with Hasler's Party. Only her intuition. She fell ill and the doctor was puzzled. Towards the end of January, Mrs Powell received a letter from Mrs Ewart in Glasgow, telling her of the receipt of the 'Missing' telegram, and later on Mrs Ewart came to visit her. Heather fell further into distress and the doctor sent her into St Mary's Hospital for observation.

Fisher, Colley and Ellery came back in the submarine before Christmas, but were not keen to stay again at 'White Heather', nor was Mrs Powell anxious to have them; all the jollity had gone out of the place.

Then, very late one night some months later, Sparks arrived at 'White Heather'. Mrs Powell came down to the door. She was relieved and delighted to see him, but, she says, he was obviously upset about something, and looking much older (as the men in the unit also thought). He would say little about what they had been doing, but when asked about the others said: 'They will be along later.' Then he asked where Heather was, and went next day to see her in hospital. When she saw he could give her no news of the others, the girl's fears were but increased and when some time later she was allowed to come home and found all the men's wardrobes empty and cold she broke down again. She went further into a decline and tuberculosis was then diagnosed. Her father came home from sea, but she was already nearing the end. To his shocked ears she told how she had dreamed that they were all dead. Without the will to fight her illness, she died a month before her seventeenth birthday.

Elsewhere in the country three mothers had news of their sons in April.

Mrs Moffat, in Halifax, received a letter from the Plymouth Division, Royal Marines, saying: 'From the information received from a German Casualty List, the body of your son, Marine David Moffat, Ply. X 108881, was washed ashore on 17 December 1942. . . .' Mountbatten himself wrote her a letter of sympathy.

Mrs Mackinnon and Mrs Conway received more encouraging news through Red Cross channels. The messages took more than three months to reach them, being dated 29 December, but they said that on that day both were prisoners. In the case of Conway, the message said: 'Have seen James last week. He is healthy and conveys New Year's greetings to you. Don't worry.' Mrs Mackinnon received a similar message.

These things Hasler learnt from the parents themselves in April, for one of his first thoughts on return was to enquire for news of the missing men in any direction that he could. It was not until the war was over that the dreadful truth – or part of it – was learnt, and the greater part, indeed, has remained hidden until these lines were composed.

After the eight missing men had disappeared from our story, we have only a glimpse of Laver and Mills. After landing just north of Blaye in the early hours of 12 December, they made very good progress for two days, but did not succeed in getting any civilian clothes. After covering about 20 miles through difficult country, they were picked up by the French police, while still in uniform, at La Garde, a suburb of Montlieu, 12 miles south-east of the hamlet of Villexavier, which Hasler and Sparks passed through that day. In accordance with Vichy orders, Laver and Mills were handed over to the German Security Police, who took them to the municipal police prison in Bordeaux.

Of Mackinnon and Conway we know a little more. Captured German documents show that, after separation from their companions at Le Verdon (for which we still do not know the reason), the crew of *Cuttlefish* carried on their mission for three days alone and undismayed. They spent 10 December on the east side of the Ile de Cazeau, only a few miles from where the others of the party were experiencing so uncomfortable a time on the very same day. At 9 o'clock that night, however, as they made off on the last lap, their canoe struck a submerged obstruction opposite the Bec d'Ambes – that sharp point of land that marks the confluence of the Garonne and the Dordogne – and was completely wrecked. Conway extricated himself from the sinking craft only with difficulty and he and Mackinnon then swam back to the island. It was cruel luck after a most creditable performance by these young marines in severely testing conditions.

What happened in the next few days is uncertain, for the recorded information is unreliable. Our next definite knowledge comes from a French source. A few days before Christmas, Monsieur Louis Jaubert, tenant of a small house near the railway line in the tiny village of Cessac, which lies some 20 miles east-south-east of Bordeaux, was looking out of a window and saw his neighbour, Monsieur Cheyrau, walking along the track followed by two strangers carrying sacks or bags. He went out and greeted them and M. Cheyrau said in a whisper: 'They are two Englishmen coming from Bordeaux.'

M. Jaubert invited them all into his house to share a bottle of wine. He was anxious to help the refugees, for he himself had a son in the French army who had been hospitably treated on being evacuated from Dunkirk to England in 1940 and who had been made a prisoner by the Boches on his return to France subsequently. He felt a strong bond with the young men, therefore, but was careful to assure himself first that they were genuine and not German police agents. Having seen their proofs, he arranged to take them in for supper, bed and breakfast, while his neighbour provided the midday meal. Mackinnon, who was wearing a blue serge suit, had a painful boil on his knee, was walking with difficulty and needed a rest. Madame Jaubert dressed the knee with fomentations.

Later the Frenchmen took the two Britons into the neighbouring village of Frontenac (famous for its own special wine), believing that in one of the cafés there they might meet a representative of an escape organization. They tried two cafés without success and returned home. Washing their clothes that night, Mme Jaubert was astute enough to look for the trademark on their underpants and saw that it was English.

In spite of his painful knee, Mackinnon was anxious to get on, both for his own sake and because of the terrible risk to which he was exposing his hosts. He disclosed to M. Jaubert that he was making for Bilbao, in north-east Spain, and asked him to find out the railway fare to Toulouse, as he and Conway had only 1,000 francs left. This proved to be ample and Mac declined M. Jaubert's offer to advance him some more.

To entrain for Toulouse, they would have to go to the town of La Réole, some 25 miles to the south-east, and on the third day of their stay with the hospitable M. Jaubert a Frenchman came forward who offered to conduct them across the line of demarcation during the night. It was arranged accordingly. 'We parted from them,' says M. Jaubert, 'with tears in our eyes and embraced them; they were such nice boys.'

Full of determination and with rising hopes, the two young marines reached La Réole in safety, but there irretrievable disaster befell. Some time afterwards M. Jaubert heard to his dismay that they had been taken prisoner. He wrote for information to the mayor of La Réole and learnt from him that Mackinnon and Conway had been admitted to a civilian hospital. There, it appears, they were betrayed, and in the last days of December a squad of Germans was sent over from Langon to seize them.

This point marks the beginning of a foul and abominable story, one only of the many unspeakable infamies committed by Nazi Germany throughout Europe. Much of the story is still veiled and all that we can do is to record the bare outlines of the facts as far as they have been gathered. First, let us look at a 'very secret' and very revolting document in which the Germans themselves, without any sense of shame, coldly record their own odious behaviour.

This is a document dated 12 January 1944 and signed by a German staff officer named Major Reichel, addressed to the Military High Command and others, reporting the action taken against British and Allied men captured in various raids. The information was disseminated for 'exploitation and propaganda purposes' as a counter-action to what the Germans called the 'Kharkov fake trials', in which the Russians had put on trial for the most atrocious massacres some Nazi officers and the Russian traitor who had driven their mobile poison-gas wagon. This disgusting document contains the following report on the Frankton operation (the italics are mine):-

> (5) Sabotage attacks on German ships off Bordeaux.
>
> On 12.12.42 a number of valuable German ships were badly damaged off Bordeaux by explosions below water-level. Adhesive mines were attached by 5 British sabotage squads working from canoes. Of the 10 who took part in the attack the following were captured a few days later:
>
> Mackinnon, Naval Lieutenant, born 15.7.21, North Argyll-shire.
>
> Laver, Albert Friedrich, Petty Officer, b. 29.9.20, Birkenhead.
>
> Mills, William Henri, Marine, b. 15.12.21, Kettering.
>
> Wallace, Samuel, Sergeant, b. 24.9.13, Dublin, Eire.
>
> Conway, James, Marine, b. 28.8.22, Stockport.
>
> Ewart, Robert, Marine, b. 4.12.21, Glasgow.
>
> A seventh solider, Moffat, was found drowned. The rest, among them their leader, Major Hasler, Marine Sparks, and Corporal Sheard, presumably escaped to Spain.
>
> The men concerned paddled in their canoes by twos from a submarine up the mouth of the Gironde. They were wearing special olive-grey garments *without any military badges*. Having carried out the explosions, they sank their craft and tried to make their escape to France with the help of the French civilian population. They met in two places on the Gironde in a bar and were brought to the demarcation line by intermediaries, with whom arrangements had been made beforehand.
>
> *Noteworthy punishable offences committed on their flight have not been discovered up till now.* All those captured were shot in accordance with orders on the 23.3.43.

The last sentence is erroneous. The Germans seem to have been able to shift their ground whenever it suited them and Wallace and Ewart, at least, were not dealt with as Kharkov 'reprisals'. The action against them was, or purported to be, in pursuance of Hitler's infamous 'Commando Order', under which all 'Commando saboteurs', were, in outrage of The Hague Regulations, to be denied all quarter or mercy and to be killed out of hand or pursued to the death. What in fact happened to Wallace and Ewart was disclosed in full detail in the war diaries of the German admirals Bachmann and Marschall, in the war crimes trial at Hamburg in 1948 of Colonel Werner von Tippelskirch and in other sources.

These showed that Wallace and Ewart, after separation from their companions at the first tide-race, proceeded doggedly on their own nearly all that night. At about 4 a.m. on 8 December, however, they were 'swept into the surf' after a severe buffeting and capsized near the Pte de Grave lighthouse. Here they swam ashore and were taken prisoner in a state of collapse by a flak battery of the Luftwaffe. Later in the day various articles of their equipment, including limpets and maps, were found scattered on the foreshore. Later still their wrecked canoe was found below low-water mark off Pte de Grave itself but could not be salvaged. The prisoners were handed over by the Luftwaffe to naval custody under the jurisdiction of the Senior Naval Officer Inshore Squadron, Gascony, at that time Captain Max Gebauer. It was he who, while dining the evening before at Royan with Admiral Bachmann, Commander-in-Chief Western France, had ordered the 'show-out' of the searchlights when the report was brought to him of *Tuna* having been located by radar.

When the report of the capture of Wallace and Ewart came through to Gebauer early on the morning of the 8th, he at once ordered a search to be made for any other British parties and he informed his admiral. Bachmann ordered the prisoners to be shot. The headquarters of Navy Group West in Paris were also informed, and from von Rundstedt's supreme headquarters in France came orders to the army to take immediate steps for the protection of the U-boat base at Bordeaux.

It happened that Bachmann had come to Royan from his headquarters at Nantes to watch gunnery practice by the coast defence batteries on the morning of the 8th and afterwards to inspect the ships of the Defence Flotilla at Le Verdon – the very ships that Hasler and his companions had had to evade the night before. After the gunnery practice, which took place while the remnant of Hasler's Party was in hiding at Pte aux Oiseaux,

Bachmann and Gebauer crossed to Le Verdon and there Bachmann ordered the prisoners to be brought before him. Wallace and Ewart were accordingly marched into his presence. He glared at the men whom he had ordered to be murdered, without saying a word. He saw, however, as Gebauer subsequently admitted, that they were in uniform, with the Royal Marines shoulder-title; Wallace's chevrons were noted in particular.

Nevertheless, Bachmann stuck to his infamous order, varying it only, at the request of intelligence officers, to the extent of allowing interrogation before execution. Wallace and Ewart were accordingly taken over the estuary and lodged in the old French fort of Royan. There they were interrogated by the naval intelligence staff in the evening – with no result.

Meanwhile the telephone wires between Royan, Paris and Hitler's 'battle headquarters' in Polish Ukraine ('the Wolf's Lair') were being kept very warm. Marschall's headquarters of Navy Group West were perturbed when they heard of Bachmann's order to execute the prisoners. They could not very well overrule the instruction, as it purported to be in accordance with Hitler's Commando Order, but this appears to have been the first case under that order, which had been circulated (solely to senior officers) only in October. It does not seem to have occurred to any of these Germans that the marines were not 'saboteurs' but just as much military persons on a military mission as if they had come in a cruiser instead of a canoe. Undoubtedly there were some Germans to whom the Commando Order was repugnant, but, under pressure from Hitler, the anxiety of Marschall's staff officers, in spite of all their postwar protestations, had little to do with any concern about their own honour; what they were worried about was that the men might be slaughtered before the utmost possible information had been wrung out of them. They were particularly keen to interrogate these valuable naval prisoners. On the score of honour, their main concern was to avoid the stain on such consciences as Hitler had left them if the execution was carried out by men of their own service – a stain that they did not avoid.

For these reasons, late that same night of the 8th, Rear-Admiral Wilhelm Meisel, Marschall's chief-of-staff, ordered a special interrogation officer (a tobacconist who had spent some time in England) to be fetched at once from Germany, and he also telephoned Hitler's headquarters in Poland. He asked to speak to no less a person than Field-Marshal Keitel, chief of all the German armed forces (the Wehrmacht). 'Sorry, he is out.' Colonel-General Jodl then? 'Sorry, he is out too; in fact, all the high officers have gone to the pictures with the Fuehrer.'

Finally, Meisel spoke to Colonel von Tippelskirch, of Hitler's headquarters staff, who was the senior officer present concerned with such matters (the Q branch). He and Meisel, who was a very excitable person, had an angry conversation, not assuaged by the differences in rank or service. Meisel, we are led to infer, thought that the men should be treated as prisoners of war, to which von Tippelskirch replied in effect: 'Why the devil do you want to rout me out at this time of night on such a trivial business? The Führer's orders are quite clear. The men must be shot at once.' He relaxed only to the extent of agreeing to interrogation.

The next morning von Tippelskirch's superior, General Warlimont, himself telephoned Marschall's headquarters and confirmed that, 'on the express orders of the Führer', the men were to be shot, after first being questioned, 'with no methods barred'. Marschall accordingly sent out the following signal to Bachmann:

> *With no methods barred*, also using the *subterfuge of sparing their lives* and the assurance of good treatment, try to obtain *before execution* the following information . . .

With this cynical admission of their own treachery and dishonour, the Germans pursued their intentions. At four o'clock on the morning of 10 December, Wallace and Ewart were turned out, taken to Bordeaux and handed over to the villains of the Security Police – the counterpart in occupied territories of the infamous Gestapo. Of what then happened to the two marines in detail we are mercifully ignorant, but we do know that, to their eternal honour, Wallace and Ewart disclosed nothing of the least value to the enemy and in particular they spoke no word of betrayal of their comrades who were even then pursuing their sure and inexorable way towards their objective. To the end the Germans remained entirely ignorant of Hasler's purpose and progress and believed that Wallace and Ewart were alone. Wallace successfully hoodwinked the Germans into believing that he was the leader of the party and that only one other canoe – the one damaged in the launching – was involved. Not until after the explosions had taken place, the hubbub begun and Laver and the others captured did the Germans suspect the truth.

Very late on the night of 11 December, just when Hasler and Laver were approaching their targets not a mile away, a small convoy formed up unobtrusively in the main square of Bordeaux. It was led by a senior thug of the Security Police and consisted in addition of Lieutenant Theodor Prahm (Adjutant of the Naval Officer in Charge, Bordeaux), a naval party of one petty officer and sixteen ratings, Wallace and Ewart, a doctor – and two coffins. At dead of night, in every circumstance of shady and felonious purpose, the convoy drove away into the heart of a forest. It turned off the road and followed a track to a remote sandpit. All dismounted. In the sandpit two posts were driven into the ground. Sergeant Wallace and Marine Ewart, unafraid, were marched up and tied to them. The headlamps of the lorries were turned full on. At the word from Prahm, the firing party formed up at a few paces' distance.

It was very cold. From a cloudless sky the stars shone in frosty brilliance. No wind stirred the dark outlines of the trees. In the crude glare of the headlamps, at half an hour past midnight of 11/12 December at the very moment when Hasler had successfully completed his mission, Prahm gave his order to fire.

Thus was accomplished this clandestine and disreputable murder, from which none emerged with any honour save the two gallant marines, whose behaviour shines out in all this record of brutality, and whom even the Germans did not forbear to describe as 'these brave men'.

After the war, Bachmann being reported as already dead, von Tippelskirch was brought to trial as having been 'concerned in the killing', but he was acquitted. No members of the German navy were arraigned. It was fortunate for at least one of them that our own Royal Navy, for reasons of sentiment that it would be unprofitable to discuss, was not keen on such trials. Von

Tippelskirch's trial took place at Hamburg in 1948, lasting from August till October. The president of the court was Colonel E. A. Howard, with Mr C. L. Stirling KC, as Judge-Advocate. There was much careful and studied lying, more than one of the witnesses apprehensive that he might himself be transferred from the witness-box to the dock. Bachmann, whom several Germans seemed to have regarded as the soul of honour, was described by the Judge-Advocate as a 'bloodthirsty ruffian'. To Prahm, he said: 'You brought the German Navy into complete and everlasting disrepute by this monstrous thing' – for Prahm could quote no order from his own superior nor any authority of any sort whatever except a casual request late at night from the Security Police to go out and shoot a couple of British soldiers.

Of the shooting of Mackinnon, Conway, Laver and Mills we know nothing for certain. The German actions, records and statements were so full of deceit and lies that the truth is still hidden. The probability, however, is that the end did not come until 23 March 1943 and there is evidence that for their final inquisition and execution they were taken to Paris. It is typical of German deceit that the burial certificates declare that the bodies were buried in Bagneux Cemetery, Paris, but no written record or physical trace of such burials was ever found, after the most exhaustive search.

It is even more typical and revealing of the Germans' own guilty consciences that the burial certificates of *all six* of these Cockleshell Heroes assert that they were 'found drowned in Bordeaux Harbour'.

19. THE RAIDER OF TODAY

The Bordeaux raid by no means closed the story of Hasler's Party. In the summer of 1943 a repetition of the same raid was considered and reached an advanced stage of planning, but very wisely it was not carried out. The unit, however, added further to its laurels in July 1944, when, after Hasler had left it to go to the Far East, Lieutenant J. F. Richards led a most successful raid against enemy ships in Portolago Bay, in the Mediterranean island of Leros. In this raid three Cockles entered the fortified harbour, full of wide-awake and chattering Italians, to attack enemy destroyers and naval escort craft. Richards was awarded the Distinguished Service Cross, and Sergeant King, with Marine R. N. Ruff, their canoe half-filled with water and actually sinking before they made their hide-out under machine-gun fire, won the Distinguished Service Medal.

When the war was over, and so many of these small units came to an end, the traditions and lessons of the RMBPD, and indeed of all other canoeing units, became inherited by the Special Boat Sections of the Royal Marines, the name itself having in fact been that of Army canoeing units formed during the war.

Today the Special Boat Sections, together with the other amphibious units of the Royal Marines, form an important tactical element in the Royal Navy's part in combined operations. They thus maintain, though in a new guise, the Corps's traditions as the soldiers of the sea, in which, under the White Ensign, they have carried the renown of the Globe and Laurel, their proud badge, into all the seas of the world. No more attractive life is open to young men with the spirit of adventure.

Tradition lives on while technique changes, and today technique in the linear descendants of the wartime raiders has made great strides. The successor of the famous Cockle is the Canoe Mark XI, and the marine who mans it is a 'swimmer-canoeist', combining his canoeing with the special new art of underwater swimming in the 'frogman's' watertight suit, fins and oxygen supply. They are all picked men, specially selected for the qualities that their task demands. A section now consists of two officers and sixteen men, and their main task still remains that of carrying out small-scale raids, though there is a special emphasis today on missions of reconnaissance of an enemy shore to discover information.

New types of small craft are being evolved and of special interest are the inflatable craft. These strange craft fold up, parachute-wise, into a small, tight bundle and on being thrown into the water they automatically inflate themselves by means of carbon dioxide bottles, performing strange contortions as they writhe and wriggle in the water in the process of assuming their destined shape. These can carry from three to ten men and can be propelled by paddle, outboard motor or sail.

The normal method of conveying a raiding force to its target area is by submarine, but coastal craft, fishing vessels or flying-boats are also used. The big new development, especially since the arrival of the inflatable boat, however, has been the conveyance of these craft and their crews close to the target area by means of parachute from the air. For this the men normally work in pairs, one dropping with the inflatable canoe strapped to his leg and the other with the paddles and other equipment needed for the operation. The Special Boat Section is thus able to operate in waters inaccessible to surface craft and submarines – the object that Hasler himself pursued for so long.

There is also now a new type of canoe compass and more advanced equipment for the navigation of small craft under operational conditions. For the frogman swimmer there are underwater compasses, torches and watches.

The limpets used for attacks on shipping are basically the same as those used on 'Frankton', but in order to save weight they can be made up specially to meet any particular 'requirement' of the target. The modern swimmer-canoeist does not, however, operate only against ships. He is trained to attack objectives ashore also, and on these missions he uses special charges designed to concentrate their explosive power against the most vulnerable part of the target.

An interesting point about all this equipment and technique of today is that it is all one-man-power. Devices such as the wartime explosive motorboat, the chariot and the midget submarine are now the business of officers and ratings RN, while their brethren of the 'Royals' depend upon the power of their own limbs to reach their target. They carry out their approach to the target *on* the water by canoe or inflatable craft, *in* the water by surface swimming, or *under* water in the frogman's suit.

These Special Boat Sections are but one of the amphibious activities of the marines today. There are, for example, the Landing Craft Squadrons, in which the marine, becoming more sailor than solider, mans entirely the assault and raiding craft that are used to land a military force over beaches. One of these craft regularly crosses the North Sea from Germany to Chatham under the command of a captain Royal Marines. There are also Naval Beach Units, which are mixed RN and RM organizations, and in which the marines provide landing-craft specialists and signallers, their jobs being to organize the unloading and turn-round of landing craft on the beach, to mark the beach and to maintain communication between ship and shore.

These landing-craft units inevitably have close relations with another new activity for which the Corps has now made itself famous – the Commandos. Whereas during the war there were Army and RM Commandos, today only those of the Royal Marines remain, trained either for amphibious raiding operations or for use as infantry units on land. In their new rôle they have blended the concept of the Commando's physical and mental toughness with a wonderful discipline and a high excellence of performance, whether in assaulting cliffs, skiing, parachuting, field craft, parade ceremonial or just keeping the peace in the troublous places of the world.

The all-round amphibious versatility of the Royal Marines was perhaps never so finely demonstrated as in the assault on the strongly defended key island of Walcheren, lying at the mouth of the Scheldt, in 1944, in the course of the Allied armies' great campaigns in the conquest of Germany. On this occasion the Royal Marine Commandos who made the infantry assaults amid floods and wreckage were brought in to the beaches in landing craft manned by men of their own Corps and supported by the fire of their own gunners from support craft.

Besides all these amphibious activities, Her Majesty's Jollies still set great store and pride in their old traditional task of providing detachments on board the larger ships of war, where they serve as the Navy's soldiers, manning some of the guns and providing infantry for duties in the ship or for landing parties. Though trained as soldiers, their integration with ships' companies gives them a naval outlook and basis which are most valuable in relation to their other functions and thus moulds them to a form distinct and set apart from any others in the service of the Crown.

APPENDICES

A. Typical navigational calculation by No. I of a canoe

He is at sea on a pitch-black night with a drizzle falling and cannot make out even large objects at more than about half a mile. A navigational buoy is visible a few hundred years away and this gives him his approximate position. If in doubt as to which buoy it is, he will paddle over and read the name on it.

He now knows his position, and can lay off a course to the next objective – shall we say, a small creek formed by a stream running into the estuary. To reach this, he has to cross the estuary, with the tide diagonally against him, and he does not expect to sight any more marks until he gets there, a distance of three sea miles.

He gets out his transparent chart case and dim red reading torch and a pencil and ivorine writing tablet. Inside the chart case is a chartlet of the area, made by cutting a section out of a full-sized Admiralty chart and drawing on it in blue pencil (a) a scale of sea miles, and (b) one of two Magnetic North lines running right across it.

The chart is held so that it cannot slip in the case, and the man first marks his present position on the transparent case, and labels it with the time . . '2341'. (The Perspex case is slightly roughened with emery paper so that it will take ordinary pencil.)

He then lays his pencil so that it points at the objective, then swings it to the right or left an estimated amount to allow for the side effect of the tide. He is helped in this estimation by the simplified tidal data which he is carrying and can refer to, or else he can just use his eyes and see the strength and direction of the tide on the buoy, and estimate how it will vary during his passage.

As the cruising speed of a loaded canoe is only about three knots maximum, tidal stream has a huge effect, and indeed it is not practicable to canoe in tides of over about two knots unless they are more or less astern. In this case, he swings his pencil to starboard about ten degrees, and notes that as the tide is diagonally on his bow his speed over the ground will be reduced to an estimated two knots.

Having adjusted the pencil to his satisfaction, he estimates the angle which it makes with one of the Magnetic North lines, and hence decides on his magnetic course, which he sets on the grid of his compass. He also does a mental calculation, dividing the total distance by his estimated speed over the ground, and decides that he should arrive in about an hour and a half, i.e. at about 0115. After noting the course and the expected time of arrival on his tablet, he puts everything away and takes up his paddle, and off they go.

Obviously, it is essential that he should not have spent more than a minute or so on the whole business, particularly if the tide is carrying him backwards all the time he is working it out. The standard of accuracy is not high, but even on a dark night he will rely on picking up visual landmarks wherever possible, and so correcting his position periodically. Sometimes a skilful navigator will introduce a deliberate error to one side when approaching, say, a shore or line of obstacles, so that he is certain which way to turn when he reaches it.

Other aids to navigation are the stars, particularly the Pole Star; the appearance of the surface of the water, which often reveals submerged shallows, etc., particularly when the tide is running; and soundings, which tell not only the depth of water but also, by leaving the lead on the bottom for a little while, the strength and direction of the tidal stream when this cannot be judged by other means. For sounding, Hasler's unit often used a fishing reel mounted on a very short rod, and a small fishing lead.

B. Outline Plan of Operation 'Frankton' as prepared by Major Hasler and Lieutenant-Commander L'Estrange and approved by CCO

Combined Operations Headquarters,
1A, Richmond Terrace,
Whitehall, S.W.1.
October 29th, 1942.

OPERATION 'FRANKTON'

OUTLINE PLAN

References

1. [Here follow numbers of the charts and maps concerned in the operation.]

Nature of Operation

2. A small party, six strong, will be disembarked from a submarine approximately 9 miles from CORDOUAN LIGHT. The party will paddle up the GIRONDE ESTUARY in Cockles Mark II, lying up by day and paddling by night to the BASSENS-BORDEAUX area, where they will carry out a Limpet attack on blockade runners in the Port. The party will escape overland to SPAIN.

Information

3. (a) *General.* Intelligence docket, air photographs, map trace of coast defences, chart trace showing lying-up places in river, chart trace showing mines laid by us, tidal charts of estuary, are available in COHQ.

4. (b) *Enemy Patrols**
   (i) Two armed trawlers maintain a permanent patrol off the river mouth.
   (ii) There is the ordinary enemy trawler traffic engaged in mine-sweeping.
   (iii) Six M-Class mine-sweepers are stationed at ROYAN or LE VERDON.
   (iv) U-Boats may be met either approaching or leaving LA PALLICE or LE VERDON.

* Further information on enemy defences and dispositions became available later.

River Patrols

(v) Whilst there is no information which shows the number or type of craft patrolling the river, it must be assumed that the river is patrolled.

Intention

5. To sink between 6 and 12 of the cargo vessels in the BASSENS-BORDEAUX area.

Forces required

6. (a) *Naval.* One submarine carrying three Cockles Mark II.
   (b) *Military.* Six All Ranks, Royal Marine Boom Patrol Detachment.

Meteorological Conditions [See Appendix A for data]

7. (a) *Moon.* No moon is essential.
   (b) *Tide.* It will only be possible for the Cockles to proceed on the flood tide or during slack water.
   (c) *Wind.* Maximum Force 3.
   (d) *Sea.* Slight.
   (e) *Swell.* Moderate.

Dates

8. (a) A period of approximately ten days in the beginning of each of the months December and January is suitable for the operation.
   (b) The operation is timed to take place.
      (i) Submarine leaves Clyde about November 25.
      (ii) Party leaves submarine, first possible night December 3/4. Last possible night December 12/13.

Passage and Route

9. The force will embark in submarine as directed by Flag Officer Submarines and proceed to position approximately 45° 10′ N., 01° 30′ W. Passage will take about 6 days.

Command

10. (a) Operation will be under the command of Flag Officer Submarines.
    (b) Naval Force Commander, Officer Commanding HM Submarine.
    (c) Military Force Commander – Major H. G. Hasler, RM.

Outline Plan

11. (a) *Naval.* The submarine after taking its position by day would, under cover of darkness, approach the coast, surface and disembark the Military party in 3 Cockles Mark II. The Officer Commanding Submarine will report time, date and position of disembarking Military Force on his return.

(b) *Military*. The Military Force will proceed up the GIRONDE Estuary, lying up by day and travelling by night for the full period of the flood tide, reaching an advanced base within 10 miles of the objective on the 2nd or 3rd night, and carrying out the attack on the following night.

(c) *Air*. It will be necessary to make arrangements that no bombing or mining operations take place in the area during the period in question. It is known that the enemy have an efficient mine-watching organisation in the area and it is essential that the mine-watchers are not put on the alert by an air raid. As the operation takes place during a period of no moon and our mining operations usually take place during a moon period, it is not anticipated that there will be any difficulty in arranging this.

Evacuation

12. The Party will escape overland through OCCUPIED FRANCE to SPAIN as per special instructions.

Cancellation of Operation

13. The operation may be cancelled:
    (i) By Flag Officer Submarines for such reasons as inability to supply Submarine.
    (ii) By Naval Force Commander in consultation with Military Force Commander for such reasons as unsuitability of weather, enemy minefields or movement of enemy surface or air forces which might prevent the disembarkation.
    (iii) By Military Force Commander when it becomes clearly apparent that the enemy position is such that the military tasks cannot be completed without seriously prejudicing the safety of his forces.

Administration

14. Special clothing and equipment, demolition stores, rations, medical stores to be provided through COHQ.

Security

15. (a) See Standing Instructions to Military Force Commanders.
    (b) No plans will be issued to party by Military Force Commander until Force is locked up.
    (c) Special instructions reference escape to SPAIN to be issued to the Force before sailing.
    (d) Special arrangements to be made reference Security in the Clyde by COHQ.

Report

16. A full report on the operation will be submitted to CCO (copy to Flag Officer Submarines) by Military Force Commander on his return.

Training

17. Special training began on October 20 and will include:
    (1) Boat practice.
    (2) Handling of limpets.
    (3) Rehearsal from submarine.
    (4) Full-scale rehearsal on British estuary (if possible).
    (5) Training for escape.

Note. Appendices of the Outline Plan are not included here.

C. The origin of the 'frogman's' suit

Before he left for the operation, Major Hasler told Captain Stewart that during his absence he wanted him to develop some method of operational swimming underwater. He thought that the Germans would very soon take measures against the direct approach by canoe, and that in future it would often be necessary to swim the last hundred yards or so. A new technique was also needed to be put in hand for the development of the underwater glider that subsequently came to be known as the Sleeping Beauty.

Hasler was, of course, thinking in terms of attacks on enemy shipping, since this was the rôle to which he had been assigned by COHQ, but it could be seen that there were other purposes for underwater swimming.

We had no equipment at that time other than the Italian swim-fins that fitted on to the feet, and we knew of the similar Californian type, and of course we had the Davis gear for escaping from sunken submarines.

In consequence of these instructions, Stewart had a series of discussions with Lieutenant-Commander Shelford, the Diving Officer of HMS *Dolphin*, to develop some form of swimming with a breathing apparatus, and at first they both visualised that the method of swimming would be the ordinary breast-stroke. Shelford and Stewart went to the Diving Committee to ask for the authorisation of a lightweight suit made from balloon fabric. The members of the Committee laughed breezily and wanted to know how the diver was going to keep warm; but they agreed none the less to give approval to the development. Shelford then arranged for Stewart to meet Mr Gorham, of Dunlop's.

Stewart and Gorham together worked on the development of a streamlined suit, but of rubber sheeting, not balloon fabric, in which the man entered the suit through the neck, put the helmet on and made a watertight joint round the neck. When the prototype of this suit had been made Gorham brought it down to Southsea, but it was still without any breathing apparatus.

By this time there had arrived in England, at the request of COHQ, a man who was soon to be regarded as 'the king of surface swimmers'. This was Lieutenant Bruce Wright, of the Royal Canadian Navy, a swimmer of Olympic standard and originator of the Sea Reconnaissance Unit formed later. He had brought over some of his own equipment and a pair of American-type fins, and had been attached to the RMBPD. The technique that he had evolved was essentially for surface swimming, which did not interest us much, but after Stewart had shown him how to use the Davis gear, and Gorham had arrived with the suit, it did not take them long between themselves to see where the answer to this problem lay. Gorham went back to Manchester to work on a new outfit that could be used with both the fins and a new oxygen-breathing apparatus. In due time Stewart went up to Manchester and he and Gorham, in a locked swimming-bath from which everyone else was excluded, carried out the vital tests. By the time that Hasler returned in April the development of the frogman's gear was virtually completed.

D. List of stores carried by canoes on Operation 'Frankton'

Boats' Gear (in each canoe)

Double paddles, Mk II (3 pairs)
Handgrips, Mk II
Bailer and sponge
Magnetic holder
Codline (20 fathoms)
Set of 5 cargo bags
Sounding reel (16 fm)
Repair bag
Log pads, containing tide tables
P8 compass and corrector
Dim reading torch (with spare bulbs and batteries)
Protractors
Camouflage net
Waterproofed watch
WT matches (2)
Tin of camouflage cream
Escape kit
Whiting line, 4 fm length
Pencil, paper and chart

Weapons and Explosives (in each canoe)

No. 69 grenades, 2
Limpets, rigid, 6-magnet, 8
Ampoule boxes, 2
Limpet spanners
Placing-rods, 2

Together with the .45 Colt automatic and fighting knife carried on the man and one silent Sten 9-mm. per Division.

Food and Medical (in each canoe)

Compact rations for 2 men for 5 days
Water-cans, ½ gallon, 5
Benzedrine, 1 box
Water sterilising sets
1st field dressing, 2
Iodine bottle
Toilet paper, 2 packets
Morphia syringes, 2
Hexamine cookers, 5
5-pint dixie
Tin of foot powder
WT ditty box
Tin of cough lozenges
Tin of laxative pills

On the Man

These are enumerated in the text.

Spare Clothing and Accessories Carried in the Bags (per man)

Pair of short pants
Toothbrush and paste
Towel
Handkerchief
Sea-water soap
Razor and blades
One shaving brush between two men
Pair of felt-soled boots, with spare laces
Pair of socks
Roll-neck sweater
Spare woollen gloves
20 cigarettes
Extra box of matches

E. Report submitted to Flag Officer Submarines by the Commanding Officer, HMS Tuna

OPERATION 'FRANKTON'

Preliminary trials in INCHMARNOCK clearly showed that it was unlikely the whole operation would take less than an hour to complete without damage to the boats. 30 minutes to assemble boats. 45 minutes to disassemble boats.

It was tentatively decided, therefore, that I should try to surface in about position 45° 27′ N-1° 35′ W to assemble boats on fore casing at full buoyancy; then trim down and approach the GIRONDE, finally disembarking in about 45° 27′ N – 1° 23′ W. This would only mean being stopped for about 45 minutes. This position was considered to be the closest possible from my point of view, and the furthest possible from the point of view of the Military Force, to the GIRONDE. It was obvious that in this position, the earliest possible night was 6th/7th, to allow for a one-mile error in position and still get far enough up the GIRONDE before the end of the flood.

The night of the 6th/7th proved impossible, as I was completely unable to establish my position with sufficient certainty and it was imperative to be dead accurate. This was unfortunate as conditions were quite perfect, a nice mist coming down immediately after dark.

I spent the whole of the day of December 7 working northward along the coast and finally obtained an accurate fix at 1345. Air activity by Me 110s, Me 109s, Arados Ju 88s, Dornier 18s throughout the day was intense, and the surface was oily calm with a long swell.

At 1800 a patrol trawler was heard and seen and it appeared to me that he was patrolling a line 130°-310° running nearly through our intended position for disembarking.

It was then decided, to the evident delight of the OC Military Force, to try and disembark close to the coast and near the RAF's badly-laid mines (outside the dotted lines to the southward). I don't think those mines could have been laid in a more embarrassing position, as they seemed to interfere with every plan of action from the very start. This plan quite evidently required extreme accuracy in navigation, even allowing for the rather touching faith of the authorities in the accuracy of the positions given by the RAF – a faith which I did not share. Further, this plan entailed coming to full buoyancy 4 miles off the coast and 10 miles from the RD/F station and doing the whole operation in one, cutting out the approach at low buoyancy. But the most important considerations were that in that position the boats had a fair tide for an extra hour, and that our position would be dead accurate.

Surfaced in position 45° 22′ N–1° 14′ W at 1917. Sea was flat calm. Patrol boat was in sight but about 4 miles away. It was a beastly clear night. Commenced the operation at 1937.

All boats were out on the upper deck by 1945, only one being damaged while coming out of the hatch. Trimmed down and disembarked the remaining five.

When the first boat was in the slings searchlights suddenly started sweeping the sea from POINTE DE LA NÉGADE and all down the coast, but there was no light opposite us. There was an uncomfortable feeling that this reception may have been due to the RD/F station plotting us, and this feeling was strengthened by the fact that the trawler was evidently closing. The last boat was waterborne (position 45° 23′ N–1° 14′ W) at 2020, and I consider now this time was remarkably fast, and reflects great credit on Lieutenant Bull and his upper-deck hands.

2022 waved 'au revoir' to a magnificent bunch of black-faced villains with whom it had been a real pleasure to work, and withdrew to the south and west.

[sgd] R. P. Raikes
Lieutenant in Command
HMS *Tuna*

PAN GRAND STRATEGY SERIES

TRENCH WARFARE 1914–1918

The Live and Let Live System

Tony Ashworth

PAN BOOKS £7.99

The story of the great battles of the First World War has been told by historians, journalists and others. The shock and slaughter of the Somme, Verdun and Passchendaele, where soldiers endured unimaginable casualties with amazing courage, is a major theme of most books. Large-scale battles, however, comprised the smaller part of soldiers' total time in combat. For 90 per cent of that time soldiers fought small-scale battles which took place between and throughout large battles. These small conflicts were violent, continual and involved complex weaponry and specialized tactics. Yet, during small battles, soldiers could and often did make choices not possible during large ones. From these choices, there evolved between enemies a curious culture of live and let live which constrained the war culture of kill or be killed in fundamental ways. It was a culture that was spontaneous, unplanned yet ongoing throughout the war, and it gave soldiers some control over conditions of their existence.

The trench warfare culture emerged from a context of mistrust between enemies, dug in within yards of each other and armed to the teeth, where both were rewarded for aggression and punished for the lack of it. It is a story which has not hitherto been told.

All Pan Books are available at your local bookshop or newsagent, or can be ordered direct from the publisher. Indicate the number of copies required and fill in the form below.

Send to: Macmillan General Books C.S.
Book Service By Post
PO Box 29, Douglas I-O-M
IM99 1BQ

or phone: 01624 675137, quoting title, author and credit card number.

or fax: 01624 670923, quoting title, author, and credit card number.

or Internet: http:www.bookpost.co.uk

Please enclose a remittance* to the value of the cover price plus 75 pence per book for post and packing. Overseas customers please allow £1.00 per copy for post and packing.

*Payment may be made in sterling by UK personal cheque, Eurocheque, postal order, sterling draft or international money order, made payable to Book Service By Post.

Alternatively by Access/Visa/MasterCard.

Card No. | | | | | | | | | | | | | | | | |

Expiry Date | | | | | | | | | | | | | | | | |

Signature ______________________________

Applicable only in the UK and BFPO addresses.

While every effort is made to keep prices low, it is sometimes necessary to increase prices at short notice. Pan Books reserve the right to show on covers and charge new retail prices which may differ from those advertised in the text or elsewhere.

NAME AND ADDRESS IN BLOCK CAPITAL LETTERS PLEASE

Name ______________________________

Address ______________________________

____

____

____

8/95

Please allow 28 days for delivery.
Please tick box if you do not wish to receive any additional information. ☐